Taming Intractable Conflicts

Taming Intractable Conflicts

MEDIATION IN THE HARDEST CASES

Chester A. Crocker, Fen Osler Hampson,
and Pamela Aall

UNITED STATES INSTITUTE OF PEACE PRESS
Washington, D.C.

The views expressed in this book are those of the authors alone. They do not necessarily reflect views of the United States Institute of Peace.

UNITED STATES INSTITUTE OF PEACE
1200 17th Street NW, Suite 200
Washington, DC 20036

First published 2004

Printed in the United States of America

The paper used in this publication meets the minimum requirements of American National Standards for Information Science—Permanence of Paper for Printed Library Materials, ANSI Z39.48-1984.

Library of Congress Cataloging-in-Publication Data
Crocker, Chester A.
    Taming intractable conflicts : mediation in the hardest cases / Chester A. Crocker, Fen Osler Hampson, and Pamela Aall.
        p. cm.
    Includes bibliographical references and index.
    ISBN 1-929223-56-0 — ISBN 1-929223-55-2 (pbk.)
    1. Conflict management. 2. Diplomatic negotiations in international disputes. I. Hampson, Fen Osler. II. Aall, Pamela R. III. Title.

JZ5599.C76 2004
327.1'7—dc22   2004043385

Contents

Foreword

Taming Intractable Conflicts: Mediation in the Hardest Cases delivers an admirably succinct and forthright assessment of the problems of mediating conflicts that are unusually resistant to resolution. The authors don't merely rehearse a list of the difficulties of mediating intractable disputes; they conduct a groundbreaking exploration of the subject, carving out a new approach that yields new insights into both the sources of intractability and the mediator's challenges. Their argument for a *strategic approach* to conflict management is arresting and persuasive, and many of the ideas they put forward are sure to provoke discussion. For instance, their contention that the first priority in working toward a settlement is "hammering out a framework of negotiation or a statement or declaration of principles," rather than tackling violence and security issues, is striking and sure to stimulate debate.

Taming Intractable Conflicts speaks with equal authority to a number of different audiences. Many books claim to span one or more of the divides between academics and practitioners, between government agencies and NGOs, and between experts and novices, but most tend to have much less crossover appeal than they hope for. Perhaps because most books are written by scholars, practitioners are especially likely to be disappointed by the content of volumes that claim broad appeal. In this case, however, the authors—one of them a seasoned diplomat—have paid particular attention to ensuring that practitioners are not shortchanged. The result is a volume that is no less accessible than it is sophisticated, and that provides solid, practical advice to current and future mediators while illuminating for professors and their students the concepts and dynamics that underpin effective mediation. The breadth of professional experience on which the authors draw goes a long way toward explaining their success in this regard. Between them, they have served—with great distinction—in government, in academia, in private foundations, in publicly funded think tanks, in the NGO community, and on the frontlines of diplomacy.

The insights and implications of this book are remarkably far-reaching. For instance, the authors criticize the tendency for mediation to be dismissed by foreign policy pundits as "social work" and for mediation experts to frown at the idea of states using mediation to promote their own interests. "It is time," they write, "for foreign policy pundits and academic commentators alike to take a deep breath and recognize that mediation can be and typically is an instrument of conflict management that should be judged on its merits as a policy tool—that is, on the basis of what it can contribute to the advancement of the mediator's conflict-related interests and goals." Such a recognition, of course, would not merely enhance understanding of the nature of mediation but also increase the readiness of governments to engage, through mediation, the parties to long-festering conflicts. At present, governments often eschew the relatively low-cost but painstaking process of mediation and choose instead simply to ignore intractable conflicts—ignore them, that is, until they generate regional instability or international terrorism, at which point those same governments are forced to respond with high-cost military interventions that do little to address the underlying causes of conflict and that require considerable investments of diplomatic resources for years thereafter. As the authors remark with typical frankness and concision, when addressing the ills bred in forgotten conflict zones, "diplomacy should be the first response, not the last."

The fact that *Taming Intractable Conflicts* can shed so much light on so many issues will not surprise readers who have opened the pages of the authors' previous volumes. Since 1996, Chester A. Crocker, Fen Osler Hampson, and Pamela Aall have put together four path-breaking edited volumes, all of them published by the United States Institute of Peace. Two of these, *Managing Global Chaos* and *Turbulent*

Peace, are remarkably broad ranging, bringing together a large, diverse, and distinguished cast of contributors to examine the varied causes of contemporary conflict and the equally varied possibilities of responses to it. Lauded by scholars and practitioners alike, both books have won substantial audiences on campuses and in the halls of government.

The other two edited volumes focus, like this book, on mediation. In *Herding Cats,* published in 1999, highly respected practitioners recount their efforts to bring peace in conflicts that involved multiple mediators working simultaneously or sequentially. Most of the cases examined in *Herding Cats* are success stories and the lessons they offer are thus clearly of great potential value. But failure, too, has important lessons to teach, and recognizing as much, Crocker, Hampson, and Aall were inspired to examine mediation in the most challenging of circumstances. The United States Institute of Peace convened a group of experts to discuss prominent cases of intractability, discussions that in turn generated two books: this one, *Taming Intractable Conflicts,* and the authors' fourth edited volume, *Grasping the Nettle: Analyzing Cases of Intractability,* which will be published in late 2004 and which combines analysis of the dynamics of intractability with in-depth assessments of eight specific cases.

These books complement not only each other but also the many other Institute-sponsored studies of the theory and practice of mediation and other forms of conflict management and resolution. The Institute is proud of both the quality and the quantity of the work it has supported in this area. Aside from the numerous grants it has awarded to researchers throughout the world to explore different facets, types, and instances of diplomatic negotiation, the Institute has published more than thirty books and dozens of reports on the subject. The books range from broad-ranging analyses such as Timothy Sisk's *Power Sharing and International Mediation in Ethnic Conflicts,* Chas Feeeman's *Arts of Power,* John Paul Lederach's *Building Peace,* and John Darby's *Effects of Violence on Peace Processes,* to case-specific studies by practitioners such as Ahmedou Ould-Abdallah's *Burundi on the Brink,* Princeton Lyman's *Partner to History,* and my own *Exiting Indochina.*

The Institute has also developed a series of studies that focus specifically on cross-cultural negotiations. This series encompasses both explorations of overarching principles and factors—for instance, Raymond Cohen's *Negotiating Across Cultures* and Kevin Avruch's *Culture and Conflict Resolution*—and in-depth examinations of the negotiating style of individual countries, including China, Japan, North Korea, Russia, Germany, and France. These volumes will soon be joined by studies of the impact of culture on Israeli-Palestinian and Indo-Pakistani negotiations.

Taming Intractable Conflicts is an important addition to these works. Crammed with down-to-earth advice for mediators, brimming with insights for policymakers, and studded with bright ideas for scholars, this book highlights the Institute's continuing commitment to enhancing our knowledge, both theoretical and practical, of the craft of diplomacy.

Richard H. Solomon, President
United States Institute of Peace

Preface

Several years ago, we edited a book entitled *Herding Cats: Multi-party Mediation in a Complex World.* That book looked at a variety of mediation challenges but focused primarily on the difficulties of peacemaking when many third parties are involved in the process. The case studies in *Herding Cats*—written by practitioners who had led or been closely involved in the mediation—concentrated in large part on successful mediation efforts, including the 1991 comprehensive peace agreement on Cambodia, the Dayton accords, and the 1995 settlement of the Ecuador-Peru border dispute. Because we were interested in pulling out lessons from these successful mediation attempts, we did not include many cases of mediation efforts that failed. In the intervening years, we have watched as peace processes have failed to take hold and fraught postconflict periods have reignited into violence. Clearly, successful cases tell only part of the story of mediation; long-enduring, resistant conflicts also have much to teach us about the complexities of mediating difficult conflicts. This realization is reflected in this book, *Taming Intractable Conflicts: Mediation in the Hardest Cases,* and its companion volume, *Grasping the Nettle: Analyzing Cases of Intractability.*

Many friends and colleagues helped us in this endeavor, In order to explore the complicated relationship between intractable conflicts and third-party mediation, the United States Institute of Peace convened a group of scholars and practitioners with extensive experience in the area. Richard Solomon, both as a member of the Experts Group on Intractable Conflicts and as leader of the Institute, provided invaluable support. We also owe the other members of the

Experts Group a great deal of gratitude for their inspiration, insights, and guidance, as well as for their conviction that intractable conflicts can yield to negotiation under the right circumstances. Many thanks go to Morton Abramowitz, Pauline Baker, Jacob Bercovitch, Diana Chigas, Jan Eliasson, Melanie Greenberg, Paul Hare, Bruce Jentleson, Richard Kauzlarich, Louis Kriesberg, Samuel Lewis, Roy Licklider, William Nash, Charles Nelson, Joyce Neu, Meghan O'Sullivan, Marina Ottaway, Robert Pastor, Harold Saunders, Teresita Schaffer, Stephen Solarz, Paul Stares, Stephen Stedman, and William Zartman.

Several members wrote papers for Experts Group meetings, as did the following specialists: Cynthia Arnson, Steven Burg, Stephen P. Cohen, Charles King, Stephen Morrison, Howard Schaffer, Scott Snyder, Shibley Telhami, and Theresa Whitfield. These papers and the discussion they engendered added depth and breadth to our own understanding as reflected in *Taming Intractable Conflicts*, while forming the core of *Grasping the Nettle*.

Among this group, special thanks are due to Jan Eliasson and Louis Kriesberg, whose wisdom, experience, and clear-sightedness inform this book and who graciously put us back on the right path where we had strayed from it.

We would also like to recognize the staff of the Institute's Education Program—Jeff Helsing, Raina Kim, Alison Milofsky, Alan Tidwell, and research assistant Naren Kumarakulasingam—for their strong support for and interest in this endeavor and their patience with its sometimes distracting nature. Dan Snodderly and the members of the Publications Program did a superb job, especially Nigel Quinney—sharp eyed, quick witted, and an editor of rare quality. His commitment to the project and authors made this volume a much better book.

Taming Intractable Conflicts

1

Introduction
MEDIATION AND INTRACTABLE CONFLICTS

IN THE 1990S AND EARLY TWENTY-FIRST CENTURY, negotiations brought an end to some of the world's most challenging and difficult conflicts. In places as varied as Mozambique, Cambodia, and Guatemala, third-party mediators played critical roles, acting independently or together to bring about a negotiated settlement between warring parties. Some of the world's other long-standing conflicts, however, have been extraordinarily resistant to negotiated solutions or mediated interventions by third parties. In the Middle East, for example, Israelis and Palestinians have struggled for years to reach a negotiated settlement with only modest results. In many parts of sub-Saharan Africa, such as Sudan, northern Uganda, Burundi, and the Democratic Republic of Congo, intense civil conflicts continue to exact a high toll even as peace efforts struggle to gain traction. In many parts of Eurasia, secessionist struggles, border disputes, and various kinds of guerrilla insurgencies ebb and flow but show few signs of receding entirely. And in Cyprus, where violent armed conflict is a thing of the past, efforts to reach a more permanent political settlement have had to overcome dogged resistance because of intense political differences that divide the parties.

Much analytical work has focused on the causes of these conflicts and the forces that contribute to their intractability (as explained below, an "intractable conflict" is one that is unusually difficult but not impossible to manage or resolve).[1] Much less attention has been devoted to how these conflicts may end and, more specifically, to the role that third-party intermediaries can play to bring about a negotiated end to the violence. Indeed, it is somewhat ironic that the excellent recent work on conflict causes has prompted the scholar-practitioner community to devote more attention to what third parties should do to *prevent* the eruption of violence in new places[2] than to how third parties should manage conflicts that are already raging.

This lack of attention to ending conflict in the so-called intractable cases has three apparent sources. The first is an obvious sense of frustration born of a litany of cases in which repeated third-party interventions apparently failed. Nobody likes failure, and the lesson that some drew from a track record of tried-and-failed attempts at negotiation is that it makes little sense for outsiders to continue to bash their heads against a wall of intransigence.

The second source is the view of some policymakers, practitioners, and scholars that it is best to give some conflicts as wide a berth as possible on the grounds that there is no compelling national interest to be served by becoming involved in a hopeless case. For these people, the risks of being bogged down in or dragged into someone else's conflict far outweigh any potential benefits conferred by the end of hostilities.

The third source is a widespread sense that because many of these conflicts have gone on for so long they have essentially become self-contained or hermetically sealed. Many believe that there is little chance that these conflicts will escalate or spill beyond their existing boundaries, because the parties are deadlocked and have neither the will nor the capacity to raise the level of violence to a new (or higher) threshold. A rather perverse, self-fulfilling logic informs this assumption: "If the parties can live with the conflict (and the violence), then, presumably, so can the international community." In those cases where violence and formal military hostilities have long since ended (e.g., Western Sahara, North and South Korea), where open warfare has ended but a final political settlement on outstanding issues has not been reached, there is also a strong sense that it is best to leave things alone and not engage in interventions that could, in fact, make the situation worse.

Each of these three lines of reasoning is faulty. In the first place, the argument that third parties are doomed to fail ignores the fact that a few intractable conflicts have in recent years yielded to negotiations, if not full settlements. In Cyprus, for example, years of impasse in UN efforts to broker a settlement to end the division of the island have yielded to hope, as Turkey redefines its national interest in an end to the conflict. Against all odds, a joint effort by three international mediators brought the Northern Ireland conflict to a negotiated agreement.[3] After many years of wheel-spinning by a range of third parties, a U.S.-led coalition of Western and African states has recently made substantial headway toward ending the civil war between the Khartoum government and the southern rebellion in Sudan, a country that has known mostly war since its independence in 1956. Even in the Middle East, the endorsement by Israelis and Palestinians of the Bush administration's "Road Map to Peace" showed that a strong desire for peace could coexist with continued indications of deep-rooted intractability, an unresolved tension that may at some point yield dividends under the right set of circumstances. And if we look back to the late 1980s and early 1990s, we can find examples in Namibia, El Salvador, and Cambodia of protracted conflicts that succumbed after many years of third-party persistence to a negotiated outcome.[4] Success stories of tough cases that cracked cry out for investigation into the reasons why negotiated third-party interventions produced positive results when they did.

Second, the notion that outsiders should avoid some conflicts because the costs of intervention outweigh any real benefits is called into question by the events of September 11, 2001. If diplomacy and negotiation had ended the brutal civil wars in Sudan and Afghanistan a long time ago, the world might look quite different today. Al Qaeda operatives would have had fewer places to hide and to plan, organize, and prepare for their attacks on New York and Washington. Our retort to those who say this is simply wishful thinking is to point out that these (and other) forgotten conflict zones have served as breeding grounds for a host of ills such as terrorism and disease exported to neighbors and around the world. In an era of globalization, it is not just global "goods" but also global "bads" that we must worry about. In responding to these "bads," diplomacy should be the first response, not the last.

Finally, the third premise—that the longer a conflict continues, the more the parties themselves learn to live with and manage its dynamics, and therefore the less likely it is to escalate beyond its existing borders or boundaries—is also questionable. The parties to a protracted conflict certainly have high thresholds of pain—if they did not, they would have greater incentives to look for a negotiated way out of their impasse. But when public passions are inflamed by terrorist acts and constant violence, political judgments often become skewed and the propensity for taking risks increases. The possession of weapons of mass destruction and weak command-and-control systems can also increase the likelihood of miscalculation with devastating consequences. The Indo-Pakistani conflict over Kashmir is a case in point. In 2001–2, the conflict between these two countries showed all the danger signs of escalation as governments, emboldened by popular opinion and a false sense that the political and military advantage lay with them, tried to exploit the conflict for their own ends. It was only severe external pressure (and mediation in all but name) from the United States and Great Britain that helped to reduce tensions by making the parties recognize the dangerous game they were playing.[5]

Even when possession of weapons of mass destruction is not the principal trigger for escalation, many intractable conflicts have the potential to undermine regional political stability. Following the speedy end to the Iraq war in 2003, governments in the region that were allies of the United States worried openly about the consequences of leaving the Israeli-Palestinian dispute untended because of the conflict's continuing radicalizing impact on public opinion in the Islamic world. In Central Africa, civil conflicts that have erupted in one country have quickly drawn in regional actors seeking to ward off hostile rebel groups that find sanctuary across the border and— often at the same time—looking to exploit the conflict for their own national or personal ends. The civil and regional war in the eastern part of the Democratic Republic of Congo has resisted various third-party attempts at mediation and has dragged in many of Congo's neighbors, with adverse consequences for political stability throughout the entire region.

THE MEANING OF INTRACTABILITY

Many scholars and practitioners use the term "intractable conflicts" to mean conflicts that can *never* be solved or effectively managed.[6] Our view of these conflicts is closer to the dictionary definition of *intractable;* that is, these conflicts are stubborn or difficult but not impossible to manage. What separates intractable conflicts from other conflicts is a difference in the willingness or susceptibility of parties to entertain political options other than violence. In a conflict, parties look to a political settlement when the costs of continuing to fight begin to outweigh the benefits. This dynamic can occur for a number of reasons: circumstances change, elites change, or the public grows weary of the violence that marks the status quo. However, in intractable conflict situations, these changes in cost-benefit calculations don't happen: elites are not very interested in considering negotiated alternatives because the conflict does not hurt them enough; a large number of people may be benefiting from the conflict; and too many entangled and entrenched interests stand in the way of a negotiated resolution.

Intractable conflicts have a number of salient characteristics. In the first place, they are typically long-standing, having lasted for years, possibly decades. As a consequence, they are conflicts where psychological wounds and a sense of grievance and victimization run very deep. Some intractable conflicts remain unresolved despite repeated attempts to resolve them—whether through the outright victory of one side or through direct or mediated negotiations. Some others remain unresolved and continue to burn because nobody, including the parties themselves, has tried (or cares) to resolve them. Intractable conflicts are also characterized either by frequent bursts of violence or, if there is a temporary cessation of the violence, by a failure by the parties to leave the danger zone of potential renewal of violence. It should be stressed that the level of violence across intractable cases is not always the same. Some intractable conflicts are essentially prolonged wars characterized by ongoing military hostilities between the parties. Others are characterized by violence that is episodic, at low levels, but recurring. Still others are "frozen" in the sense that violence has ended, but no permanent settlement or resolution is within reach of the parties. Sometimes the conflict continues because nobody has seriously tried to help the parties deal with their differences in a negotiating forum.[7]

Third parties often have difficulty acquiring traction in intractable conflicts because the parties to the dispute are not seriously interested in considering negotiated options that would lead them out of their current situation. This is not to say that the barriers to negotiation are insurmountably high, but they are higher than in other conflict settings, where third parties have been able to coax the parties to the table.

In intractable conflicts, political extremists—on all sides of the dispute—often dictate the terms of any potential resolution of the conflict. Those terms may be a violent resolution of the conflict in which one side crushes the other. Or, if a potential solution is expressed in political terms that are (theoretically) amenable to a negotiated result, the solution may be one that leaves no room for compromise or major concessions to the interests of the other side.

What makes a conflict intractable? What factors and forces raise the barriers to negotiation in an intractable dispute? There is no simple answer to these questions. One of the most important factors contributing to intractability is leadership. Leaders may have a vested interest in continuing the fight because their political careers and personal wealth depend on it. Individual leaders may have a strong personal identification with and commitment to the ideals and goals of the "struggle," a commitment that outranks other aims. Leaders may also fear for their personal safety if peace becomes a reality. Any one of these factors may prevent the leadership from viewing negotiation as an acceptable alternative to continued fighting.

Another way of looking at this problem is to think of intractable conflicts as conflicts that are essentially led by spoilers.[8] Spoilers may be individuals (or groups) for whom negotiation is but a breathing space before the next campaign, people who perceive that ongoing conflict offers greater security than the uncertainties of peace, or leaders who believe there is nothing to negotiate about because unconditional victory is the only acceptable and conceivable

outcome. Militants and revolutionary leaders who exhort their followers with the battle slogan, "To Continued Struggle, To Certain
Victory," no doubt believe they are only doing what committed freedom fighters must do—locking themselves into a position where there
is little to discuss except the terms of the other side's handing over
power. When the raised fist of revolution meets an equally powerful
force determined to hang on to power, the scene is set for an
intractable conflict. The obvious challenge for third parties in these
kinds of situations is to distinguish the spoilers from those individuals and groups who might become interested in exploring the negotiation option.

There are, however, many other factors promoting intractability.
These include a lack of resource constraints on the parties; internal
fragmentation or weakness of one or both sides, making compromise and risk taking impossible; uneven or absent linkages to external
partners, to third parties, or to regional security mechanisms that
could support negotiated outcomes through the provision of credible
guarantees, confidence-building measures, verification, and monitoring; and the interest of outside actors in keeping conflicts alive.

A common assumption about intractable conflicts is that they
lack a clearly identifiable resolving formula—that is, there is no obvious solution to the conflict that offers benefits to both parties. Less
well recognized are those instances in which a resolving formula does
exist but has already been discredited or rejected by the parties.[9] In
such an instance, negotiation has already been tried and has failed
(perhaps more than once). Getting the parties back to the table
becomes even more difficult than getting them to negotiate initially,
because their past experience leads them to expect failure once again.

Finally, it is noteworthy that intractable conflicts often occur in
regions with inadequate or ineffective regional security mechanisms
and poor connections to better-endowed regions. These conflicts often
occur in societies in which civilians have few means of controlling or
influencing the armed parties, which dictate or dominate the political arena, and they often occur in poor societies. In sum, intractable
conflicts are created through the interplay of variables at the elite,
societal, regional, and global levels.

THIRD-PARTY RESPONSES TO INTRACTABILITY

This book is a study not about the causes of intractability but about what third-party mediators—be they a superpower such as the United States, other powerful states, middle powers such as Norway and Canada, international organizations such as the United Nations, or nongovernmental organizations (NGOs)—should do when confronted with an intractable conflict.[10] In considering the causes of intractability, we are therefore looking to solutions. A useful point of departure is to contrast our own perspective on the problem with what others have said about the challenges of mediation in problematic conflict situations. These approaches can be summarized as (1) let it burn; (2) engage only when national interests clearly dictate; (3) engage wherever there is violent conflict; and (4) leave it to others.

Let It Burn

Some argue that intractable conflicts should be allowed to burn themselves out.[11] There is no point, the argument runs, in meddling in the internal affairs of others if they are not interested in seeking a negotiated way out of their difficulties. These experts believe in giving war a chance in order to bring the parties to their senses. Indeed, according to this logic, the best possible outcome for a conflict may be the decisive victory of one side over another. In the eyes of the proponents of this view, unquestionable victory would certainly lead to a much more preferable state than an uneasy, negotiated cease-fire, in which the parties use the breathing space to rearm before resuming violence with even greater intensity and loss of life than before.

This argument ignores an increasingly important characteristic of contemporary warfare. The battlefield itself does not necessarily lead to a durable peace except in fairly unusual—and, arguably, increasingly unobtainable—circumstances: when the victor wins overwhelmingly and then rigorously assimilates (or annihilates) the loser, who gets little support from any quarter; when the victor is magnanimous in co-opting and sharing with the loser; or when the weaker side has the foresight to sue preemptively for a deal. These are not common conditions in the modern era. Losers and victims in an era of globalization are less isolated and have more friends, enabling their causes to be sustained and reopened.

Engage Only When You Have To

A variation on the "let it burn" argument is the contention that big, powerful countries such as the United States should scale back their global commitments and focus only on interventions, including mediated ones, that are of extremely high strategic importance.[12] Because the conflict presents a direct threat to the intervenor's national security, responding to it becomes a natural part of the intervenor's foreign policy. The benefits to the intervenor of a conflict's successful resolution are clear from the start, and therefore the intervenor will find it much easier to establish priorities and to gain popular support for the intervention. This approach also diminishes the temptation or pressure to become a global supercop, a role that demands a huge amount of resources, resolve, and willpower.

It is, however, exceedingly difficult to parse the world into conflicts that meet some imaginary A, or B, or C list in the ranking of U.S. strategic priorities, especially in a post-9/11 world, where traditional C-list countries, such as Afghanistan and Sudan, have suddenly moved into the major league of U.S. and allied concerns. Lists such as these have often ignored the fact that ongoing conflicts have been breeding grounds for forces that have challenged regional and international stability. The stubborn reality is that wars in these and other places serve the interests (however defined) of those who choose to fight them. Choosing to ignore these wars on the grounds that they will burn themselves out or that no compelling national interest is involved to warrant intervention is no longer a risk-free option.

Intervene Wherever Fighting Is Taking Place

Another third-party approach to intractable conflicts is to intervene in every conflict to the extent possible.[13] This is an approach associated more with international organizations and NGOs than with large states. International organizations such as the United Nations are under considerable pressure to agree to engage if the conflict parties request such help.[14] If this engagement has only tepid support from the Security Council or powerful member-states, the institution will have only limited resources to devote to the intervention. This was the United Nations' situation in East Timor before the Australians decided to launch a muscular peacekeeping mission to protect the East Timorese from the Indonesian military. Although the United Nations had a presence in Dili and Jakarta, it was a very weak one, incapable of bringing the parties to the negotiating table and serving mainly to demonstrate international irresolution about responding to the mounting crisis.

Unlike the United Nations, NGOs are not obliged to respond to crises, but they often stand accused of becoming involved in conflicts without compelling reasons to do so. Their critics accuse them of parachuting in to deliver some conflict resolution services and disengaging as soon as funding runs out.[15] The resulting interventions are weak and unsupported, and usually not connected to any other ongoing effort to make peace in that conflict. Unless there is close coordination and support between the "track-two" (i.e., unofficial) and "track-one" (i.e., official) negotiation channels, these efforts will not generate the requisite political momentum or lend traction (and public support) to a formal negotiation process once the latter gets under way.[16] And a congestion problem may well arise if there is too much uncoordinated activity at the track-two level and parties are buried with invitations to participate in problem-solving workshops, dialogues, and other kinds of activities hosted by well-intentioned players following their own agendas.

Leave It to Others

If great powers will not engage, and NGOs and international organizations cannot do so, they can always hope that others will fill the breach and shoulder the peacemaking burden.[17] The trouble with this approach, of course, is that someone else rarely takes up the challenge, and as a consequence the conflict becomes forgotten. In addition, internal wars have qualities that push them toward stalemate. Chechen and Dagestani warlords began battling Russians during the reign of Catherine the Great; Sudan has been at war for most of the past fifty years, Colombia for much of the past forty; the conflict in Kashmir festers more or less on its own except for rare bursts of external "meddling." As we argue later in this book, the lack of responsible third-party engagement in intractable conflicts can serve to reinforce their intractability until it seems as if these conflicts will never end.

Strategic Engagement

Three of the four above approaches—let it burn, engage only when it is impossible not to, and leave it to others—might be said to demonstrate a *laissez-faire approach* to intractable conflicts. Our own view of the intractability problem is that a laissez-faire approach to these hardened cases of international conflict is neither a desirable option nor, ultimately, a sustainable one. This is because the parties to an intractable conflict have already amply demonstrated that they are incapable of reaching out to each other and devising negotiable solutions to the issues that divide them. If the parties can't do it themselves, leaving them to their own devices in the hope that negotiations will one day suddenly emerge is the height of wishful thinking. And as we have argued above, letting a conflict fester risks spreading the contagion to others, infecting whole neighborhoods, with potentially devastating global consequences.

A laissez-faire approach by great powers toward other intermediaries, such as small powers or NGOs, on the grounds that it is best to "let a hundred flowers bloom" in the hope that some of these efforts to launch dialogue may bear fruit, is also unwise. Although there is much to be said for encouraging helpful fixers in the absence of alternative intermediaries, they will not help matters if they trip over one another and subject the parties to endless rounds of dialogue that lead nowhere and that could discredit both the negotiating process and the ideas needed to end the fighting.

In this book we argue for a *strategic approach* to conflict management, especially when dealing with intractable disputes. We argue that mediation is an important instrument in the foreign policy toolkit of state-based mediators and that it can serve broader national and

international interests when it is used wisely and judiciously. Moreover, a strategic approach to mediation also belongs in the best-
practice toolkit of international organizations and NGOs. For all
parties, a strategic approach requires careful research, planning, and
preparation before the effort begins. It demands a clear articulation
of goals. It involves reaching out to potential allies and engaging
stakeholders, including those who may act as spoilers. It means recognizing that intervening in an intractable conflict, be it interstate or
intrastate, has regional and international ramifications that should
be understood and, if possible, managed by the mediating party.

We also argue in this book that mediated interventions in intractable conflicts require a clear sense of strategic direction from
those who are in a position to make the parties see the costs and benefits of continued fighting in a different way. In some circumstances,
the third party may change the equation through coercion—the threat
or use of sanctions and military force. In many circumstances, however, the third party will help the antagonists recalculate the costs
through persuasive means. Mediators may persuade the parties in
an intractable dispute to come to the negotiating table through a
process of incremental, trial-and-error learning that elicits trust and
builds confidence in the negotiation process. They can help the antagonists make difficult decisions by being willing to provide a road
map, share the burdens, and lessen the risk of the journey ahead.
They can introduce resolving formulas that package and sequence the
handling of difficult issues in new and acceptable ways. Moreover,
they can coax, cajole, and browbeat with various inducements and/
or threats that help secure and sweeten the prospects of a deal. Just
as important, they can devise creative ways to strengthen confidence
in the process and in the resulting settlement, enabling parties to
make credible commitments for peace.

A strategic approach to mediation does not mean that mediation
is a sport for the privileged few based on their rank in the international system's hierarchy of power. It does not mean that mediation
is the sole province of the U.S. government or former imperial powers
such as France or Great Britain. In some cases, a strategic approach
might advise that an international organization, an NGO, or a small

state get the negotiation on track before the United States or another major power gets involved.[18] The same reasoning may hold for mediation attempts following earlier failure by great powers, especially in cases in which presidential reputations have been involved. A collective approach may be particularly appropriate for intractable conflicts because it is unusual for one mediator (state-based or otherwise) to possess all of the qualities—influence, leverage, relationships, staying power, political stamina, and resources—required to sustain a negotiation process over the many months or years that it may take to reach a negotiated settlement. That said, it is vital that this orchestra have a conductor—whether drawn from the ranks of government, the United Nations, or the NGO community—who can persuade the independent members of this group to play in harmony.

MEDIATOR, KNOW THYSELF

The words *gnothi seauton* ("know thyself") were inscribed in gold letters above the entrance to the Temple of Delphi in the ancient Greek world. Pythagoras's injunction, which Greek philosophers from Plato to Aristotle viewed as the first and most important step to achieving genuine knowledge, has special salience for the international mediator. An important theme in the chapters that follow is that in order to be effective, mediators must understand themselves, their motives, and their resources in order to avoid exporting their own confusion, incompetence, and political baggage into the conflict zones in which they work. Although this precept applies to third parties in any conflict situation, it is more important in the intractable cases because one of the major sources of intractability may be the deleterious impact of previous unsuccessful attempts to reach peace. A critical self-awareness of what went wrong, of failed strategies and initiatives, and of the suspicions and antipathies that resulted is essential to any hope of success when mediation attempts begin anew.

Some conflicts, such as the Israeli-Arab conflict, rouse passions far beyond their national borders or regions. A special challenge faces mediators dealing with these conflicts. Groups outside the conflict zone can derail a mediation effort as they pursue their own interests. Diaspora groups can provide funding that keep a conflict alive. Mediators who represent thriving democracies in which citizens and groups with strong passions lobby their governments and rally public (and foreign) policy in their favor must be alive to the risks that these partisans present. So, too, must the mediators' political masters, who, by currying favor with special interests, may undermine with sudden, catastrophic result the flexibility, autonomy, and credibility that a mediator must have to conduct high-level negotiations and fulfill his or her mandate.

"Knowing thyself" also means that the designated mediator has to assemble the requisite resources, including bureaucratic and political support on the home front, before trying to engage the parties to the conflict. Mediators who come to the realization that these core elements are not in place are well advised to spend their time getting their own mandate and line of responsibility in order before launching negotiations. The same logic and advice apply to NGOs, special representatives of small states, and other actors that choose to offer their intermediary services.

Mediators also have to go into a conflict with a plan and a commitment to see it through. They must be realistic about their limitations in extraordinarily difficult circumstances. At the same time, they must keep their eye on the final goal of a genuine settlement. Focusing on short-term measures will signal to the parties that negotiations are not grounded in a real sense of purpose on the mediator's part and, therefore, that the parties have little to lose by resisting initiatives or playing games at the negotiating table.

OUTLINE OF THE VOLUME

Because of their nature, intractable conflicts will rarely end in a fight to the finish. The parties are too evenly balanced—even if their power springs from very different sources—and the resources necessary to sustain the conflict too accessible. Intractable conflicts, more than other conflicts, call out for help from the outside. But that help must be competent and appropriate to local conditions. In many cases, mediation may be the answer. There are many lessons to learn from examples of tradecraft in which mediators successfully brought nasty, prolonged wars to a negotiated end. There are also lessons we can learn from cases of inept meddling and bungled mediation in which outside help made a problem worse and undermined later peacemaking efforts.

The chapters that follow are grouped into two parts, both of which examine mediation in an intractable conflict from the mediator's point of view. Part I explores the context in which mediation occurs: chapters 2 and 3 investigate why mediators choose to become involved with a conflict and what happens when no one does, and chapter 4 reviews the mediator's environment and the kinds of challenges mediators face not only in their "home" environment but also on the ground as negotiations begin. Part II is devoted to examining the actual tradecraft of mediation in an intractable conflict at different stages: at the beginning of the engagement (chapter 5); when the going gets very rough (chapter 6); during the settlement negotiations (chapter 7); and in the postsettlement implementation stage (chapter 8).

Our purpose in writing this book is to help mediators in intractable conflicts think through and plan their mediation strategies. It is also to help students of international conflict management understand the important lessons of statecraft and the policies and bargaining strategies that mediators invoke to help bring these devastating conflicts to an end. These conflicts are resilient, stubborn, and ruthless in nature, but they are not hopeless cases. And sometimes—in fact, often—it is thoughtful, well-executed third-party interventions that make the difference.

Part I

Understanding the Context

2

When Powerful
States Mediate
MOTIVES AND RESULTS

T HIRD PARTIES COME IN MANY SIZES AND SHAPES, and they play a wide range of roles in conflicts to which they are not a direct party: ally, patron, strategic-military partner, trading partner, strategic adversary, imposer of sanctions, witness, observer, mediator, provider of good offices, kibitzer, peacekeeper, humanitarian aid provider, diplomatic busybody, and self-anointed activist. Among the most important of these roles is that of mediator, a term which is generally understood to mean an actor who renders assistance in the quest for a negotiated settlement when conflicting parties cannot find one by themselves. Mediators, it should be borne in mind, typically are not driven solely or even chiefly by altruistic motives. Mediation is undertaken for a range of motives that may include a broader strategy of conflict management; sometimes it is based on motives that are as much political as they are strategic.

In this chapter, we look at the interplay between the motives and the interests of powerful states that choose to become involved as mediators of intractable conflicts. The discussion focuses on the impact and possible consequences of mediator actions that are driven by those motives and interests. The objective is to heighten awareness among both practitioners and analysts of mediation of the choices states face so that mediation is recognized for what it is: a foreign policy tool. The chapter explores the sometimes ironical effects of mediators' interests and motives, effects which in some situations produce powerful positive results but in others can distort or aggravate a conflict.

The focus in this chapter is largely on powerful state actors, because they have a great deal of independence in determining whether or not they will act as peacemaker in other people's conflicts. The United Nations does not have the luxury of that choice; on the contrary, it faces powerful pressures to become involved if the combatants request it and the leading members of the Security Council are not opposed. As for NGOs, they may wish to act as a mediator but are likely to lack the necessary resources and international clout to play a principal role. Small powers have more resources than NGOs, and somewhat greater freedom of choice than the United Nations, but, as we will see in the next chapter, their natural niche lies in those conflicts in which powerful actors decline to engage.

Why do actors with the possibility of choice in fact choose to engage as mediators in intractable conflicts? The answer to this question will be relevant to other mediators, whether they represent international organizations, medium-sized or small powers, or NGOs. But the picture will be clearer if we focus on the group—powerful states —with the greatest capacity to act on its decisions. Subsequent chapters take up the contributions of other actors, especially in circumstances where major powers do not engage.

MEDIATION'S LINK TO FOREIGN POLICY

Attention to mediation has increased over the past decade as the practice of it has increased compared with previous periods. This increase has come about for many reasons: the explosion of vicious civil and regional wars at the end of the Cold War; a heightened willingness of a number of official institutions to intervene in conflicts and a generalized lowering of the barriers to entry for mediators seeking to play their role; the growing appreciation of the complexity and multidimensional nature of peacemaking; the evolution and expansion of nonofficial approaches to conflict resolution; and, at times, a rising interest in political settlements by the warring parties themselves.

It is now generally accepted that third parties have been helpful —if not vital—in resolving certain conflicts. But the intractable cases represent an enduring and glaring blot on mediators' track records, raising questions about the suitability of mediation for handling the really tough cases. Prospective mediators who wish to notch up a stellar record of success would do best to concentrate on the easy, or "tractable," cases, rather than those we are focusing on here. Why are the hard cases so hard for mediators to grapple with? Is it possible that certain conflicts in some circumstances become intractable as a direct result (or as an unintended consequence) of actions and policies of third parties? Do these cases persist despite the best efforts of the most powerful and committed third parties, suggesting the need for fresh approaches and still greater efforts? What can be done to improve the mediators' track records and explain the apparent irony that mediation has become something of a growth industry, even though the list of intractable cases appears to change only slightly year after year?

Mediators are a special type of party to the conflicts in which they become involved. Indeed, it could hardly be otherwise. Mediation is an inherently triangular political process: the parties to the conflict seek to position themselves in reference both to each other and to the mediator, while the mediator seeks to nudge them both toward decisions neither is able to make alone or to persuade them to engage in direct, bilateral negotiation. Debate continues over the extent to which a mediating entity should be neutral and unbiased in relation to the conflict parties, and over the strengths and weaknesses of different types of mediators. But there is little debate that powerful states bring with them motives and interests. They bring resources and capabilities, on the one hand, and biases or preferences and interests, on the other.[1]

For most track-one actors (national governments and interstate groups such as international and regional organizations), mediation is a tool of strategy and policy. Mediation is not typically undertaken in a political vacuum, divorced from other policies and other instruments for pursuing interests. Rather, it is properly understood as a strategic tool of conflict management, parallel to certain other tools, but also unique in many respects. Interestingly, this central point is more clearly recognized in the mediation literature[2] than in foreign policy writings, which often seem uncomfortable discussing the place of a mediation process or a peace process. Foreign policy writers often set themselves up either as champions of foreign policy as a contact sport or as champions of foreign policy as social work, a polarization that overlooks the fact that there are other roles played by powerful actors in world affairs—peacemaker, policeman, fireman, arbitrator, and problem solver. Mediation experts, in contrast, while quick to recognize the role that interests and motives may play, often question the legitimacy of interest-based mediation.[3]

It is time for foreign policy pundits and academic commentators alike to take a deep breath and recognize that mediation can be and typically is an instrument of conflict management that should be judged on its merits as a policy tool—that is, on the basis of what it can contribute to the advancement of the mediator's conflict-related goals and interests. Just as conflict parties are not interested in achieving peace at any price, so, too, powerful mediators have clear preferences about the kind of settlement they will support. Having said this, it is also time for a clear-eyed recognition of the difference between policies that contain, freeze, or settle an intractable conflict and those that may escalate and prolong a conflict, contributing further to its intractability.

The significance of this point can hardly be overstated. It means, first, that we need a clearer grasp of the reasons why powerful international actors decide to become involved as mediators. In making this decision, they may be motivated by any number of goals and objectives. They may become engaged for foreign policy reasons: to accomplish core objectives such as strengthening regional security in a strategically sensitive region. When this is the case, the results can be impressive. The role played in the early 1990s by the United States in the settlement of the Cambodian War is an example of a powerful international actor engaging in mediation and negotiation in the pursuit of the larger goal of regional stability, in this case in Southeast Asia.

However, the linkage of mediation to foreign policy also means that there are times when broader, strategic factors dictate that states and interstate coalitions view conflict management, rather than a mediated settlement, as the primary goal. They may judge, for example, that a mediated settlement is simply out of reach and that they should focus on containing a conflict, using mediation efforts and other diplomatic tools to keep it from escalating or expanding. They may use their influence to maintain military balances, level the playing field, and deter others from manipulating the conflict for their own ends. They may use their influence to freeze a conflict and impose a form of coercive peace, believing that this is the best of the bad alternatives available, at least for the time being. U.S. policy in Bosnia and Kosovo in the mid- and late 1990s fits this description.

All these forms of conflict management can be viewed as interim alternatives to mediation initiatives aimed at achieving an early settlement. Conflict management of this type is self-interested in one sense, but it may also be the only feasible course of action. Besides, conflict freezing or containment can be a way station or initial step on the road toward a final settlement, creating conditions for future efforts. Balkan policy debates of the 1990s raged around these questions of sequence and whether or not it is legitimate simply to stop the bloodshed. Such considerations are especially pertinent in the special case of the United States, which has at its disposal a wider range of policy instruments, including coercive diplomacy and the use of force, and more far-flung strategic and foreign policy interests than other political actors.

At the same time, it must be acknowledged that achieving an end to the conflict is not necessarily the first priority from the perspective of the third party: it depends on the terms and implications of the settlement. In this sense, it is entirely possible that mediators' policies may inhibit or undercut the chances for settlement, whether this is acknowledged or not. Third parties may obstruct mediation because they prefer the status quo to an outcome that would require a friend or an ally to make significant concessions in a negotiation. Or, in another variant, a third party may judge that its *other* bilateral interests with one of the parties take precedence over its interest in reaching a negotiated settlement of the conflict. The potential tension between perceived third-party strategic interests and the generic goal of ending intractable conflict is evident.

A second complicating aspect of the mediation–foreign policy linkage occurs when states engage in mediation for essentially political reasons (both domestic and foreign), introducing extraneous political influences into the mediation process. Such situations distort the mediator's perception of a conflict and have the potential to aggravate a conflict's intractability in certain circumstances. Once again, third-party action may be based on the proposition that there are higher priorities than achieving a mediated settlement in the abstract. But when this happens, intractability increases. The problem is further compounded when—for essentially political or bureaucratic reasons—a number of rival, overlapping, or uncoordinated mediation efforts are launched, sending mixed or contradictory signals to warring parties and, thus, fueling intractability.

In sum, third parties typically have a wide range of interests to consider when they weigh their options in reference to a conflict situation. While these interests—and the muscle and resources that accompany them—can lead mediators to major success in ending conflicts, such interests may also help explain why other cases drag on interminably. Furthermore, third parties may contribute to intractability when they mediate for the wrong reasons and in the wrong ways—or (as we illustrate in the next chapter) when they fail to mediate at all.

Another point to be acknowledged is that not every violent conflict is suitable for mediation. Sometimes, what is called for is old-fashioned imperial policing or robust coercive diplomacy to suppress and contain a conflict, possibly helping to lay the groundwork for subsequent efforts to settle it.[4] Containment of a conflict may be a phase leading to subsequent mediation and settlement. It is thus important to identify when mediation may be the correct policy response to an intractable conflict and when other tools and techniques of conflict management may be more appropriate.

In some cases, a stalled mediation may be salvaged by temporarily freezing the mediation process in hopes of preserving it for a better day. But, when mediators opt out or pull out of a stalled effort, conflicts become "orphaned"—that is, their intractability flows at least in part from the absence of external help. We will look at this phenomenon more closely in the next chapter. In this chapter, we now explore those cases in which mediators do elect to engage and the interaction between mediators' interests and the goal of settling intractable conflicts.

Foreign Policy and Strategic Reasons to Mediate

States and interstate groupings may decide to engage in mediation of an intractable conflict under the guiding motive of obtaining a settlement. We identify three distinct types of substantive rationales for mediation—humanitarian, strategic, and regional security/governance—though we recognize that the distinctions between them are not watertight and that overlapping rationales are common.

Humanitarian Motives

A state may undertake the role of mediator for *humanitarian purposes* in situations where there is a strong public voice and ethical imperative for action to end civilian suffering and forestall further disasters or atrocities, even if the state's strategic interest in the conflict is slight or nonexistent. The logic here is that a mediation initiative may create a viable negotiation process leading to a settlement that would end the fighting and the suffering occasioned by warfare. Even in the absence of a comprehensive solution, an ongoing mediation process may offer opportunities to contain or scale back the fighting and to press for greater respect for humanitarian law and values by the warring parties. Once a mediation has begun, each party is likely to see the advantages of holding the moral high ground, both as a public relations exercise and to obtain the mediator's support and understanding while wrong-footing the adversary party. When motivated in substantial measure by humanitarian considerations, the mediator may be able to establish interim goals that are explicitly linked to saving lives—for instance, establishing safe havens for refugees, demilitarizing relief corridors, and arranging pauses in the fighting to permit relief agencies to bring succor to the needy.

Whether such interim measures aimed at creating humanitarian "space" amidst a hot war are effective can be hard to judge.

Mediators need to carefully weigh the risks of being manipulated by warring parties, which may be eager to be seen (not least by the international media) cooperating with humanitarian agencies or to play one-upmanship games over humanitarian issues while they quietly prepare for further war. In conflicts as varied as those in the Balkans, Afghanistan, Sudan, and Congo, external actors have typically found themselves in the position of having a greater interest than the combatants in saving local civilians—a situation in which mediators are likely to be diverted from their primary agenda and to lose much of their leverage on the warring parties. At another level, humanitarian mediation efforts could distract attention from the main agenda of peacemaking. If they succeed, they might make the conflict more tolerable, giving the parties a breathing space to rearm, re-equip, and get ready for the next round of fighting. At the same time, when a conflict rages without letup for years, it is hard to argue against doing whatever can be done to improve conditions facing innocent civilian victims on whom the armed parties impose unspeakable burdens.

This point is reinforced by considerations of economy and domestic public support. A democratic government providing significant relief assistance year after grisly year in the world's uglier war zones may be faced with impatience, "humanitarian fatigue," and demands for bolder action to bring the war to an end—a dynamic that could drive powerful third parties to consider shortcuts and more drastic measures. Faced with such cross-cutting pressures, a mediator needs to decide before launching a fresh initiative whether the purpose is principally to alleviate suffering as quickly as possible or to end the underlying conflict that causes it. The latter, more ambitious, approach is the only serious response to the really intractable conflicts, but it requires a level of political commitment and staying power that is difficult for outsiders to muster.

This assortment of challenges perfectly captures the dilemma facing Western policymakers over Sudan in recent years. On the one hand, policymakers in the United States, the United Kingdom, and certain Nordic and other Western European countries face important domestic constituencies deeply concerned about the plight of the southern Sudanese. For years, southern Sudan has been afflicted by a nutritional and health crisis and the effects of a particularly brutal form of communal strife, including the capture and trade of persons, and has been caught up in direct fighting between government forces and allied tribal militias and the forces of the Sudanese People's Liberation Army and other southern factions. Western governments have channeled substantial humanitarian assistance resources to Sudan, sustaining affected populations on both sides and, in certain cases, turning a blind eye to the reality that armed factions derive certain tangible benefits from these resource flows as well. When millions of people are dying or being internally displaced by war, the case for assistance becomes irresistible even though such aid is unlikely to bring peace any closer. On the other hand, serious-minded peacemaking initiatives require a basis for testing the interest of the parties in addressing the underlying conflict issues of group identity, constitutional structure, self-determination, and the relationship of Islam to the Sudanese state. As U.S. officials and envoys learned in launching a fresh peace initiative in 2001–2, they must face rather than fudge the choice between short-term humanitarian gestures and building a sustainable peace process.[5]

Strategic Motives

States may decide to become mediators for *strategic reasons* involving geopolitical relationships or regional security considerations. In such cases, mediation is a method for advancing and defending national or allied interests in a zone of conflict. The logic is that an intractable conflict cannot be neglected because it is too volatile. For example, the long-term Middle East conflict. between Israel and its Arab neighbors and the Palestinian population of the occupied West Bank and Gaza always has the potential to expand geographically or technologically, to stir the passions of domestic constituencies and diasporas, to complicate Western links with the oil-producing states of the Gulf, or to be exploited by a strategic adversary (as, for example, the Soviet Union exploited it during the Cold War). Since the Six Day War in 1967, the U.S. interest in doing something about the Middle East conflict has included an element of determination to lead the region's peace diplomacy—in order to shape it, to steer it in

directions favorable to American views of how matters should be
resolved, to deny the lead role to other Western powers or the United
Nations, to exclude or check Soviet influence, and to manage the
conflict's impact on U.S. relations with the Gulf states. Through
seemingly endless vicissitudes and periodic achievements or interim
accords, the name of the game for Washington has been to manage
and contain the conflict.

Washington's strategy has included containment of the conflict,
control and leadership of regional diplomacy, mediation as circumstances permit of an overall peace framework, and strong security
links with key friends and partners. The mediating role complements
and goes hand in hand with the full panoply of parallel U.S. policies:
arms supplies and training relationships, security guarantees, close
cultural ties, and major development and macroeconomic assistance
programs. These policy tools are designed, above all, to ensure U.S.
primacy in a strategically sensitive region—the Middle East—and
to guarantee the security of Israel, Egypt, Jordan, Turkey, and the
Gulf oil producers. At certain junctures, the best available option
has been to contain and freeze the conflict's basic parameters using
this combination of policy instruments. Over time, however, the
mediation of a settlement has emerged as an increasingly central, even
indispensable, instrument for containing and managing the conflict.
In other words, a purely process-driven approach—going through
the motions of diplomacy in order to maintain the outward appear-
ance of a peace process that, in reality, is going nowhere—is no
longer sufficient to control and contain the conflict.

While there have been third-party roles for other actors—for
example, the European Union, Norway and other individual European states, and, in limited areas, the United Nations—the Americans
have worked to orchestrate the region's war and peace diplomacy.
The unique U.S. relationship with Israel has given Washington its
dominance and its capacity to veto competing efforts. Particularly
interesting is how this strategic motivation includes a dual element:
to build peace based on certain core principles (rejection of the use
of terrorist violence, recognition of a wide range of Palestinian rights,
including statehood, return of Arab territories conquered by Israel,

recognition of Israel's right to exist within secure boundaries), on the one hand, and to reject or obstruct any attempt to resolve the region's affairs on any other basis than this, on the other hand. This Janus-faced strategy clearly demonstrates how conflict management includes, but is not limited to, mediation. Over time, other U.S. strategic interests have included discouraging regional escalation, deterring the entry of additional military parties, using diplomatic and other means to counter regionwide terrorist activity, sustaining strong security assistance and arms sales relationships (with all their strings, terms, and conditions on end use, transfer to third parties, and the like), and maintaining deep and productive ties with like-minded regional and adjacent states.

This is not to say that U.S. conflict management/mediation strategy has "succeeded" in the Middle East. But it has produced significant partial, interim results and certain core building blocks of an ultimate peace framework. And it has worked better, in the view of a series of administrations from both major political parties, than the alternatives. Despite disappointments and shortcomings, it would appear to have worked better than available alternatives from the perspective of the warring parties as well. Arguably, the job of Middle East peacemaking is partly completed—if one considers Israel's agreements with Egypt and Jordan, the substantial movement achieved on the Israeli-Syrian track during the 1990s, and the apparent convergence on some key issues in the Israeli-Palestinian negotiations. This is the fruit of three decades of talks brokered primarily by the United States.

Even though the guns have not yet been silenced and the shape of the final deals remains unclear, the Middle East conflict illustrates how mediation-as-conflict-management serves the interests of both a powerful third-party actor and the direct parties to the conflict. As the Israelis and Palestinians descended into an abyss of violence in 2001–2 and the American regional posture faced new challenges after September 11, 2001, the nexus between mediation and conflict management was further dramatized. The U.S. decision in early 2001 to back off from both mediation and conflict management served only to fuel local and regional instability. Such American passivity was not sustainable. The year 2003 witnessed a fresh determination to take the lead in defining the basis for an ultimate settlement, suggesting that visible U.S. engagement in mediation has become an indispensable tool both for prosecuting the war on terrorism and for containing the bloodshed between Israelis and Palestinians.[6]

In the Middle East, the strategic interests of the mediator are served when the parties make tangible progress; conversely, those interests suffer from stalemate and escalation between the warring sides. But the stars do not always line up this way, as the example of Cyprus demonstrates. In this case, conflict management has included an element of mediation by various American, British, and UN figures over the course of nearly forty years. But third parties have not always been willing to elevate the goal of achieving settlement to the number-one priority in their relations with the Greeks, the Turks, and the Cypriot entities with which they were dealing. The primary strategic interest of the leading Western powers has been to contain the conflict, forestall outside meddling (by Moscow during the Cold War), and prevent an eruption of fighting between two NATO members in the strategically sensitive eastern Mediterranean.

Until the late 1990s, Western diplomacy, UN peacekeeping forces, British strategic bases on the island, and Western naval deployments in the area were all directed toward these objectives. Suppressing and freezing the Cyprus conflict while giving low-key diplomatic support to UN efforts to mediate a settlement was the preferred course. The United Nations' problems in trying to reach a negotiated settlement have been compounded by this hands-off attitude by the United States and other permanent members of the Security Council, which were unwilling to choose between Athens and Ankara or even to define the meaning of the terms embedded in the mandate supporting UN peacekeepers since 1964. Following the island's invasion by Turkey in 1974 and its de facto partition, the issue of Cyprus was managed but not resolved for the simple reason that the United States and other major powers were more interested in overall regional stability and their relations with Turkey and Greece than they were in solving the conflict on Cyprus. Mediation will not

flourish in an environment where the major powers—for understandable and strategically cogent reasons—have other priorities.
The Cyprus tail was not allowed to wag the NATO dog.[7] In the past
few years, however, the Cyprus question has become tightly linked
with the issue of admission of new members to the European Union,
as Greece has pushed the admission of Cyprus as a means of pressing Turkey to lean on the Turkish Cypriots in the intercommunal
talks. In effect, broader questions of EU enlargement, Turkey's role
in Europe, and the post-9/11 geopolitical climate have changed the
external political dynamics and provided a fresh impetus to the
Cyprus peace effort.

The Cyprus case perfectly illustrates how and why mediation
exercises tend to become embedded in broader geopolitical policies
and to be affected by overarching strategic shifts. But it is not unique
in this respect. Efforts by various Western nations (the United
States, France, Sweden, and Italy) to facilitate a resolution of the
Nagorno-Karabakh conflict in the 1990s were inevitably influenced
by Russia's overwhelming proximity and superior levers of influence and by the refusal of the former to elevate this dispute to the
top of their list of priorities in their relations with Moscow. From
Russia's perspective as a core member of the negotiating group on
Nagorno-Karabakh, it made strategic sense to use the mediation process to steer developments toward an outcome favorable to Russian
regional interests in the sensitive Caucasus region. Other third parties
would not be able to ward off Russia's heavy-handed influence with
the local Armenian and Azeri parties unless they were prepared to
escalate the issue bilaterally in Moscow.[8]

The case of the Western Sahara conflict in northwestern Africa
reflects a similar pattern. Over the years since the territory's contested decolonization by Spain in 1975, neither the United States
nor France, the most important external powers in Maghrebi politics,
has been prepared to make the fate of the Sahrawis the defining
touchstone of its relations with Algeria and Morocco. UN peacekeepers have been inserted and UN-led mediation, assisted by former U.S. secretary of state James A. Baker III, has pressed for

implementation of a UN Security Council plan for a referendum on final status of the contested territory. But the key powers have been reluctant to let the Saharan conflict dominate regional politics. However sensible this may be as a matter of policy, it is also a classic formula for sustaining an intractable, if largely suppressed, conflict.

Regional security considerations have decisively shaped the view of key external players toward conflict management and mediation in Bosnia. American views of engagement in Bosnian mediation evolved as the security and diplomatic stakes evolved. After it failed to prevent the breakup of Yugoslavia, the United States adopted a hands-off posture, leaving the Bosnia-Herzegovina crisis to unfold before the horrified, if paralyzed, gaze of Washington's European allies. When the Europeans eventually teamed up with the United Nations and assembled a third-party mediation team led by former British foreign secretary David Owen and former U.S. secretary of state Cyrus Vance, the George Bush administration offered cautious, qualified support for the resulting Vance-Owen plan. But the incoming administration led by President Bill Clinton moved quickly to distance itself from the plan and floated alternative ideas designed to bolster the position of the weaker, Bosnian Muslim, side.

Washington, in other words, refused to support proposals made by its European allies, which had forces deployed on the ground as UN peacekeeping troops, but it stopped short of offering serious alternatives: Bosnia remained, in the U.S. view, a European quagmire rather than a place of U.S. strategic interest. Domestic political influences dictated measured support for the Bosniac victims of brutal ethnic cleansing, but for several years the extent of domestic interest was limited, a situation that perfectly suited the limited enthusiasm of the administration for doing anything substantive about the problem.

Rival U.S. and European instincts over the conduct of mediation and humanitarian intervention played out for almost four years, until 1995, when public criticism of the U.S. administration's policies reached a crescendo following the Srebenica massacre and a mortar attack on the marketplace in Sarajevo. At this point, Washington finally became fully engaged in negotiated efforts to end the war in conjunction with coherent allied military moves to heighten pressure on the Bosnian Serbs and acquire the leverage required for mediation. This process culminated with the signing of the Dayton accords in late 1995, a complex package that—interestingly—stopped the fighting and created a series of new and somewhat ambiguous political structures, but that purposefully did not sort out the main outstanding issues of power and sovereignty. Mediation was used in Bosnia to manage the conflict, contain it from spreading, suppress active fighting, and buy time for the possibility of a gradual trans-formation away from the militarized and nationalistic politics of the early 1990s. It was not used to settle or solve the basic issues, many of which remain unresolved to this day.[9]

These examples illustrate the ways in which geopolitics and conflict management can intersect and point up the role that medi-ation can play, depending on broader factors in the strategic con-text as perceived by powerful third parties. In some cases, mediation closely paralleled dramatic geopolitical shifts in the international system. As the Soviet Union collapsed, a number of states, including the United States and Sweden, played a critical role between the new authorities in Estonia and Russia to ensure a peaceful transition of power in the Baltic state and a negotiated departure of Russian forces. The United States similarly played a key role in ensuring the denu-clearization of Ukraine, Belarus, and Kazakhstan. U.S. mediation also served as a catalyst for a broader international effort to end the fighting in Cambodia and get foreign forces out of that country as the USSR collapsed and China and Vietnam normalized relations. In this case, the United States and others used mediation to end an intractable conflict. Such geopolitical shifts may represent some of the best opportunities for third parties to manufacture moments for intensive peacemaking, using contextual fluidity to press warring parties to leave their entrenched positions and abandon their worst-case scenarios of the outcome of negotiations with the other side.

But such opportunities are not always taken. For example, U.S. officials saw no apparent reason for sustained mediation over the factional fighting in Afghanistan once Soviet forces withdrew from the war that former president Mikhail Gorbachev had termed Mos-cow's "bleeding wound." Managing this conflict no longer appeared

to be strategically pressing, a viewpoint that proved to have disastrous longer-term consequences when the resulting failed state came
under Taliban rule in 1996.

Geopolitical interests and power dynamics explain why in certain cases third parties may perceive a higher interest—as well as
lower risk—in managing the conflict than in attempting to resolve it.
That is, they may prefer to freeze or suppress the conflict in order to
contain its spread, check the risk of escalation, deter an adversary
or rogue power, and limit the potential regional damage of continued
conflict. For many years, the United States has stationed its troops
in South Korea because deterrence is seen as the best conflict management strategy for the Korean peninsula. In contrast, a mediated
settlement that entails engagement and negotiation with the North
Koreans would involve significant risks—not least in terms of America's relations with its South Korean ally and other allies, which
could see compromise with the North as a troubling precedent for
America's future dealings with China. Some third parties have such
strong geopolitical or strategic interests in a region that its conflicts
become "impacted" in their interests and off-limits for mediation
until their interests shift. Korea may be such a case.

Other examples can be cited of instances in which regional or
global powers have preferred the status quo of sustaining their side
in a drawn-out conflict over supporting a negotiated compromise:
Cuba in Southern Africa until the late 1980s; Vietnam and China in
Cambodia until the early 1990s; Russia in the Caucasus conflicts after
the collapse of the USSR. These examples are not cited to justify such
behavior by powerful actors but to point out that these actors sometimes decide that mediation is not the right answer. Clearly, a dog-
matic adherence by outside parties to damage-limiting strategies may
blind them to opportunities for successful mediation efforts; such
opportunities can emerge from shifting circumstances, crises, leadership changes, and other developments.

Regional Security/Governance Motives

The payoff of some peacemaking efforts has less to do with advancing direct, immediate national interests or upholding case-specific

humanitarian values than with *building a more stable and secure regional and world order*. The third party faces neither a strategic nor a humanitarian imperative to mediate or undertake other forms of conflict management. Rather, it works for the public good of a settlement for broader reasons: to harvest the benefit of acting (and being seen to act) in the common interest; to enhance its international reputation and standing; to support popular norms related to transparency and good governance; and to combat generic evils—for instance, terrorism, criminal mafias, and failed states—that tend to germinate in intractable conflict zones.

When considering this category of motives, one may well ask whether all intractable conflicts do not warrant some form of third-party engagement. The reply must clearly be "no," at least for any specific third party and, in particular, for the United States, which already shoulders more international burdens than it can bear politically, economically, and militarily. In cases where a conflict has been effectively frozen or removed from the list of hot wars, the case for engagement is politically and bureaucratically hard to make. Where the human toll is low and the regional consequences are tolerable, a conflict simply may not make the cut for the attention of the White House and cabinet-level officials. This judgment, however, leaves plenty of opportunity for others—lower-level U.S. officials, other major powers or coalitions, medium-sized powers, UN and regional envoys, and nonofficial bodies—to play third-party conflict management and mediation roles.

An interesting example—examined in more detail in the next chapter—of successful mediation by such actors came in Mozambique in the early 1990s. After nearly fifteen years of internationalized civil war, a geopolitical shift in Southern Africa away from regional violence coincided with a low-key initiative by the Italian Catholic lay organization Sant'Egidio, which was working in parallel with the Italian government and a number of other Western and African regional governments. Peace accords concluded in 1992 set the stage for a successful transition to elections held under UN auspices. In another illustration, the government of Norway, in collaboration with influential NGO leaders, has pursued mediation and conflict management in a number of "discretionary" cases of this kind (that is, cases where the third party elects to become involved for motives unrelated to geopolitical interest). In addition to their work that paved the way for the Oslo accords, Norwegians have played a quiet but sustained and professional role in such places as Colombia, Sri Lanka, and Sudan. Norway does not publicize its motives, but they include its desire to continue its self-conscious and highly popular international role as a good citizen and practitioner of humanitarian solidarity. The engagement of a medium-sized or small power (or of a group of such states) in mediation typically derives from a commitment in principle to peaceful settlement and the rule of law. A powerful state such as the United States also shares these values, but since it cannot be everywhere, it generally concentrates on cases linked in some way to larger strategic interests.

POLITICAL RATIONALES FOR MEDIATION

Just as mediation intersects with broader strategic interests, it can also become linked with politics — both domestic and foreign. In this regard, mediation is no different from other instruments of foreign policy. Mediators sometimes battle to buffer their efforts from volatile *domestic political winds,* and they may find themselves overwhelmed if those winds grow too powerful. But mediators also may face *external political forces* that are capable of distorting the conflict arena and aggravating an already intractable situation. We now examine several concrete scenarios.

The first scenario involves the impact on policy decisions of domestic public opinion regarding a gruesome conflict in a country of only moderate strategic importance. In response to atrocious conditions in ill-governed Sudan, U.S. legislators and interest groups demand that their government "do something," whether it involves helping victims, leveling the playing field between the government and the rebels, or denying normal relations with the offending government. U.S. officials may attempt a more dispassionate approach, recognizing that only peace can bring about an end to the outrageous conditions, that civilians suffer from the exactions of both the government and the rebels, and that symbolic help for the weaker side in a decades-old conflict guarantees only continued fighting. Mediation in such circumstances risks becoming a political football as domestic lobbies press their government to take sides and eschew a balanced approach by intervening in support of the weaker side.

A mediation launched in such a domestic political environment (of the third party) has the advantage of strong domestic interest but the disadvantage of potential interference from the political arena. Generally speaking, mediation works best when an effective firewall screens the mediator from such pressures and enables the mediator to operate according to the merits of the conflict itself, engaging both sides in a search for a balanced framework for negotiation and testing them both to face up to the decisions required for a settlement. If this approach is not politically possible, the mediation risks becoming a charade whose rationale is to be seen doing something constructive while tilting in practice toward the favored party. The challenge of insulating the mediation from such pressures can be addressed only when the mediator is a unitary actor whose top decision makers are determined to support the mediation politically in the face of domestic cross-currents.

At times, mediators will face direct intrusion by legislators or other domestic groups into a mediation. This may take the form of demands that an administration shift its proposals or realign its diplomacy by cutting off discussions with a particular political entity or by denying it a role in a transitional process or final settlement. Such pressures faced U.S. mediators at key junctures of the Cambodian settlement process in the early 1990s over the participation of the Khmer Rouge in the emerging agreement. The public tends to applaud mediators who moralize publicly and define every conflict in terms of good guys and bad guys, even if such posturing is counterproductive to the task of ending a conflict; and the public has a low tolerance for the uncertain, hard slogging often required to achieve an agreement and bring about substantive change on the ground. A mediator, however, cannot easily select which parties to talk to in a hot conflict: ignoring the men with the guns or with the capacity to block a deal will not work unless one has the power literally to coerce the sides to closure—a rare circumstance. Middle East diplomacy offers multiple illustrations of the role of domestic politics in pushing officials to adopt public postures at odds with the serious pursuit of negotiated solutions. The very intractability of the Middle East conflict also illustrates how domestic politics can generate resistance or reluctance to mediate because of the potential risk that mediation failure will undermine presidential prestige, tempting subsequent leaders to disengage. The Haitian crisis of the early 1990s offers another example of a mediation driven in major part by the internal political imperatives of the United States and other outside states anxious to take the perceived democratic side and to avoid an exodus of emigrants.

Some actors in the political arena would rather see the bad guys bleed than settle and will oppose any deal to which an especially odious party would agree. Domestic actors may engage in their own separate, "third-party" diplomacy with a favored side, coaching it and pressing it to resist compromise proposals coming from their own government. Alternatively, domestic actors may press for sanctions or for breaking relations with one side while initiating direct support for the other. Such patterns were evident in relation to the protracted U.S.-led diplomacy aimed at achieving South African withdrawal from Namibia and Cuban withdrawal from Angola in the 1980s. Illustrating the political nature of the terrain, opposing U.S. movements brought pressures to bear on the executive to take actions that would simultaneously punish the South African, Angolan, and Cuban regimes—the very parties with which the mediator was working.

Another scenario reflects a generalized desire among the domestic public that their government "do something" about a conflict. The public, which may not favor one or another side on the field of battle, may be motivated purely by an ethical or humanitarian concern. Democratic governments are the first to experience such pressure, and their diplomacy often reflects it. Mediation initiatives are mounted amidst public fanfare. Senior-level travel is intentionally hyped and meetings are carefully choreographed for the media, with jackets buttoned, handshakes arranged, and stray wisps of hair slicked back into place. The emphasis in official press guidance is placed on process and atmospherics.

Mediation conducted in this style may be aimed at providing suitable diplomatic cover for a genuine negotiating process; after all, even the most difficult compromises require protection until the final trade-offs are worked out. In many cases, however, a preoccupation with process signals that nothing much is happening in the negotiations. At its worst, the "process" mentality encourages the warring parties to play the same game and to conclude that outside mediators are interested only in appearances. Everyone involved in the negotiating process can play this game of make-believe, a game whose victims are not at the negotiating table and cannot schedule photo-ops.

External politics can also influence the conduct of mediators who become motivated to act for reasons unrelated to the substance of the conflict. For example, allies or members of a regional grouping may value group solidarity over the substance of the issues. For some members, continued participation in the mediating group may rank high enough to make it worthwhile to submerge intragroup divisions and maintain mutual support, at least at the rhetorical level. This leads to a paradox: group solidarity is a good thing for the overall health of a multiparty mediation effort, but it may place disproportionate clout in the hands of the most determined or most powerful group members. Alternatively, the quest for solidarity may lead members to paper over their differences and conceal fundamental divergences, leading to agreements that are subsequently abandoned or bog down in the details of implementation. Elements of both these problems bedeviled African states (and their tacit partners at the United Nations and in Western capitals) attempting to broker an agreement in the months leading up to the Lusaka accords of July 1999 aimed at bringing about an end to the internationalized civil war in Congo. The resulting accords were a perfect reflection of the subregion's unresolved differences.[10]

For some mediating bodies—both official and nongovernmental —garnering the international status and prestige accorded to the role of mediator may be the principal motive for becoming engaged in the first place, a motive that can hardly be a good thing for the mediation itself. In a number of post–Cold War cases, there have been multiple, competitive, and overlapping mediation attempts, creating congestion in diplomatic channels and confused messages that add to intractability. When the price of entry into a mediation process is shaped by such considerations or, worse, when the warring parties are in the driver's seat in deciding who may mediate, the exercise is probably doomed in advance. Regional organizations—as well as international bodies such as the United Nations—may be especially vulnerable to the operation of these dynamics; breaking ranks runs counter to the prevailing institutional culture in most intergovernmental groups, especially those comprising weak states that seek strength in numbers. Even a powerful state will on occasion defer to others in the overarching interest of sustaining and protecting the group's role. By shifting influence from mediators to parties and distorting the focus of the diplomacy, such role anxiety contributes directly to intractability.

Another illustration of external political motivation occurs when mediators consciously shape their initiatives with a view to aligning themselves with—or distinguishing themselves from—the policies and preferences of other major actors. This may happen when participants in a group mediation process tailor their contribution not in accordance with the conflict's own requirements but on the basis of more highly valued bilateral interests with other members. Western participants in the OSCE's Minsk group, an effort to mediate the Nagorno-Karabakh dispute, are reported to have pulled their punches during the early and mid-1990s in some measure due to their overarching political interests with Russia. The latter had the greatest direct leverage on the ground and had no intention of permitting this group mediation to undercut its own interests, and Russia used its seat at the table to steer the mediation accordingly.[11]

These examples of the impact of extraneous political factors on mediator performance underscore a basic point: mediation is a foreign policy instrument and is subject to the same kinds of influences that affect other such instruments. It can hardly be surprising, then, that mediation initiatives often fall short of their mark. They are not always conducted on the merits of a given case; they are sometimes conducted for ancillary or even "wrong" reasons; and they are at times subject to irresistible pressures that divert and distract mediators from the course that might otherwise have been taken. This cautionary note is especially pertinent in the case of the United States, whose constitutional arrangements and political realities can complicate the pursuit of strategic objectives. Such considerations may translate into initiatives that are weak and ill focused. They may produce self-serving diplomatic interventions unrelated to realities on the ground. And they may offer the warring parties multiple opportunities to outmaneuver and manipulate third parties, turning the initial intervention ironically into a form of support for one side or the other.

CONCLUSION

In this chapter, we have identified circumstances in which powerful third parties may contribute to intractability. We have seen examples in which strategic as well as political motives for mediation can have this effect. Clearly, it would be preferable if this potential source of intractability were minimized or neutralized. In a perfect world, political distortions of mediation would be avoidable, but in the real world, harried officials, especially in democratic polities, face multiple pressures from varied constituents and may not be able to resist. Mediators may find it helpful, however, to recognize the issue explicitly.

In the chapter that follows, we explore the obverse of the problems reviewed here: the particular problems that arise when conflicts are forgotten, orphaned, or overshadowed by larger, external political dynamics. Instead of acts of commission, we look at how acts of omission occur and how they can affect a conflict's intractability. Since it is both inevitable and understandable that major states will ignore certain intractable cases, we also explore the opportunities created for international and nongovernmental bodies to play the role of mediator in such cases, offering, at least in some measure, a form of compensation or remedy for the problems we have identified here.

3

Out of Sight, Out of Mind
THE FATE OF FORGOTTEN CONFLICTS

THE PREVIOUS CHAPTER focused on mediators' strategies, priorities, and motives when they elect to engage in peacemaking. This chapter looks at what happens in intractable conflicts when third parties fail to become involved as mediators or withdraw from the effort. Without some outside assistance to help the parties enter into negotiations, these forgotten conflicts run the risk of consuming the societies they spring from. The consequences can spread far beyond the national borders of the conflict, as the past decades in Sudan and Afghanistan illustrate clearly, where prolonged forgotten conflicts resulted in failed states. Failed states provide a permissive environment for particularly nasty leaders, thugs, criminals, and terrorists. Although international engagement cannot guarantee that a state consumed by conflict will move to a negotiated settlement, it does improve the odds.

In the 1990s, much attention focused on the success or failure of international intervention in the many conflicts that broke out after the end of the Cold War. At the same time that the Balkans and Northern Ireland were front-page news, however, a number of conflicts burned on without attracting significant international attention. Sierra Leone, Sri Lanka, Kashmir, and Afghanistan all experienced active warfare or high states of tension during the 1990s. All saw a prolonged period in which no outsider was sufficiently interested to try to change the status quo of the ongoing conflict. The reasons for this lack of interest differed from one case to the next, but the consequence was the same: a lack of consistent peacemaking assistance from the international community.

This is not to say that major states have no impact at all when they neglect conflicts. Sometimes, as examples in this chapter illustrate, they contribute to intractability by holding conflicts hostage to their own foreign policy goals. The lack of sustained international engagement in mediation or other peacemaking efforts allows these conflicts to remain as captives and dependents of more powerful states, just as the lack of international attention to orphaned conflicts allows them to burn on indefinitely.

The result of this absence of international interest is hard to measure. But if the alternative to settlement is continued fighting, and parties show little talent for making peace by themselves, then a reasonable working hypothesis is that the presence of third-party mediation heightens the chances of a negotiated—and lasting—agreement. And perhaps the opposite is true: the absence of third-party engagement in peacemaking heightens the chances that the fighting will continue. Just as bad tradecraft or poorly conceived interventions can aggravate conflict, the absence of available third parties can help ensure intractability.

This chapter identifies five varieties of "forgotten" conflicts: neglected conflicts, orphans, captives, dependents, and wards of the system. These categories are flexible and respond to fluid conditions within or outside the immediate conflict arena. In the discussion of how these conflicts evolve and why their forgotten status contributes to intractability, we note that conflicts often "migrate" between different forms of forgotten status and, under certain circumstances, may gain (or regain) the assistance of effective third parties who can lead the way to settlement.

We argue that the lack of purposeful, sustained third-party engagement may be an element of these conflicts' intractability. Forgotten by the international community, they are more likely to burn on, mostly unattended, like an underground fire. The absence of third-party engagement may actually aggravate these conflicts, increasing the odds that they will evolve in damaging ways domestically, regionally, and even internationally. Afghanistan, after all, became intractable in the wake of big-power disengagement, creating conditions for a failed state and its takeover by local political forces prepared to franchise their state to a global terrorist alliance.

The identity of the third party or parties and the nature of the assistance they render may be very different in situations where historically there has been little third-party involvement. The third-party challenge in interacting with these conflicts involves a different set of tasks than taking on, for instance, the Israeli-Palestinian conflict, which for decades has directly engaged powerful outside actors. When major states engage in mediation, they generally do so for compelling reasons. The conflicts we are examining in this chapter did or do not present compelling reasons for engagement by powerful third-party actors. Often, the first challenge facing third parties that do become engaged in these forgotten conflicts is to put them on the map. Getting the world to take notice, marshalling the requisite resources for peacemaking in the face of international indifference, convincing the parties that outside involvement can help—rather than hinder—their cause, exposing the parties to the procedural considerations and negotiation skills involved in conducting talks: these tasks often involve working around the conflict to put the necessary pieces in place for mediation to occur (an undertaking that scholar-practitioner Harold Saunders calls "circumnegotiation").[1]

These are not tasks usually undertaken by major states when they intervene diplomatically in other countries' conflicts. They are, however, well within the capacities and reach of other official and nonofficial institutions—NGOs, international and regional organizations, and small states—that can act alone or in collaboration with higher-profile efforts by larger states to build the conditions for peacemaking in forgotten conflicts. These actors and agencies should not be viewed as a substitute able to fill the empty chair left by absent powerful third parties. But there are certain things they do very well, and it makes sense to look more closely at the interdependence and interaction between such intervenors. Hence, we conclude by arguing that more attention be given to fostering layered and sequenced interventions based on a conscious division of labor.

VARIETIES OF FORGOTTEN CONFLICTS: NEGLECTED CONFLICTS, ORPHANS, CAPTIVES, DEPENDENTS, AND WARDS OF THE SYSTEM

In a forgotten conflict, antagonists are left to fight it out among themselves.[2] Forgotten conflicts often take place in or between countries somewhat removed from strategic hot spots. They seldom appear in major national newspapers, even on the back pages, and rarely rate a mention on broadcast news. Despite their obscurity, these conflicts can be vicious, with constant high levels of violence, endless cycles of provocation and reaction, or dangerous spikes of bloodletting and revenge. They also go through periods of quiescence, making it seem as though the conflict is under control until violence suddenly explodes and destroys the illusion of peace.

Given the variety in nature and circumstance of forgotten conflicts, we have divided them into five categories:

♦ *Neglected conflicts:* conflicts that fail to appear on the radar screens of major states and are, to all intents and purposes, invisible in the eyes of the international community.

♦ *Orphans:* conflicts that once enjoyed a significant level of third-party interest but, due to intervening circumstances, have lost the outside world's attention and willingness to provide assistance.

♦ *Captives:* conflicts in which one or more interested parties resist or veto third-party involvement.

♦ *Dependents:* conflicts that appear to be caught up in external events, struggles, and forces beyond the control of the immediate protagonists.

♦ *Wards of the system:* conflicts that attract the willing attention of no major state actor but nevertheless become the charge of the United Nations and other international organizations, which may not be given the resources to do much more than furnish emergency assistance.

These categories are not hermetically sealed, and a forgotten conflict may move among them. A conflict's place in our typology will vary over time due to a range of factors such as regional or global political changes and shifting trends in the readiness of major states to become involved in particular types of wars or specific regions. These categorizations will also vary with the observer's point of entry and the specific time period being observed. Nonetheless, they do provide a framework for considering when, why, and with what result the international community forgets a conflict.

Neglected Conflicts

Neglected conflicts compose the largest body of forgotten conflicts. Most conflicts, except in the most strategically sensitive areas, are neglected at their outset. They may be viewed by the international community as part of a process of state building or state consolidation, or as a temporary spilling over into violence of issues that the parties will eventually resolve. At this stage, these conflicts are not intractable, positions have not hardened, and the violence is at a relatively low level—the perfect opportunity, in fact, for a concerted strategy of preventive diplomacy by one or many third parties. And yet, despite the clear warning signs of impending large-scale violence, in these cases the international community often does little or nothing to prevent the conflict from continuing.[3] Left alone, some of these conflicts may persist for years, in the process becoming resistant to resolution.

The confrontation between the minority Tamils and majority Sinhalese in Sri Lanka has been a neglected conflict over large periods of the country's history. Since its independence in 1947, Sri Lanka has attempted to deal with the issue of political and cultural rights of national minorities. In the early days, government policy was at times relatively inclusive, recognizing Tamil as an official language and according Tamils full political rights. More often, however, the government did not recognize these rights and instead developed exclusionary policies that reflected a growing nationalism and anti-Tamil sentiment among the Sinhalese. The status of the Tamil population became a contentious political issue in democratic Sri Lanka. As frustration at their exclusion from full national recognition mounted among Tamils, support for the tactics of the radical Liberation Tigers of Tamil Eelam (LTTE) also grew through the 1960s and 1970s.

During this period, however, the outside world viewed majority-minority relations within Sri Lanka as a domestic political affair, something that the Sri Lankans would have to work out for themselves.

In the 1980s, Sri Lanka ceased to be neglected. Communal riots in 1983 led to many deaths—estimates range from four hundred to three thousand deaths—and caused the displacement of over one hundred thousand people, many of whom fled to southern India. These riots made Tamil rights a political issue in the southern Indian province of Tamil Nadu. Domestic political pressure spurred the Indian government into action, and between 1983 and 1990 India took on the role of mediator. India at first seemed to succeed, bringing the rebels and government together at the Thimpu talks in 1985. No agreement was reached, however, and as talks progressed, it became evident that India's role was as much party to the conflict as mediator. Its tacit support for the Sri Lankan Tamils over the years became more overt as the Sri Lankan government troops made headway against the Tamil rebels. Its provision in the mid-1980s of humanitarian support to the Sri Lankan Tamil population in defiance of a Sri Lankan blockade was seen in Colombo as an antagonistic gesture.

A concerted effort to improve the badly deteriorating relations between the two countries led to new talks, this time between India and Sri Lanka. The result was the Indo–Sri Lankan peace accord of 1987, which set the stage for a cease-fire between the government and rebel groups, featured a pledge by the Indian government that it would not support the rebels and promised eventual devolution of power to a Tamil region in Sri Lanka. As part of the accord, India agreed to provide peacekeeping troops in order to facilitate the implementation of the agreement. India's status both as peacemaker and as a party to the conflict was ambiguous, and India's approach met with a great deal of resistance both from Sinhalese, who saw India as an invading force, and from the radical LTTE, whose movement toward independence was curbed by India's actions. Despite the presence of between 75,000 and 100,000 troops, India was not able to disarm the LTTE and became the object of both political and physical attacks. Rajiv Gandhi's assassination in Tamil Nadu by

Tamil extremists in 1991 was seen as a direct result of the Indian peacekeeping effort and led promptly to its termination.

With India's withdrawal, Sri Lanka was again left largely alone to solve its problems. For the next nine years, despite efforts by some international NGOs to improve the climate for negotiation, various attempts to launch talks between the government and the Tamil separatists failed to produce results. Finally, in February 2000, the government announced that it wished to hold mediated peace talks with the rebels. This time, the mediator was not a regional power, as it had been in 1983, but the government of Norway, which had good ties with the Tamil Tigers and a long history of aiding development in Sri Lanka as a whole. For the moment, it seems, Sri Lanka found the outside intermediary it needed. This embryonic peace process has continued—albeit in fits and starts—led by a small power and strengthened by support from the United States and other international actors.

Another example of a neglected conflict is the interethnic struggle in Rwanda that ultimately erupted in genocide in 1994. Former assistant secretary of state Herman J. Cohen's account of the buildup to the genocide explains that Washington neglected the conflict in the early 1990s in part because "the United States did not expect the conflict in Rwanda to get out of hand" and in part because the United States was preoccupied with attempts to promote negotiations in Angola and Ethiopia and to bolster the prospects for peace in Sudan, Mozambique, and Liberia.[4] Yet, had Washington looked a little harder, it would have found several warning signs of impending disaster. Cohen points to a number of signs of military buildup and societal breakdown that should have alerted the international community to the probability of renewed conflict, and he concludes that the United States should have joined the French government as early as 1990 in pressuring Uganda to withdraw support from the Rwandan Patriotic Front. "Instead of selecting these options, we engaged in 'rote diplomacy,' calling routinely for a cease-fire and negotiations. The Rwanda crisis taught us this option can sometimes do more harm than good."[5] Nonetheless, the approach taken by Cohen's successors made clear that the lesson was not learned.

At times, neglected conflicts do elicit, if not action, then at least acknowledgment. The internal fighting in Nepal is an example of a neglected conflict that has been acknowledged by the international community. Since February 1996, a Maoist insurgency group has actively challenged the government. The murder in June 2001 of the king and other members of the royal family by the crown prince coincided with an increase in the level of violence in the internal conflict. Although the government imposed a state of emergency on the country, the "people's war," as the Maoist group calls it, continues. This situation has the hallmarks of a protracted conflict in the making: an insurgent group with possible cross-border links to two very powerful neighbors (China and India), a weak state, a declining economy, a potentially explosive region, and an international community focused on a long list of seemingly more compelling dramas. Unlike some other forgotten conflicts, Nepal joined the ranks of recognized cases as the war on terrorism opened the eyes of the previously distracted international community to the dangers of ignoring conflicts in South Asian states. In 2002, the United States, India, and Britain pledged military aid to the Nepalese government for its battle against the insurgents, and China—whose support for the Maoists would have certainly prolonged the war—also sided with the government. The massive post-9/11 change in the international system and a consequent reordering of priorities in the United States and elsewhere served to rescue this conflict from being completely forgotten, although how long the international interest will be sustained and how effective outside support will be are open questions.

Orphans

Some conflicts do attract international attention and serious assistance for their resolution, only then to lose that third-party interest. The reasons for disengagement are varied. The third party may decide that its job vis-à-vis the conflict is over. Domestic political backlash may force the third party to disengage, as the United States did in Somalia after the public uproar over the death of eighteen U.S. Special Operations soldiers at the hands of Somali militiamen in October 1993. The operation may become too expensive or consume too many resources to justify its continuation. Or the parties or other actors in the international system may lead the third party to understand that its services are no longer needed, that the parties can make peace by themselves, or that another agency—the United Nations, a regional organization, or a powerful state—may be more acceptable to the antagonists.

The third party may become distracted, discouraged, and incapable of continuing in its role. In the 1990s, the United Nations struggled to keep up with the many demands on its peacekeeping capabilities, as conflicts exploded in Somalia, Haiti, Bosnia, and Rwanda and neighboring states of the Great Lakes region of Africa. As civilian slaughter became a common weapon of war, the United Nations found itself playing the role of an unarmed policeman in a gangland shootout. Not only could it not offer protection to the civilians under its care, but its very presence under these circumstances made a mockery of international engagement in peacemaking.

Third parties may abandon conflicts for reasons that have nothing to do with the conflict at hand. The end of the Cold War produced orphans all over the world, some of which, such as Cambodia, were adopted again at a later date. At times, the third party withdraws because of a strategic decision that its interests are better served by exiting from the peacemaking efforts. In chapter 6 we discuss a number of examples of this strategic disengagement, including the U.S. withdrawal from the Kashmir mediation in the early 1960s and the Australian decision to hang back in the Bougainville mediation in the 1990s.

Whatever the reason for the third parties' disengagement, orphans are often created at a transition point, when a conflict is moving from one stage to another. Third parties that are active in trying to prevent conflict from breaking out are often disinclined or unable to mount and sustain a serious mediation effort after conflict has erupted. Another transitional point occurs after a peace settlement is signed and the process enters the implementation stage. It is not uncommon for outsiders that played a central role in successfully mediating a conflict to walk away from the implementation stage. But even when outsiders remain involved in the implementation stage, they may be as concerned with designing an exit strategy that will allow them to go home as they are with building a durable peace. Military planners may establish benchmarks based on the end of fighting and an improved security environment in order to set a departure date. Diplomatic third parties may see free and fair elections — or some close approximation — as their signal to depart. There is nothing inherently irrational about these third-party decisions, but they reflect an utter failure to appreciate that transitions are by nature unstable. During these periods, peace can be derailed by spoilers, miscommunication, or a lack of will and capacity on the part of the belligerents to move ahead without third-party assistance. Peace can also be derailed by a failure of will on the part of the lead external actor.

Afghanistan after the Soviet withdrawal offers a classic case of an orphaned conflict. The U.S. government and its regional collaborators began pouring resources into the mujahideen resistance shortly after the Soviet invasion in 1979. Starting with $30 million in 1980, this U.S. aid rose over the years to reach $630 million in 1987.[6] The aid financed the military resistance, but it also flooded the country with sophisticated weapons and enormous supplies of money, as useful to protecting the illegal drug trade and supporting rival candidates for power as they were to funding the opposition to the Soviet-backed regime. As the Soviet troops withdrew in 1988 and 1989, the sense of wartime unity among the resistance leaders broke down, and they began to build up their own personal empires as warlords and political rivals.

Although on-the-ground conditions were becoming more chaotic, the United States and the Soviet Union did have the basis of a plan to manage the transition from war to peace in Afghanistan, a plan that was overtaken by the demise of the Soviet state. As Afghan specialist Barnett Rubin notes, "The United States and the Soviet Union would ask the Secretary General's Office, in accord with General Assembly resolutions, to sponsor an interim government; the superpowers would use their influence with the regional states and with their Afghan clients to assure implementation of the plan and promote stability. With the dissolution of the USSR, however,

one superpower disappeared, the other disengaged, and cooperation between them became moot."[7] Abandoned by both the Soviet
Union and the United States, Afghanistan was rent by internal fighting until the Taliban—a radical Islamic group with strong support
among those Afghans tired of the corruption and violence of the
mujahideen—gained control of most of the country in the late 1990s.

Imposing a strict Islamic rule that returned Afghanistan almost
to a preindustrial age, the Taliban managed to keep Afghanistan
free from contact with outside states. Although unofficial groups in
the United States remained slightly engaged during this period,
worsening relations between the Taliban and the U.S. government
strictly limited official contact.[8] As Rubin concluded in 1995, "What
failed in Afghanistan was not just the Afghan state, but the international system that had first sustained and then undermined its
rulers."[9] Afghanistan became an orphan in the international system,
a situation which ended only with the aftermath of September 11,
2001, and with the ensuing military campaign led by the United
States with local and external allies to destroy the Taliban and help
build a functioning and democratic society out of the ruins of over
twenty years of war. The painfully slow transition in Afghanistan
serves as a reminder of how important and how difficult it is to remain engaged in the postconflict reconstruction period.

Captives

If neglected and orphaned intractable conflicts suffer from a lack
of third-party attention, the next two categories—captives and
dependents—suffer from too much attention from the wrong quar-
ters. In these situations, the conflict is fueled or frozen by entities
that are not direct parties to the conflict in the sense of being combatants but nonetheless exert a great deal of influence over the parties and the course of the conflict.

Captives are conflicts in which outside parties play a determining role in the conflict. These parties make it possible for the conflict
to continue: they keep the goal of victory within tantalizing reach,
reduce the likelihood of a negotiated settlement, and trap the parties
in a conflict that cannot end without their acquiescence. Most of the

time, these outside parties are states with strong interests in the outcome of the conflict, but sometimes conflicts are held captive by nonofficial forces.

The Cold War provides a number of examples of captives. In this period, when many countries were making the transition from colonial status to independence, both the United States and the Soviet Union had a strong interest in the outcomes of struggles over governance. Proxy wars, in which opposing sides fought each other in their own right but also acted as surrogates for the two superpowers, were common. The conflicts between North and South Korea and between North and South Vietnam are classic proxy wars. In these wars, each combatant had its outside patron whose support allowed the fighting to continue well beyond the antagonists' own capabilities. Without the patronage from powerful outsiders, it is likely that these conflicts would have ended more quickly, in most cases as the result of the victory of one side over the other.[10] Instead, these internal conflicts became captives of the larger military and ideological confrontation between the United States and the Soviet Union. As noted in the previous chapter, there are times when conflict management takes precedence in the priorities of a major power such as the United States. That has certainly been the case on the Korean peninsula, where the challenges to regional stability have not only outlived the Soviet Union but also become enmeshed in the global effort to contain weapons of mass destruction in the hands of rogue regimes.

Today, big-power proxy wars have been replaced by something less structured but just as entangling. In some cases, an external government supports one side in a messy civil war that targets civilians and encourages predatory behavior. In other cases, the external involvement may take the shadowy form of private entities (sometimes with links to neighboring governments) that engage in arms trafficking and resource looting in collaboration with rebel movements. This is the pattern that lay at the root of the intertwined conflicts in Liberia and Sierra Leone in the 1990s.

Some especially interesting cases have developed in areas that were formerly part of the Soviet Union, areas where Russia now plays an important role. In his comparison of the conflicts between the separatist regions of Abkhazia, South Ossetia, Nagorno-Kharabakh, and Transnistria and the metropolitan states of Georgia, Azerbaijan, and Moldova, regional specialist Charles King notes that, since the USSR began to break up, the Russians have provided peacekeeping forces or arms supplies in all four conflicts.[11] With significant numbers of ethnic Russians in Georgia and Moldova and continuing ties between Armenia and Russia, the former superpower has considerable interest in the outcomes of these conflicts. Weak as the Russian government has become, the successor states of Georgia, Azerbaijan, and Moldova are far weaker, and consequently Russian support for the territorial separatists has been a major factor in allowing them successfully to challenge and resist the authority of the recognized governments. For Abkhazia, South Ossetia, and Transnistria, the relationship goes beyond ethnic solidarity and military support to include economic ties and preferential Russian visa and passport treatment for citizens of the separatist territories.

These conflicts in the former Soviet Union have become deadlocked because in each case the separatist territories—with considerable Russian help—are as viable as independent entities as the states from which they are trying to separate. This balance of power makes these conflicts difficult to resolve without some major change in the capacities and resources of one party over the other. A withdrawal of Russian troops—as began to happen in Georgia and Moldova after the 1999 OSCE summit in Istanbul—might provide that change. The relationship between Russia and the separatist territories, however, continues to be very strong, and as long as Russia feels it has an interest in promoting autonomy or independence in these separatist regions, the conflicts will not be resolved.[12]

Dependents

Dependent conflicts suffer from violence and instability in a neighboring country or region. In these cases, outside forces can intensify a conflict without holding it captive or even fully intending to have an effect on it. For instance, states can fuel conflict in other states through their inability to control their own borders and manage their own problems—problems that might include the unwelcome presence of rebels from a neighboring state or a flourishing illegal arms trade conducted by homegrown criminals. In Central Asia, Uzbek rebels use Tajikistan's territory as a staging ground for their activities against the government of Uzbekistan, a situation that serves to intensify Tajikistan's own conflict and lawlessness.

In many instances, however, states deliberately promote conflict in other states to further their own strategic interests or to retaliate for the actions of neighbors. For instance, Uganda and Sudan have both been engaged in protracted civil wars. The Sudanese conflict revolves around the challenge of the Sudan People's Liberation Army (SPLA), an insurgent rebel movement based in southern Sudan, to the Islamist government in Khartoum. This conflict has attracted a good deal of regional and international attention over the years. The Ugandan conflict has attracted much less attention. In Uganda, the rebels are situated in the north, in and around an area that has a long history of involvement—often on the losing side—in the country's power struggles. The strongest force among Ugandan rebels is the Lord's Resistance Army (LRA), known best internationally for kidnapping thousands of children as recruits for LRA forces.

Since the mid-1980s, reciprocal meddling and cross-border intervention in these internal conflicts have generated a high level of hostility between Sudan and Uganda, fueling and entrenching the domestic conflict in each country through the provision of direct aid and safe refuge to the rebels of its neighbor. These are dependent conflicts in the sense that they rely in some measure on Uganda-Sudan hostility and could change substantially if one or the other conflict was brought under control. Active intervention by the Carter Center starting in 1999 led to agreements between the two countries to cease assisting rebel groups, thus breaking the cycle of dependency, at least in theory. That the internal conflicts in both cases continued after the agreements were signed, however, is a sobering reminder that intractable conflicts may have multiple sources of fuel.[13] Removing one source may lower the temperature for a while but will not necessarily extinguish the conflict.

Although states are often the agents that perpetuate or spread conflict in these situations, private nonofficial groups also can hold a conflict captive or make it a dependent. This is especially true in conflicts that have produced a large diaspora population that can provide funding for one or more parties to a conflict. Removed from the day-to-day aspects of the conflict, these diaspora groups may harbor very hard-line views about tactics and possible outcomes of the conflict. The diaspora may limit the settlement options of the parties to the conflict, both by providing resources to keep the conflict alive and by threatening to withdraw their support if conflict leaders deviate from a certain path. Among the strongest supporters of the Irish Republican Army, for instance, were Irish Americans whose direct connection to Ireland may have been a few generations old but who believed in the cause of Irish unity with a radical fervor. For years, these outside groups fueled the conflict by providing funds and arms to the IRA, encouraging notions of an eventual armed victory, limiting the maneuvering room available to bridge-builders within the republican community, and complicating the role of the U.S. government in peacemaking. A similar pattern complicates the U.S. role in the Middle East and Cyprus, the Canadian position in Sri Lanka, and the French role in Algeria—to mention just a few examples.

Wards of the System

There is a final set of conflicts that are forgotten in the sense that they often end up as wards of the system, adopted by an international institution, most often the United Nations, because no one else wants to take the lead in managing or resolving them. At times, adoption by the international system is a happy event. The long wars in Mozambique, Namibia, El Salvador, and Guatemala, for instance, benefited enormously from UN involvement. The OSCE has played a very constructive role in a number of European conflicts. The Organization of Islamic States has provided the impetus for continuing talks between the Philippine government and rebel groups in Mindanao. It is, however, also important to recognize the liabilities involved in becoming a ward of the system.

Because of its charter, the United Nations is more or less obliged to respond to urgent appeals for help—provided there is some measure of support for doing so among member-states—whether or not it has the resources and capabilities to be effective.[14] Alvaro de Soto, the UN secretary-general's representative in the El Salvador, Cyprus, and Western Sahara peacemaking efforts, referred to this phenomenon when describing the United Nations as a "hospital emergency room," which gears up to save the desperate patient before investigating whether he or she is covered by insurance and has a family member who will assume responsibility and provide posthospitalization care.[15] During the 1990s, the United Nations was barely capable of responding to the multiple demands of adopting conflicts in Somalia, Bosnia, Mozambique, Rwanda, Congo, Angola, El Salvador, Guatemala, and Kosovo. Its record in this period is very mixed: Mozambique and El Salvador, for instance, could be counted as successes, but Bosnia, Rwanda, Congo, and Angola demonstrated the weakness of an underresourced and undersupported warden of war-torn states.

The problems besetting the United Nations are also experienced by regional organizations. The Liberian civil war, for instance, was neither neglected nor orphaned, as there was significant regional engagement in the form of a predominantly Nigerian peacekeeping force (ECOMOG). Although both the United Nations and the Organization of African Unity (OAU) gave support to the ECOMOG mission, this support was understaffed and underfunded. As Adekeye Adebajo writes, "the reduced strategic value of Africa after the end of the Cold War, coupled with international opposition to military rule in Nigeria (the key contributor to ECOMOG), resulted in the international community, particularly the United States, failing to provide the necessary logistical and financial support for the intervention."[16] As a consequence, the ECOMOG effort was weak; it was further undermined by regional resentment of the Nigerian force, which became a factor in the peacemaking venture and resulted in turning the peacekeeping force into a party to the conflict. In this case, the attention that the conflict and the ECOMOG intervention had from the international system was perfunctory and failed to include measures that would support the effort to end the fighting.

From Orphaned to Captive to Adopted

The above categories capture a conflict at one particular stage in its cycle. For some conflicts, that stage lasts for many years. Other intractable conflicts, however, move swiftly from one stage to another during the cycle of violence. When fighting breaks out in a conflict, the outside world make take a while to react, and until it does, the conflict may be neglected or orphaned. As the conflict continues, it may become the captive or dependent of outside forces that stoke the violence and bolster the combatants' capacities for continued military action. During this time, a conflict may be adopted by an interested peacemaker, but the fact that there are internal and external sources of conflict increases the complexity and makes an effective intervention difficult to design and manage. The complexity may lead the third-party peacemaker to disengage, orphaning the conflict, or it might lead to heightened engagement in a regional peacemaking effort, which in the end may result in a settlement.

Returning once again to the case of Rwanda, we have an example of a conflict that followed a tragic course in terms of third-party engagement. The United States and major European states played an important role in efforts to bring peace to Rwanda as it experienced cross-border incursions, state failure, and ethnic militancy in the early 1990s. This engagement, however, proved to be superficial and short-lived; after the initial flurry of Western concern, the Rwandan conflict became orphaned as international attention waned. The United Nations stepped in to help implement the 1993 Arusha accords, while Western powers maintained a hands-off watching brief, and Rwanda became a ward of the system. At this moment, the United Nations was especially overtaxed with peacekeeping responsibilities given to it by the Security Council, whose leading members — grown cautious after the peacekeeping disasters in Somalia — failed to provide robust support for the United Nations' involvement in Rwanda. By refusing to recognize or respond to rapidly deteriorating conditions in Rwanda in the ensuing months, these states and the UN system itself created conditions for the wholesale slaughter that occurred in early 1994. The UN Security Council's failure to provide sufficient troops to keep the peace was followed by the decision to pull out the modest peacekeeping contingent on the ground, and the abandonment of Rwanda was complete. After most of the damage had been done, the United States and France mounted separate, brief military actions to create humanitarian enclaves for refugees fleeing the Hutu-Tutsi strife. But from this point on, Rwanda and Central African politics would be dictated by the men with the guns. In the aftermath of the Rwandan genocide and the ensuing scrambles for power in Congo in the mid- and late 1990s, the Western powers largely took a backseat to African or UN initiatives, offering only sporadic backing for these measures. Thus, in a few short years, the Rwandan conflict had moved from adopted to abandoned to a UN wardship to abandoned to barely adopted again.

Like Rwanda, some cases limp into the international emergency ward but re-emerge to attract the attention of other actors at a later point, as happened in 2000–2001 in Sierra Leone, when the British displayed significant interest in this small, long-neglected West African nation. Joint British-UN leadership of peacemaking in this case included both political/diplomatic and military components and a willingness to tackle the regional destabilization mounted from Charles Taylor's Liberia. The United Kingdom's determined and focused actions turned around what would otherwise have been a major UN peacekeeping failure and created conditions for considerable success in reversing the regional rot spreading from Liberia. In the process, Sierra Leone moved from being a neglected conflict to being a dependent on neighboring Liberia's turmoil and then to being adopted by the United Nations and a leading member of the Security Council.

WHY DON'T OUTSIDERS GET INVOLVED AND WHAT HAPPENS WHEN THEY DON'T?

A variety of reasons explain why the international community ignores in some cases both the conditions that lead to violent conflict

and the violent conflict itself. Among the strongest reason is the tradition of respect for national sovereignty and the strong prohibition
against interfering in the internal affairs of an independent state.
This reluctance to engage in domestic matters may have played a
role in the lack of external engagement in conflicts such as those in Sri
Lanka, East Timor, and the Democratic Republic of Congo, putting
these countries off-limits for much of their conflict histories. For instance, various states deplored the harsh Mobutu regime in Congo or
Indonesia's blatant dismissal of East Timor's claims for independence
or self-determination, but they could not—or would not—openly
challenge these governments' legitimacy, partly from fear of receiv-
ing the same treatment themselves from other members of the international community. Respect for national sovereignty, after all, is a
two-way street: once national sovereignty has been successfully challenged in one or two cases, the door opens to similar challenges to
other states. This reluctance by states to question sovereignty is
even more pronounced in certain intergovernmental agencies, which
of course are tools of states.

Until the early 1990s, the assertion of state control and respect
for national sovereignty hampered nonofficial organizations such as
human rights groups and humanitarian agencies in their efforts to
attract international attention to the human suffering that can be both
a cause and a consequence of conflict. These organizations might
have been able to publicize human rights abuses if they could get into
a country to witness the misery, but they rarely could gain access.
When they did, they rarely could gain the ear of powerful decision
makers in other countries who might put pressure on the offending
regimes to improve domestic conditions. With official organizations
reluctant to act and nonofficial organizations powerless to do so, a
number of conflicts were effectively denied any outside assistance in
the areas of conflict prevention and peacemaking.

Other factors that limit the interest and ability of outsiders to
get involved in a peacemaking effort include

◆ the difficulty outsiders face in gaining entry into a conflict,
  because a party resists outside interference or because a neighboring major power prevents it;

◆ the complexity of internal politics, which may discourage engagement because third parties are wary of assuming the potential responsibility of undercutting an existing regime and find
it hard to identify leaders with sufficient legitimacy to become
valid negotiating partners;

◆ the failure of previous third-party efforts to aid in peacemaking,
which may prompt the third party to pass on an opportunity to
intervene;

◆ a level of violence insufficient — in the eyes of reluctant third-
party states — to warrant intervention;

◆ a judgment by the international community that the conflict is
containable and does not merit engagement;

◆ a calculation by potential intervenors that the objective of stopping the conflict may be less important than other strategic
objectives; and

◆ the prevalence of the belief that this conflict is someone else's
problem.

Although it is difficult to generalize about the consequences of
the absence of third-party involvement in a peace process, it is possible to identify some costs. Many costs spring from the inability of
the conflict parties to establish any kind of relationship with their
enemies that might lead to negotiation. Attitudes harden, lines of communication break down, and hostile responses to any reconciliatory
gesture from the other side become habitual. At this point, the lack
of trust between parties can extend to refusing to recognize each
other's leaders as legitimate negotiating partners, as has often happened in the Middle East. In other cases, parties are able to continue
to negotiate, or at least to send signals to the other side, but the repeated breakdown of talks or agreements leads both — or all — parties
to use past negotiations as a political weapon for attacking the adversary and to dismiss possible solutions out of hand.[17] Bases for agreement become worn-out or discredited and cannot be resuscitated
by the parties themselves. Once these potential solutions have been
discredited, each party may perceive the risk of reviving them to be

intolerably high, and lacking third-party help to reframe the issues, parties become trapped by their previous actions and statements.

WHAT IS TO BE DONE
ABOUT FORGOTTEN CONFLICTS?

This chapter has argued that the absence of third-party assistance can accentuate intractability and, conversely, that its presence can mitigate intractability. This chapter has also explored a variety of types of forgotten conflicts and examined how a conflict may migrate between these states of being as events unfold outside and within the conflict. The question remains of what can be done about forgotten conflicts. Some would argue that direct and forceful intervention by major states is the only third-party remedy for intractable conflicts, forgotten or not, because only major states possess the resources and capacities to stay the course and provide the incentives and disincentives necessary to change the behavior of the parties to the conflict or change the situation on the ground. According to this view, UN or nonofficial engagement is only a second-best alternative to intervention by a major power.

There are major shortcomings with this approach in the case of forgotten conflicts. As chapter 2 pointed out, a major power is not a neutral third party but acts out of perceived self-interest that may or may not match the interests of one or more parties to the conflict. The recognition that some connection exists between managing or resolving a conflict and its own national interests is key to explaining the willingness of a major power to commit high-level staff and considerable time and money to brokering peace in someone else's conflict. In the case of forgotten conflicts, it is precisely this recognition that is lacking: no major state or grouping of major states finds a compelling reason to become engaged with the peacemaking process. In such situations, nonstate actors or international organizations may be the only available third parties—and thus the debate over whether they are second best is irrelevant. It is arguable, in fact, that in the case of forgotten conflicts, these intergovernmental and nongovernmental organizations bring resources and capacities particularly suited to addressing intractable situations in forgotten conflicts.

The United Nations and other international organizations are in the forefront in terms of attempting to rescue forgotten conflicts. Indeed, as is recognized by the term "wards of the system," the United Nations and regional organizations typically adopt forgotten conflicts as part of their mission. This is not to say that the results of UN action will necessarily be helpful. On the contrary, the consequences can be disastrous in terms of bringing peace to troubled zones. Margaret Anstee's account of the neglected and underfunded UN attempt to implement the 1991 Bicesse Accords in the Angolan war makes clear the trouble that the United Nations can get into when the members of the Security Council are not seriously engaged in the mediation effort.[18] Nonetheless, the involvement of the United Nations does serve to focus international attention on forgotten conflicts and to give the third-party role greater legitimacy—at least in the eyes of the conflict parties, and often in the eyes of the member-states—than the involvement of any other organization can confer. When the United Nations engages, an obscure conflict may remain in the shadows, but it is no longer forgotten. Through his ability to appoint a special representative to a specific conflict, the secretary-general can rescue a forgotten conflict, as was the case with the Western Sahara when Kofi Annan appointed former U.S. secretary of state James Baker III as his envoy. When the Security Council backs a peace process, the United Nations can move a conflict from violence to settlement, as happened, for example, in the early and mid-1990s in the case of El Salvador. In the arena of forgotten conflicts, the United Nations can play a distinctly powerful role, but it is not the only organization that can assist an ignored or orphaned conflict and help it move to negotiation.

The Mozambique conflict illustrates a number of different roles that nonofficial organizations can play: communicator, facilitator, and mediator.[19] While this is an unusual story—examples of direct mediation by nonofficial organizations are relatively rare—it is still instructive to examine how an Italian Catholic lay organization managed to gain entry and serve as an intermediary in an inaccessible intractable conflict. In the 1970s, Mozambique descended into internationalized civil war for a number of reasons: a wretched colonial history that left no legacy of robust or even nascent state institutions and governance structures to manage the transition to self-rule and democracy; the abrupt departure of Portugal, the colonial power; an unstable regional climate, with Southern Africa on the verge of major turmoil because of the struggle being waged against apartheid and because of extensive foreign intervention; and a deeply divided international system.

Portugal's withdrawal from its African colonies in 1974 left Mozambique suddenly orphaned while setting the stage for vicious regional power struggles. The outside world, distracted by many competing demands for its attention, did not react in any consistent way to these conflicts for several years. The mid-1970s was a time of rapid change in Africa, as the United States and the Soviet Union squared off in proxy wars, the struggle against apartheid in South Africa intensified, and the liberation movements in Rhodesia challenged the pariah Smith government. Because of these changes, the unsettled and fragile internal situation in Mozambique was quickly internationalized and transformed into a devastating civil war. The white Rhodesian regime and then the South African regime chose to support regional and ethnic elements disaffected from the new Mozambique government controlled by the Marxist-oriented Frelimo liberation movement. In time, this resulted in the emergence of a militarily potent but politically opaque opposition movement known as Renamo. The Soviet Union and its allies provided support to the new government, while the leading Western nations, including the United States, sought to broker improved regional relationships across the borders of Mozambique, South Africa, and Rhodesia (Zimbabwe, from 1980). With the engagement of these outside actors, newly independent Mozambique moved from being orphaned to becoming a captive of the surrounding southern African struggles. Its captive status lasted for approximately fifteen years.

Throughout the 1980s, the Soviet Union, the United States, other major Western nations, and neighboring Zimbabwe provided support to Mozambique's government, while South Africa assisted

Renamo. A number of U.S.-sponsored agreements between Mozambique and South Africa fell apart as elements within the South African government continued to harass the Mozambican government. With this outside encouragement for the rebels, and with both sides determined to win a military victory, the parties had little incentive to settle. The end of the Cold War and the beginnings of fundamental change in South Africa released Mozambique from this captivity, reduced the level of outside resources that had sustained warfare, and presented an opportunity to end a conflict that had left more than one hundred thousand people dead and more than four million displaced. At this point in the Mozambique story, however, the outside mediator was not a powerful state but a Catholic lay charity that previously had focused largely on helping the poor in Italy.

Why was a nongovernmental organization with few of the attributes that we normally associate with successful mediation able to play the role of principal mediator in this brutal and protracted war? First, the organization, the Community of Sant'Egidio, entered the conflict slowly, at the invitation of a local, highly respected figure, the bishop of Beira. Over time, it established relationships with both parties to the conflict. Second, serving initially as an intermediary between the Catholic Church and the government of Mozambique, Sant'Egidio gained the trust of both parties, in part through its own network of relationships in Italy. Third, in addition to representing the powerful moral force of the Vatican, Sant'Egidio also benefited from the intercession of Enrico Berlinguer, the head of the Communist Party in Italy, who was recognized by the Mozambican government as an influential international figure. Together, these factors gave Sant'Egidio legitimacy and a good deal of intangible clout.[20]

Sant'Egidio also, however, created allies among states that could provide leverage. It worked closely with the Italian government, which hosted two years of peace talks in Rome, gave financial support, and provided a role model of a democracy built on contending forces. Sant'Egidio kept the U.S. government informed about what it was doing. U.S. support was important, but because the United States was not acceptable to the Mozambican government as a mediator, it was also important that the United States was willing to take a backseat. American officials offered technical expertise on military, legal, economic, and institutional issues in the negotiations. In addition, neighbors such as Zimbabwe, South Africa (by the early 1990s undergoing rapid internal change), Malawi, and Kenya, as well as the British, Portuguese, and French governments and the Vatican, also offered support for the process. Through these strategic alliances, Sant'Egidio was able to borrow leverage and power and broaden the base of its mediation. Whether it would have ever asked for the application of hard, coercive power and, if it had asked, whether the states involved would have ever granted it, is another question. What is important, however, is that this NGO placed itself at the center of a network of sources of power it could employ. Far from being a powerless institution, it was endowed with considerable, if intangible, resources and backed by allies with an ability to supply or withhold incentives to the parties.

The Mozambique experience highlights the vital importance of relationships; the unique ingredients (including hard work) that go into developing these relationships; and the need to build a larger network that can sustain the mediation at rocky periods that all peace processes—but especially in intractable conflicts—go through. This case underscores what can be accomplished when an NGO clearly understands its capacity as well as its limits and works openly to build relationships and to attract the cooperation and support of major international actors.

Other important roles that nonofficial actors can play in forgotten intractable conflicts include

- ◆ publicizing conflicts in national capitals and through the news media so that they are harder to ignore;

- ◆ building local capacity for peacemaking by improving negotiation skills;

- ◆ facilitating contact between influential (although not necessarily official) members of the contesting parties;

- ◆ serving as the eyes and ears of the international community in a conflict; and

◆ bolstering an official peace process (whether state based or led by the United Nations) through collaborative programs and building support for peace in the larger community.[21]

Most of the activities listed above serve to bring into focus a conflict forgotten by the international community. Sometimes, however, the low-level, quiet diplomacy that nonofficial organizations can engage in is as important as their role in publicizing forgotten conflicts. A good illustration of this quiet diplomacy is the part played by a nonofficial Norwegian research institute in the Middle East peace process. Although the conflict between Israelis and Palestinians could never be called forgotten, in the early 1990s it was deeply stuck and as intractable as it had ever been. In 1992, aided by its long-standing ties to Israel, urged by its Swedish neighbors, and supported cautiously by the United States, the Norwegian government made possible the first direct negotiations between Palestinians and Israelis. As a third party, Norway did not attempt to influence the content of the negotiation but provided the means for these talks to occur. In this effort, the government was aided by the Institute for Applied Social Sciences (FAFO), a Norwegian research institute that had been conducting standard-of-living studies in the West Bank and Gaza, where it had developed good ties with the Palestinians. No less important, the research institute also had strong ties to the Norwegian government, improving the chances for good communication and coordination among the Norwegian third-party institutions.

In this case, the value that the research center brought to the process was not through its contribution to the peacemaking strategy, although through its director, it was an active partner of the Norwegian government. Its contribution came instead through its long-term, nonpolitical relationships in the area, which made it an appropriate interlocutor for the parties, and its ability to provide an excuse—"cover"—for the many flights to and from Oslo that the parties had to make. This cover, and the successful efforts of the Norwegian government to preserve the secrecy of these controversial meetings, allowed the parties to deny, if necessary, that direct talks were proceeding or that there had ever been direct talks.[22] The research institute's involvement allowed the parties to conduct secret, unofficial talks and, thus, to take risks inherent in direct talks that they would not take in well-publicized, official negotiations.

CONCLUSION

The example of the Oslo process shows that an NGO and a state with resources can work together to create the opportunity and means for parties to an intractable conflict to engage in direct talks for the first time. The Mozambique example also highlights the importance of collaboration among key third parties—in this case, Sant'Egidio and the governments of major powers and neighboring states with interests in resolving the conflict in Mozambique. In this conflict, the same supportive relationships among third parties, this time between the key states and the United Nations, characterized the peace implementation stage.

Collaboration among third parties is essential for successful mediation, no matter whether the conflict is protracted or recent, acknowledged or forgotten. As we note elsewhere, long-term combatants know how to manipulate outsiders for their own ends. Offer these seasoned fighters the opportunity to set one third-party solution against another, and they will make the most of it. The lack of a common objective and game plan on the part of the third parties also dilutes the pressure on the parties to make hard decisions. Working together, third parties can create a plan to move a peace process along and can give the plan momentum, layering their efforts even as they each work in their own area of comparative advantage.[23]

In the cases of intractable conflicts, however, collaboration is crucial, as few outside parties can or will engage in trying to help the parties achieve peace. Nonofficial organizations, smaller states, and international organizations bring strengths to these situations—long-established relationships with the conflict parties, training programs that improve negotiation and dialogue skills, educational seminars that expose the parties to different ideas and different ways of framing the conflict—that are not usually found in the repertoire of powerful states. And yet, these strengths are important contributions to the capacity to make peace—a capacity that must be in place before serious talks can begin.

This work in support of peace processes extends beyond engagement with the belligerent factions to include other social groups and constituencies, as well as external actors. Just as parties to a conflict benefit from a reframing of the issues and options available, so, at times, do powerful peacemakers. Given the many factors inhibiting major powers from taking the lead in intractable conflicts, these powers sometimes need facilitators and other agents that can reframe the issues, build international consensus, and point out options for intervention.

The importance of these activities for the forgotten conflicts cannot be overemphasized. Neglected, abandoned, and inaccessible conflicts run a heightened risk of remaining intractable because the parties receive no constructive outside help in resolving the issues that divide them or even in starting negotiations. If and when a conflict eventually makes it onto the international agenda, the final intervention may be the work of powerful states or of the international community acting in concert. Before this stage is reached, however, much work needs to be done. Persistent engagement by nonofficial actors, international organizations, or small but committed states can focus attention on these forgotten conflicts and the possibilities for doing something about them. The chapters that follow offer advice that is as relevant to these actors as it is to major state actors.

4

The Mediator's Environment

THE ATMOSPHERE OF AN INTRACTABLE CONFLICT may be charged or indifferent, hopeful or fatalistic, but it will certainly bear the marks of a long, entrenched fight and many previous attempts at reconciliation. The mediator will have to deal with attitudes and conditions created by the intractable nature of the conflict as well as those created by the conflict itself. In a long conflict, the parties know each other very well. They know how the other side will react to specific proposals even before those proposals are put on the table. They know how much leeway their opponents have to compromise before hard-line supporters withdraw their support. They know how to manipulate the various third parties in order to play one off the other. They know how they benefit from continued fighting and what they would lose from acceding to peace. By this time, the world, in the guise of informed outsiders, also knows a lot about the conflict. It knows the issues and the players, and how the players' identities are caught up in the conflict. It knows that the conflict can be contained, that it is not such a big threat to regional or international security as to demand intervention. It knows about the many failed third-party efforts to do something about the conflict, and it thinks it knows why each failed. Welcome to the mediator's multifaceted environment.[1]

How much control the mediator has over this environment depends in part on what institution he or she is representing. Mediators representing significant powers providing the kinds of incentives and disincentives that move along a peace process may be able to do a great deal to shape an intervention effort. When Richard

Holbrooke brokered the Dayton accords, the history of NATO bombing and the determination of the United States to use both carrots and sticks to stop the fighting formed the backdrop to the mediation. These were elements of the mediation environment that the mediator had control over and could deploy to an end—whether to halt the violence, to stymie its regional spread, or simply to manage the situation until better moments for negotiation opened up. If the significant power is also a democracy, however, the mediator will be subject to open criticism of his or her efforts and will face the ever-present possibility that the peace process will become politicized, not just in the area in conflict but in the mediator's home environment.[2]

If the mediator represents the United Nations, other conditions apply. The United Nations confers international legitimacy on an intervention, separating the mediation effort from the foreign policy concerns on any single state and freeing the mediator from the constant task of convincing government colleagues and international allies of the wisdom of banking on this mediation effort. The United Nations, however, is an intergovernmental organization and as such brings its own set of constraints: dissension among the permanent members of the Security Council, contending agendas between the Security Council and the secretary-general's office, a mammoth bureaucracy, and very limited resources.

In contrast, if the mediator represents an NGO, he or she may have a great deal of freedom of movement but will also have few points of leverage and almost no ability to induce or force the parties to the conflict to change their behavior. In order to shape the mediation, NGO mediators must rely on persuasion, help from other third parties, and luck.

Even in situations in which the mediator can shape some part of the intervention effort, however, much of the mediator's environment reflects circumstances and dynamics that lie outside of his or her control: the robustness of institutional support, the play of international politics, the stability of the conflict region, and, most important, the nature and interactions of the conflict itself.[3] While mediators representing states may have a greater ability to influence the conflict situation than do those representing international or nongovernmental organizations, all mediators operate in uncertain, complex environments. As in every complex situation, there are many layers to this environment, including the individual mediator's personal situation; the mediator's institutional base and the political context within which it operates; and, of course, the on-the-ground environment — the history, nature, and dynamics of the conflict itself.

PERSONAL CIRCUMSTANCES AND CHALLENGES

A lively debate among educators and diplomats centers on whether good mediators are born or made. The particular characteristics of quick-wittedness, firmness, flexibility, high tolerance for ambiguity, and a grasp of what motivates people are without doubt traits you are born with. A deep knowledge of the conflict and a personal history or standing that draws the trust of the conflict parties, however, is a combination of individual characteristics, education, professional calling, outside circumstances, and blind luck. Somewhere in this combination, an ability to craft a strategy and understanding of the potential tools play a part. Looking at the experience of effective mediators, it is clear that both nature, in the form of personal characteristics and at times family ties, and nurture — for instance, opportunities, education, and experience — are important.[4]

No matter what their background, most mediators are doing something else when they are tapped to undertake a peacemaking effort. Senator George Mitchell was preparing to retire from the U.S. Senate and enter private life when asked by the White House to put together a trade conference for Northern Ireland. This request eventually resulted in his appointment as chairman of the Independent Body, a three-person mediating team for Northern Ireland. Aldo Ajello was assistant secretary-general in the UN Development Programme — far from the halls of political activity — when he was tapped to oversee the implementation of the peace treaty between Frelimo and Renamo in Mozambique. Landrum Bolling was a private person, a former university president who was asked by the Quakers' American Friends Service Committee to assess possible roles for that institution to play, when he became involved in the

Middle East peace process. There are, of course, exceptions: some mediators become involved in a process precisely because of their professional affiliation, as was the case with Middle East coordinator Dennis Ross during the Clinton administration.

For all of these individuals, lives had to be put on hold as they grappled with their assignments. Drawn into regions of conflict for weeks if not months, they became absorbed by the demands of the specific circumstances, issues, and actors they had to deal with. Most mediators do not intend to become so engaged. One practitioner account after another notes that the mediator thinks that his or her involvement will be a six-month commitment at the most. Ahmedou Ould-Abdallah, the Mauritanian special representative of the UN secretary-general to Burundi, thought he would be finished in three months rather than the two years he devoted to the simmering Burundi conflict. David Owen was assured by Cyrus Vance that their joint tenure as cochairs of the Steering Committee of the International Conference on the Former Yugoslavia would last six months, not the thirty-six months that it actually lasted. George Mitchell's first reading of his assignment in January 1995 was that it was part-time and would entail only a few months' work. The Good Friday Agreement, signed on April 10, 1998, turned out to be the result of three years' intensive negotiation. For those who take up the challenge of mediation, all aspects of personal life are affected: family, friends, professional aspirations, plans not undertaken. Like waging war, mediating an intractable conflict requires a large commitment of time, energy, and other resources.

A common perception is that mediators become involved in a conflict because they have special knowledge of the issues and parties involved in, and of the circumstances surrounding, the conflict. This does, indeed, often hold true—as, for example, in the cases of Maître Alouine Blondin Beye, a well-respected jurist from Mali who was appointed UN special representative in the Lusaka process in Angola, and of former South African president Nelson Mandela, acted for years as mediator for the conflict in Burundi. However, mediators are also selected because of other characteristics: an international reputation, a proven ability to facilitate agreements, and acceptability in the eyes of an important domestic constituency. For instance, John Danforth was acceptable as President George W. Bush's special representative in Sudan to Christian groups in the United States because Danforth is not only a former senator but also an ordained minister.

All mediators, whether they have special knowledge or not, face a personal challenge in mastering the volume of information surrounding the conflict: the facts and perceptions that undergird the conflict, the parties, the issues and how they have been articulated, changes in negotiating stances, internal and external circumstances that might influence the outcome of negotiations, and the benefits that continued violence brings and the identity of the people who reap them. A characteristic of any conflict is the construction of a mythology of the war, built up carefully over time. The role of the third party is to listen, interpret, and somehow move the parties beyond their intransigence. An intractable conflict, however, exacerbates the problem of getting adequate, accurate information, because each party to the conflict has its own version of important events, a version that presents its case and grievances in the best possible light and those of its enemies in dark shadows. No matter how good the intelligence available to a mediator, he or she may find it impossible to judge a case on its merits.

When President Bill Clinton made his first visit to Northern Ireland, he met Ian Paisley, head of the Democratic Unionist Party and a fierce supporter of continued union with the United Kingdom, and Gerry Adams, head of Sinn Féin and an equally fierce supporter of a united Ireland. "Paisley immediately launched into a unionist point of view. It was a fascinating story, well told, totally one-sided, and yet persuasive if the listener knew nothing else about Northern Ireland. . . . Paisley and his group left, and a few minutes later Adams came in with his entourage. . . . Almost exactly the same thing happened. Adams delivered the history of Northern Ireland for the nationalist point of view. It was a fascinating story, well told, also persuasive."[5] Whose story was right? These litanies of injury and resentment were so interwoven with myth, emotion, and subjective interpretation that it was hard to pick out the threads of actual fact, and it took three years of Mitchell's life to untangle them to the point where parties were willing to set them aside (not, however, to discard them) and consider signing a peace agreement.

Although the need for this kind of education is more acute for mediators who are not expert in the specific conflict, nearly all inter-mediaries—especially if they do not come from inside government— require briefings. Surprisingly, these are not always forthcoming, even from the mediator's home institution. Ould-Abdallah's experi-ence in the United Nations is not uncommon: "I was told by the under-secretary-general for political affairs to take up my new post within forty-eight hours. When I asked for a briefing . . . I was given instead only a thin file with the latest news dispatches on Burundi."[6] He finally turned to his own resources and arranged for a briefing through friends at the French and Belgian foreign min-istries. Sant'Egidio, the private Italian charity nominated for the 2002 Nobel Peace Prize, had no experience in political facilitation and had not worked at the political level in Mozambique before it became involved with that conflict. The mediators had guidance from the bishop of Beira, a close associate who had made the original re-quest for Sant'Egidio involvement, but much had to be learned on the job through nonofficial contacts, without the benefit of classified reports or expert briefings.[7]

Major disruptions to everyday life, substantial commitments of time and energy, and great difficulty in mastering a complex brief and understanding the story behind the conflict are personal challenges that mediators experience when engaging with an intractable con-flict. Equally challenging is the institutional home of the mediator, which can be helpful or hurtful—or typically both at the same time.

INSTITUTIONAL BASE AND POLITICAL CONTEXT

Outside mediators in any conflict have an institutional base—a gov-ernment, a multilateral organization, an NGO—from which they draw staff, financial resources, and credibility. Important as these home institutions are in any mediation process, they are critical in dealing with the high-risk environment of intractable conflicts. Two elements are especially valuable. The first is the willingness and ability of the institution to commit to a long-term process. Sponsors need to be prepared for a marathon—though they need not necessarily convey this recognition to other audiences. Given the complexity of the issues and the deeply ingrained attitudes of the antagonists, intervention efforts in intractable conflicts are rarely single episodes or short engagements. Even so, preserving the ability to set time limits may be an effective tool for the mediator, and thus signals from the home institution about how long it is prepared to support the third-party role can complicate a mediator's life. The second key element is the capacity of the institution to offer incentives and disincentives in support of the peacemaking effort. These incentives and disincentives are often helpful in moving the parties to a conflict from violence to political negotiation. Sometimes, these carrots and sticks are tangible and involve the promise of aid or the threat of sanctions. At other times, they are intangible and involve the approval or censure of the international community. In order to make a long-term commitment and to muster the necessary incentives or disincentives, an institution must be ready to mediate, a topic to which we will return in the next chapter

When mediation is undertaken as a stopgap measure or, worse still, for the sake of appearances, the sponsoring institution may offer little support to the mediator. Even when the sponsoring institution intends to give its full support to a mission, things can go wrong. In an intractable conflict, the mediator has many third-party predecessors, each of whom may hold very strong views on the conflict, the peace process, and what does and does not work. Many of these predecessors may come from the current mediator's home institution and may find themselves unable to resist publicly criticizing the new mediation effort or predicting its results. When it was announced in June 2001 that George Tenet, director of the Central Intelligence Agency, would meet with Israeli and Palestinian security forces in an attempt to breathe life into a shattered Middle East peace process, one State Department official immediately responded critically. "You're either in or you're out," said the Middle East specialist. "This is neither."[8] Lack of support from colleagues who have themselves experienced rounds of intractability can be just as debilitating as being undercut by the parties to the conflict.

Mediators, especially when they represent the interests of a superpower such as the United States, also have to be concerned about the reaction of domestic constituencies and bases of political support to the offer of third-party services in intractable conflict settings. When different domestic groups mobilize in favor of or against a peace process, the reverberations can be felt at the highest levels. Looking back on the Camp David talks between Israel and Egypt that were led by President Jimmy Carter, William Quandt notes, "Besides understanding the Palestinian issue less well than the Egyptian-Israeli dispute, Carter also found that the constraints of the American political system came into play whenever he tried to deal with the Palestinian question. Even to refer to Palestinian rights or to a Palestinian homeland could set off shock waves within the American Jewish community. These would be instantly felt in Congress and relayed back to the White House. Before long, Carter learned to say less in public, thereby giving the impression that he was backing down under domestic pressure."[9]

The issue here is not just that domestic politics can interfere with or complicate a mediatory role. That is potentially true in all conflicts. In intractable conflicts, however, the sheer duration allows outsiders to develop strong and sometimes polarizing views of the various issues and actors that reflect their own political positions. When this polarization and extreme characterization occur, third-party elites may find it difficult to engage in any peacemaking activity because one or both of the conflict parties are politically controversial or divisive. For instance, U.S. officials who mediated in the Northern Ireland, Palestinian, and South African cases were targets of political criticism at home for dealing with representatives of the IRA, PLO, and ANC.

The news media play a significant role in shaping these political attitudes, but they also affect the mediator's environment in other ways. On the one hand, they can choose not to cover a conflict, as was the case with the conflicts in Georgia, Central Asia, Sri Lanka, and, until September 2001, Afghanistan. On the other hand, they can turn a spotlight on a conflict, as they did in Somalia and Rwanda, forcing policymakers to commit to action or to explain their inaction. Whatever role they play, they will be a constant companion to the mediator, second-guessing the strategy and critiquing the results while uncovering new facts and perspectives. Consequently, arranging quiet contact between parties — opportunities for leaders or their surrogates to explore grounds for starting talks — is less and less an option for most mediators, especially if they represent a powerful state or the United Nations. Norway managed to provide this service to the Israelis and Palestinians who laid the groundwork for the Oslo accords in 1993, but only thanks to a good dose of subterfuge and more-or-less outright lying.[10] Nonofficial intermediaries may have an easier time remaining below the media's radar and protecting the parties to the conflict from premature exposure, but even for them, the instantaneous relay of information and the growing use of electronic technology to transmit stories, events, rumors, and criticisms color the environment in which they work.

Finally, a critical element in political support is the willingness of other actors in the international community to back up the mediator's effort. Other actors could include states with strong interests in the outcome — for instance, Russia in Eurasia — or the United Nations, or the international human rights community. The cast of characters may change over time, but the likelihood in a protracted conflict is that the interested outsiders will become as entrenched in their attitudes toward the conflict as the direct parties and will greet any new peacemaking initiative with a mixture of skepticism and hope.

THE ON-THE-GROUND ENVIRONMENT

Describing his tenure as secretary of state, James A. Baker III recollects, "the last thing I wanted to do was to touch the Middle East peace process." He saw the Arab-Israeli dispute as a "pitfall to be avoided" and with remarkable candor remembers about his past experience, "[It] left me rather cynical about the Mideast quagmire and, moreover, chagrined that I had not followed my original instincts to steer a wide berth." Nevertheless, in 1991 he decided to press for a new round of diplomacy to help resolve the Arab-Israeli dispute. Three weeks after the end of Operation Desert Storm, he saw that the liberation of Kuwait by an American-led coalition of forces had transformed the geopolitics of the region, providing "a dramatic new opportunity to press for peace in the Middle East."[11]

His image of a quagmire and his reluctance to engage with the Middle East, however, strike a familiar chord among mediators who get involved in intractable conflicts. What do third parties face in terms of a mediation environment when they try to establish the context for negotiation between parties that have fought each other for years? As a conflict drags on, participants—both leaders and the wider public—become inured to the conditions produced by the war. Many people learn to profit from the conflict. Fighting becomes a normal way of life, and the identities of both leaders and combatants become wrapped up in the conflict. Over time, barriers to negotiation arise, barriers that have little to do with the original causes of the conflict. Some of the barriers are psychological, some are political, cultural, and economic, and some grow out of the parties' long experience of negotiating with mediators.

Psychological Barriers

In intractable conflict settings, all parties to the dispute typically harbor a sense of victimization that reduces their desire (and motivation) to seek any kind of negotiated solution. As a consequence, the parties will procrastinate and refuse to engage the other side(s) in any sort of negotiated process that would explore alternatives to the status quo. A good illustration of this is the conflict in Northern Ireland. Paul Arthur, who has both studied the conflict and acted as a nonofficial mediator, explains that this conflict has been characterized by "an intimidatory culture; factionalism within the different communities; and the problems of memory." Delays in reaching any kind of solution have been plagued by "a political culture denoted for its sense of victim-hood and fatalism. . . . the desire to seek a negotiated solution was low on the list of priorities in both communities until the 1990s."[12]

Ingrained cultural or religious beliefs can also substantially raise the perceived costs of negotiated alternatives to the status quo. In reviewing the course of negotiated efforts to end the ongoing civil war in Sudan in the late 1980s, Ann Mosely Lesch observes that aside from problems posed by factional struggles and high levels of mistrust between the parties, there were religious belief systems that raised the costs of negotiated concessions and made it difficult to discuss any kind of settlement in spite of the escalating economic and political costs of the conflict to the Sudanese government. The goal of the Sudanese People's Liberation Movement (SPLM), which had emerged in the south, was to establish a "nonreligious, non-ethnic government in which all the diverse peoples of Sudan would have an equal share." However, this was not the goal of the central elites in Khartoum, who felt that the rebellion in the south could be contained by only minor concessions. This was because "the well-organized political force embodied in the NIF [National Islamic Front] adamantly opposed negotiations with the SPLM that would dilute, much less revoke, Islamic law and would weaken the Arab-centered identity of the country. . . . The government was willing to accept economic devastation and military loss for the sake of its ideology. Unless one side made an about-face in its negotiating stance, no negotiations would be meaningful."[13]

This example brings up the difficulty of unraveling the causes of conflict from the causes of intractability. The jury is still out on whether conflicts involving religion are inherently more intractable than other conflicts, whether religious-ideological issues make it harder for warring elites to compromise without being seen as betraying their principles, and whether religious disputes have a zero-sum quality that other disputes lack.

Political, Cultural, and Economic Barriers

One of the most obvious obstacles to reaching a negotiated settlement is that the parties to any intractable conflict don't want to talk to each other—at least not directly—and may even have grave reservations about entering into any kind of negotiation or discussion through a third party. As Secretary Baker recounts, even though circumstances changed dramatically immediately following the Gulf War, he realized that it was going to be an uphill battle to engage the parties in U.S.-mediated talks and to overcome what he calls the "taboo of direct talks."[14] The fact of the matter was that, since the creation of Israel in 1948, neither side wanted to talk directly to the other. Although the Egyptian-Israeli Peace Treaty of 1979 was a breakthrough of sorts, the taboo still held firm in most Arab capitals and in Israeli-Palestinian relations.

There are many reasons why the parties to an intractable dispute may refuse to talk to each other. Entering into direct negotiations may be seen as conferring legitimacy on the claims of the other side of the conflict. If sovereignty and legitimacy issues lie at the core of the conflict, the very act of entering into direct negotiations will be viewed as a major concession to the other side, a concession that not only has high (perhaps unacceptably high) costs associated with it but also carries real risks. And even if the parties agree to direct talks, the mediator may be faced with the difficult question of deciding who talks. In intractable conflict settings, when one (or more) of the parties to the conflict is highly factionalized, who speaks authoritatively for the interests of that side? Designating a representative may privilege the interests of one group over others, posing another barrier to direct negotiations.

Mediators also have to deal with the tactical habits and cultures of parties who will try to manipulate the negotiating environment to serve their own ends. Every statement or utterance by the mediator will be scrutinized by the parties, who will then leap to the airwaves to put their own spin on what is being said. The parties will try to put words in the mediator's mouth. They will resist new ideas and the messengers who bring them. These are games with a purpose. In intractable conflicts, they serve as a self-protective mechanism so that nothing serious ever happens. The parties are comfortable with the current situation; they view conflict as a way of life. These games make it impossible to move the negotiation process forward because they litter the road with tactical and procedural minefields and traps. Describing the confusion surrounding the ongoing efforts by various third-party mediators to try to negotiate an end to the conflict in Burundi in the 1990s, Fabienne Hara observed, "No protagonist in Burundi seems to want to end the search for an accord; it is a comfortable situation since it offends no one but does not necessarily require the factions to make significant compromises involving their fundamental interests. This cult of consensus, this frenzied activism, spares us from confronting the violence of conflict of interests, as expressed in the Great Lakes conflicts."[15] A similar pattern of resistance, tactical manipulation, and confusion occurred during the efforts in the 1980s to negotiate an end to the conflict in Southern Africa: "The Angolans viewed us [the mediators] with both respect and fear; they would explore our diplomacy and test our capacity to deliver the other side. Their allies, in the background, would do what they could to discredit and block us."[16]

Another barrier, especially when political groupings and movements are highly factionalized, is the tendency of political elites to "play to the demos"—that is, to cater to extreme positions and refuse to make concessions or consider negotiated options because they fear that they will undermine the political bases of their support. Again, the experience of Northern Ireland is instructive. "Politicians tended to perceive their constituents as more extreme than they really were and hence, the elite took on complementarily extreme positions in order to gain reelection." But "[t]he consequence was circular . . . electors assumed conditions were worse than they imagined and politicians matched these perceptions with ever more intransigent positions."[17]

The breakdown of the Oslo peace process in the Middle East followed a similar pattern after Prime Minister Yitzhak Rabin's assassination at the hands of a political extremist. Although U.S.-sponsored negotiations continued under the new Likud government headed by Benjamin Netanyahu, these negotiations were affected deeply by domestic political changes in Israel. Electoral reforms allowing for the direct election of the Israeli prime minister paradoxically enhanced the power and influence of minority parties in the Knesset. As a result, Netanyahu found himself in a relatively weak position politically vis-à-vis his own parliamentary coalition. Although no fan of the Oslo process, Netanyahu nonetheless found his own freedom to maneuver to be quite limited at the negotiating table and relations between Israel and its Arab neighbors worsened.

In an attempt to shore up political support, leaders at times display in political settings a ferocity and desire for military victory that seem to deny completely any possibility of a negotiated settlement until the enemy is subdued. As violence continued to mount in the Middle East during the winter of 2002–3, the mutually hostile rhetoric also mounted. Prime Minister Ariel Sharon, speaking to reporters on March 4, declared, "If the Palestinians are not being beaten, there will be no negotiations. The aim is to increase the number of losses on the other side. Only after they've been battered will we be able to conduct talks." Later that same day, Sharon told the Israeli parliament, "we are in a bitter war against a cruel and bloodthirsty enemy. We are fighting for our home and we will prevail." Hamas leader Sheik Ahmed Yassin, in a televised statement, responded, "The Zionist enemy will learn the price of aggression against our people."[18] A mediator's task of convincing leaders to retreat from their determination to beat the enemy is common to every peacemaking effort but is aggravated by the constant repetition over many years of the same threats and intransigence. The theatrics of "struggle talk" serves to rally domestic supporters, rattle the enemy, and make it difficult to remember — much less address — the original causes of the conflict. In these situations, parties settle into a ritualistic dance of "getting" the other party, baiting it politically as a corollary to the military campaign.

Finding a way for leaders to back away from this stylized conflict is complicated in societies that accept the possibility of compromise, but nearly impossible in cultures that do not. In some political cultures, issues of status and accountability can contribute to the reluctance by political elites to negotiate or make concessions out a fear of appearing to be "weak" in the eyes of their followers or constituents. Raymond Cohen refers to this as "the-loss-of-face" problem — negotiators are unwilling to sit down with the other side and/or engage in concession-making negotiations because there are higher cultural and political rewards in standing firm and sticking to one's principles than in moderating one's position in order to engage in genuine dialogue with one's adversaries. As Cohen explains, "High-context cultures [cultures in which group identity is more important

than individual identity] are also shame cultures. Standing, reputation, and honor are paramount. Outward appearances are to be
maintained at all costs. Thus the high-context negotiator has an
abiding nightmare: loss of face."[19] In high-status cultures, intractability is ineluctably wedded to political elites' own psychological
sense of vulnerability, where bargaining concessions or a change in
one's political position may be associated with personal and political weakness unless a way can be found to offset the symbolic, cultural costs that are associated with concession-making bargaining
behavior.

Disarming—particularly the disarming of rebel forces—is also
a difficult topic to address in intractable conflict settings. Even if the
parties do agree to enter into some kind of negotiations, they fear
losing negotiating leverage if they give up violence and the resort-
to-force option. Senator Mitchell calls this "the armalite and the ballot box" problem. He notes that in Northern Ireland, the IRA used
"the political process to make what gains were possible, and at the
same time maintain[ed] the use, and the threat, of violence to move
the political process along. Indeed it was an article of faith among
some republicans that the British government would change its
Northern Ireland policy only as a reaction to violence, especially in
Britain. The unionist nightmare was that they would be forced to
enter into talks with Sinn Féin while a heavily armed IRA waited
outside the door; at the first sign that Sinn Féin wasn't getting what
it wanted in the talks, the campaign of violence would resume."[20]

In his tale of the peace effort in Northern Ireland, Paul Arthur
highlights another element of difficulty: the intimidatory political
culture.[21] This dynamic is widely recognized in literature on ethnic
and revolutionary conflicts, in which armed elites impose discipline
on their own people through intimidation and readily use deadly force
to eliminate the political "middle" or the doves within their ranks.
Any hope for the growth of a moderate voice in ending a conflict is
easily killed by this intimidation.

The environment of intractable conflicts often includes potent diasporas and/or resettled refugee communities on one or both
sides. These external constituencies—for instance, Armenians, Irish

Americans, and Cubans in the United States, Tamils in Canada, Kosovar Albanians in Europe, Sudanese in the United Kingdom and the United States—may fuel conflict by channeling support to hard-line factions. Refugee communities in Arab lands surrounding Israel, in Pakistan, in Thailand, and in Rwanda and Congo have not only held on to the hope or illusion of eventually regaining their homelands but also played a role in committing host countries to such goals as the only means of eventually dispensing with the burdens and costs of playing host.

In many of today's intractable conflicts, we also have to recognize that the-armalite-and-the-ballot-box problem is a problem not just of motivation and strategic calculus but also of vested interests and a political economy that sustains the widespread availability of arms through transnational criminal networks and the illicit market for arms. These networks are sustained by an international financial system that makes it relatively easy for warlords and other racketeers to make deals and purchase arms on the open market. The challenge for third parties is not just to change the strategic motivations and calculations of the parties but also to halt or at the very least reduce the flow of weapons into the arena of conflict.

The Barriers Posed by Multiple Mediators

Since the end of the Cold War, many institutions have found themselves, if not ready, at least willing to undertake mediations. As a consequence, the number of outsiders that get involved in the conflict management process in any given conflict has risen sharply, resulting in a crowded field of third-party institutions that each mediator must deal with. Jacob Bercovitch and his colleagues have identified about four hundred distinct instances of mediation in the Balkans since the beginning of the wars that have marked the area since the early 1990s.[22] European neighbors, the United Nations, the United States, Russia, the OSCE, and myriad NGOs have launched efforts to create or consolidate peace in the region. Some of these intervention efforts have built on previous initiatives; others have been simultaneous and often competitive. This situation, repeated in many hot spots around the world, underscores an important characteristic of the mediator's environment in most intractable conflicts: the presence of multiple mediators, all trying to bring peace to the same troubled area. Multiparty mediation has advantages and disadvantages and as such presents both opportunities and costs to the principal mediator.

Benefits of multiparty mediation include the ability to facilitate third-party entry at different stages of the conflict through different mediatory institutions. An NGO may be able to gain entry at periods in the conflict when attitudes are softening or when other institutions are not interested in engaging or have been locked out by the parties; a powerful state may be able to convince or induce the parties to shift their positions at times when the United Nations or NGOs have no influence. Multiple mediators working in concert can open new avenues for dialogue, create leverage, isolate spoilers, share costs, divide risks, and, by working at both the international and the local levels, put in place the necessary elements to transform the conflict into a platform for political negotiations.

In addition to benefits, however, multiple mediators can bring serious problems, problems that can compound a conflict and add to its durability. As mediators compete for the parties' attention, they can deliver mixed messages about the international community's willingness to back a negotiating process and confusing signals about which negotiating process it is willing to back. At the same time, apparent discordance among the mediators encourages "forum shopping" among the parties to the conflict. In this situation, parties will seek to work only with those mediators that seem to favor their side and will want to change mediators as the political winds shift. Achieving smooth handoffs between mediators is a particularly challenging aspect of multiparty mediation, as much valuable information, history, and perspective can be lost in the transition from one mediator to another. In addition, the presence of a clutch of mediators allows each one to pass on to others the responsibility for defeat, thereby avoiding the stain of failed mediation and the pain of analyzing what went wrong.

No matter how the individual mediator views multiparty mediation or how well he or she understands the particular advantage of the various potential mediators, one thing is clear: in today's messy conflicts, there will always be more than one mediator. Third-party congestion is an ever-present hazard in third-party intervention, especially in long-enduring conflicts.[23]

CONCLUSION

Understanding the mediator's environment and the opportunities and constraints it presents is an understudied but important part of assessing whether an intervention is likely to be effective in any given conflict. It is, however, just a part of this assessment and as such forms a backdrop to the more obvious tasks—discussed in the next chapter—of mastering the issues at stake in the conflict, engaging the actors, and designing and implementing a mediation strategy. It is worth noting, however, that this backdrop affects every part of a mediation strategy in an intractable conflict.

While these tasks may not be substantially different from mediation in more tractable conflicts, they become more complex because of the constant or recurrent lack of ripeness within the conflict.[24] Just as this lack of ripeness contributes to fixed attitudes among the parties to the conflict, it can also lead to a fixed judgment among outside parties: "This conflict will never end because it is intractable. Were it tractable, it would have ended by now." Never mind that this reasoning is circular; it is too useful to discard. It offers an explanation for many of the long-enduring conflicts in the world today and provides an easy excuse for outsiders to do nothing. The challenge to the mediator in an intractable conflict is to encourage movement forward where possible, working on the environment within a conflict in order to make a space for political dialogue to occur. At the same time, the mediator must also develop support for the peace process within his or her own institution and in the larger political environment. The next chapters take us inside this complex set of tasks as the mediator engages in a peacemaking effort, devises strategies for the inevitable breakdown, structures an agreement, and shepherds to safety an implementation process.

Part II

Crafting the Response

5

Building a
Negotiating Strategy

SOMETIMES, THE EVENTS LEADING UP TO THE LAUNCH of a new mediation initiative are dramatic. At other times, mediation initiatives are launched quietly or even secretly, reflecting the preferred operating style or sensitivities of contending parties anxious to avoid drawing attention to an outsider's role in their dispute. In such cases, the public becomes aware of a new initiative only after something significant happens: the mediation fails, fighting escalates, or it becomes apparent that a settlement is at hand. Whether the engagement is quiet or high profile, there is a general assumption that the mediator, once appointed, will have little trouble gaining access to the feuding parties and little trouble constructing a strategy.

Reality is quite different. There are a limited number of moments, or "entry points," at which the clay of a violent conflict is soft enough to work with. These moments fall into four categories, each associated with a particular kind of development. First, a geopolitical shift in the external environment may directly impinge on the calculations of the parties and their allies. Such a pattern affected the contending parties in the Middle East after the 1991 Gulf War, in Cambodia and neighboring Indochina as the Cold War ended and the Soviet Union collapsed, and in Sri Lanka and Sudan after the events of September 11, 2001. Second, a dramatic shift may occur in the conflict's internal dynamics as a result of a sharp escalation in fighting or the prospect of descending into a deeper and bloodier abyss. Such a pattern was evident in the decisions made by key parties in the Namibia-Angola conflict in the late 1980s and in the Croat offensive preceding the Dayton summit of 1995. Third, a major change in the leadership structure of one or more parties may create openings for vigorous mediation initiatives. Just such a change appeared to play a role in the Norwegian diplomacy in Sri Lanka in 2002–3 and in the initial effort of the nongovernmental Centre for Humanitarian Dialogue in the Indonesia-Aceh conflict in 2002.

The fourth type of entry point occurs when a new mediator arrives on the scene with the skills, ideas, resources, connections, and creativity to get the warring parties' attention. This moment is our focus in this chapter. Mediators rarely inherit a viable and well-thought-out peace process and negotiating structure. The new mediator requires a fresh approach, both to distinguish this new effort from past, stalemated efforts and to utilize the potential leverage inherent in a new beginning. The stakes in getting it right are high. Failure to analyze and understand the conflict, to capture the parties' attention, to develop appropriate alliances, and to secure international backing for the mediation may lead to an early breakdown. The mediator starts by recognizing that leverage is necessary to move the parties from their current preference for conflict, and that leverage comes in many forms and shapes.

LEVERAGE

Before starting to analyze the specific dimensions of the particular conflict, the prospective mediator should begin by identifying the sources of leverage that may be available to move the parties from violence to negotiation. These potential sources of leverage may flow from the following.[1]

- ◆ The support of other states or groups of states, especially those that can help to neutralize potential opponents of the mediation, who could assist the parties in resisting or blocking a negotiated outcome.

- ◆ The balance of forces in the conflict itself, a form of influence that the mediator effectively draws from a stalemate in order to persuade recalcitrant parties that there is no military or unilateral solution.

◆ The mediator's bilateral relationships with the parties, bearing in mind at all times the necessity of keeping *both* parties under pressure to move toward settlement and avoiding imposing forms of pressure on one side that reduce or remove the pressure on the other side.

◆ The mediator's ability to influence the parties' costs and benefits, as well as their fears and insecurities. This type of leverage comes from reassurances, external guarantees, intelligence sharing, commitments to see the settlement through to full implementation, and a readiness to mobilize international resources for the dangerous transition to peace.

◆ The mediator's capacity to place a continuing series of hard questions and tough choices before the parties so that they are obliged to provide answers to the mediator. Such answers may take the form of conditional approvals from one side that can be used by the mediator to obtain mirror-image conditional approvals from the other side. Such questions may relate to the security issues inherent in winding down the conflict; confidence-building measures aimed at creating a more positive political climate and testing the sides' ability and readiness to work toward a negotiated outcome; and the political quid pro quos that lie at the heart of the political settlement, sometimes referred to as a "platform" or a "framework" of agreed-upon principles.

◆ A proposed settlement formula or package. Such leverage is typically based on selling ideas to one side that—if accepted conditionally—offer the basis for obtaining movement from the other.

◆ Donors and other third parties that are prepared to help underwrite the costs of achieving a negotiated settlement and ensure that the levels of humanitarian, social, economic, and development assistance are sufficient to effect change once a negotiated process is under way and a negotiated settlement is within sight.

STRATEGIC ANALYSIS

Recognizing that every conflict is unique, the first step in building a
negotiating strategy is an exhaustive analysis of where matters stand
in the conflict and what accounts for its intractability. Such analysis
is the essential starting point regardless of whether the mediator is
invited by the parties to enter the fray or decides to seize the initiative.
There is much to analyze: the history of the conflict and previous
efforts to resolve it; the principal actors and the nature of the issues
in dispute; the level of violence and the balance of power; conflict
dynamics and trend-lines; the external context of the conflict, including other third parties with a stake in it; and, not least, the principal
attributes, relationships, and liabilities that the mediator may have
in relation to the conflict. This last topic is worth underscoring at
the outset: mediation is a three-sided political process in which the
mediator builds and then uses relations with the other two parties to
help them reach a settlement.

A strategy is only as good as the analysis that underlies it. The
prospective mediator will have to devote considerable energy and
effort to the task of *getting to know the case.* This entails investing in and
acquiring requisite expertise from many sources: veterans of past
efforts undertaken by one's own institution or by other institutions;
country and regional specialists knowledgeable about the military,
cultural, and political circumstances of the case; seasoned observers
and close political friends of the parties who can interpret the parties'
perspective; and well-placed networkers in the diplomatic, cultural,
media, and NGO communities who are connected to the parties. The
mediator, as has been noted, will often receive little outside help in
gathering the necessary information unless he or she explicitly solic-
its such help; even then, individuals, organizations, and governments may be reluctant to share intelligence or analyses.

There is little point in considering entry in an intractable case
unless the mediator is prepared to master the negotiating brief in this
fashion. The mediator must get inside the minds of the parties and
become intimately familiar with their negotiating histories, their
taboos, and their redlines, as well as their interests and vulnerabilities,

if he or she wants to be taken seriously. The conflict is a matter of life, death, and livelihood for the people across the table from the mediator. That is why the conflict continues.

Knowing the case means mastering six basic dimensions of the conflict: parties, issues, balance of forces, timing/ripeness, history and status of negotiations, and external context. Once mastered, this information should be used to answer three questions that all prospective mediators, no matter what the size, nature, and strength of the mediator's home institution, must squarely face: Why have others failed? What's been missing in efforts to create and assemble the elements necessary to reach a deal? And am I ready to take on this task and well placed to move the parties forward toward settlement?

Parties

Knowing the parties is the first building block in the analysis. A mediator starts by identifying the *primary parties,* those directly engaged in the adversarial relationship, starting at the inner core with the armed parties responsible for (and capable of controlling) the violence. These core parties (e.g., governments, liberation movements, and warlord militias) typically are not monolithic, and thus the mediator should study their internal components, factions, and tendencies. The internal splits and fissures within the parties will become inexorably magnified by the peacemaking process; the mediator needs to assess and grasp these fault lines and their political significance.[2] Moving out from this inner core, it is necessary in many cases (especially in civil wars) to examine other political actors and constituencies with significant influence on the core parties' decision making. Such actors include interest groups such as labor, business, and religious communities. In addition, it is wise from the outset to clearly identify the *indirect parties,* such as patrons, allies, and clients, that may influence the core parties' decisions or be directly affected by such decisions and are likely, therefore, to have friends inside the core structure itself. Sometimes, these multilevel relationships are so intimate and overlapping that it is not altogether clear how to define and limit the parties, a problem that becomes operational when the time comes to figure out whom to talk to, who sits at the table, who speaks for whom, and who signs an ultimate agreement. Without answers to these questions, a mediator will only spin his or her wheels during endless rounds of circular talks.

To illustrate: A mediator will correctly identify the Indian and Pakistani governments as the core parties when looking at the conflict over Kashmir. But within and outside of this core are various factions and interests within Kashmir itself, all seeking to be heard by the mediator. These "voices" are linked in a variety of ways — historical, economic, and cultural — to a range of constituencies in India and Pakistan. A major source of the intractability of the Kashmir dispute is precisely the complexity of these relationships and the lack of any consensus on whether the Kashmiri voices should have a seat at the negotiating table and a right to approve or disapprove of proposed settlement packages. It is challenging indeed to create a mediation process in circumstances in which, one, the identity of the core parties is unclear or contested and, two, excluded voices may favor outcomes that are unacceptable to included voices. Mediation is complex enough when the third-party mediator is working exclusively with two highly centralized parties. Broadening participation guarantees procedural complexity and leads inevitably to additional substantive obstacles. Often, a mediator will need to resort to the device of "consulting" with a very wide range of actors while negotiating with the narrowest range of parties capable of making war-and-peace decisions.[3]

What is it that a mediator needs to know about these parties and actors? The short answer is: everything relevant to understanding them and becoming capable of bringing influence to bear on them. A mediator needs to grasp their political culture and decision-making systems, their leadership hierarchy and key factional elements, the distribution of power internally, and the identity of those individuals with whom it would be most useful to negotiate. A mediator also needs to know how internally coherent the parties are and to what extent party leaders are capable of making tough decisions and ensuring that they are respected by key leadership cadres and the broader society.

The simplest thing to discover about the parties is their formal, stated positions. These must be courteously acknowledged and understood as the parties' declaratory policy. Sometimes, such positions acquire totemic status and may, deliberately or otherwise, constrain leadership flexibility, thereby contributing potentially to intractability. For the mediator, the question is how to move beyond and around such positions to identify the parties' underlying political requirements and interests that may be served or threatened by continued warfare. An essential focal point is ascertaining who gains from the struggle and who would gain from its end. This analysis includes assessing tangible costs and benefits (e.g., rent-seeking and predation), as well as power, status, security, and identity considerations. A mediator will not make much progress without understanding what really motivates the parties, what they fear and perceive themselves to be vulnerable to, and, above all, what could move them out of the stalemate. In other words, the interests of the parties may, in fact, be quite different from their stated positions, and disentangling the two is a central challenge in any mediated enterprise.

Issues

Every conflict has a shape or structure consisting of the issues over which the parties are struggling. The issues tell us not only what drives the conflict but also what needs to be settled for the conflict to cease. Because they are a reflection of the parties' interests, the issues may become the basis for a tradeoff. However, the parties may articulate the issues in terms that mask rather than reveal their underlying priorities. To give three examples: The demand by one side for an end to violence or to hostile propaganda before talks can proceed may signal a lack of interest in negotiation, because it is a demand designed to be rejected. The demand that the other side's forces be demobilized and placed under external monitoring during a political transition may be an attempt to publicly emasculate the enemy. And the demand for a referendum permitting a fundamental change in the status of contested territory (for example, secession or independence) may mask a party's preference for maintaining the status quo unless that party can be guaranteed in advance control of the new entity.

The decades-long struggles for control of rural land in Colombia illustrate these points. Both the leftist-oriented guerrilla movements and the officially tolerated paramilitary groups live off the assets and agricultural production of civilian populations they coerce and control. Techniques of struggle differ, as do the combatants' declared agendas, but the guerrillas and paramilitaries occupy competing space on the Colombian food chain and do not wish to place at risk their current roles and revenue streams. The opaque quality of their political demands and their often obscure negotiating behavior can be interpreted as a broad hint that the status quo is tolerable for the elite leadership of these armed entities.[4]

Leaving aside situations in which the stated issues serve as camouflage for another agenda, the issues in a negotiation typically form the touchstones of a possible settlement. They frequently make up the agenda of the mediation process. Since they derive from the demands and interests of parties, the issues may be of asymmetrical concern to the parties—a mediator certainly hopes so: mutually exclusive interests (e.g., who controls the government, who gets the oil revenue) are hardest to handle, whereas nonintersecting interests and overlapping ones give the mediator something to work with. A key judgment to be made in the starting phase is whether a compromise deal can be reached on the basis of the issue tradeoffs available to the parties. If the issues are defined in terms that appear to exclude the chance for a dignified and balanced package, intractability is certain.

The mediator entering a stalemated, intractable conflict needs to change—through one means or another—the negotiating agenda. Deciding what issues belong on the agenda is a major challenge, not least because a mediator must define and then sell the resulting issue structure to the parties. The purpose is to frame issues so as to attract the parties by offering each of them something of value that can only be obtained from the other in the context of a package deal developed through the mediation. Accordingly, in the start-up phase, the mediator must exhaustively review ways of coming up with fresh incentives (conditioned, of course on each side's readiness to reciprocate) to attract the parties to a reinvigorated or restructured process of negotiation. If the mediator succeeds in responding to their highest-priority needs and fears, this will enlarge the pool of issue tradeoffs from which "balance" (meaning fairness or apparent equity), compensation, honor, and tangible benefit can be derived. Examples of this technique in action can be found in the fresh approaches brought to long-standing conflicts by U.S. administrations in the cases of Namibia (1981), Northern Ireland (1994–95), and Sudan (2001–2).

Power Balances

The mediator's start-up analysis continues with a deep examination of the balance of forces at play in the conflict. Mediation, like other forms of negotiation, takes place in a context, not a vacuum. A major component of that context is the balance of power between the parties, and there is a range of things important to know about this balance. First, it is essential to identify what forms of power matter the most in this particular conflict—military power, external diplomatic and political support, the financial wherewithal to sustain a struggle, international legitimacy or isolation, "soft-power" resources (e.g., domestic legitimacy and cohesion, and legitimacy in the eyes of the international community), or skilled manpower and able leadership—and, then, to assess how they are distributed among the parties. Assessing the balance in a conflict typically requires weighing and measuring a balance comprising different kinds of power, of which strictly military power may or may not be the most important. Different kinds of power are often distributed asymmetrically, requiring the mediator to assign subjective values and come up with a crude sense of a balance and of which party has the upper hand today, which is most self-sufficient, which has the most effective allies, which has the greatest staying power, and so forth.

Power balances (or imbalances) may also mask other strengths and weaknesses in the parties. Leaders may be unwilling to take risks for peace because they are reluctant to antagonize or lose the support of key internal (domestic) constituencies. Weak leaders may be much harder to deal with than strong ones, who can deliver their domestic constituencies at the negotiating table.

The next most important question is to establish whether there is a clear trend-line in the balance of forces. Is the power relationship dynamic or relatively stable? Whose side is time on and which side appears to playing a long game? How well informed are the parties about their real positions? Would they accept the mediator's analysis, or would only one party or even neither party accept it? Does their behavior at the negotiating table up to now reflect the overall balance of forces? If not, why not?

These questions open up a range of additional considerations to be weighed by the mediator. For example, while the pain and suffering of each side's population may continue to mount, ordinary civilians may have little capacity to hold decision makers accountable. In this situation, a hurting stalemate may exist between the two warring societies but not between their decision-making elites, who may be comfortable with a wartime status quo and feel little internal pressure to settle. Such an assessment may lead the mediator to develop initiatives that focus less on the power balance between the sides and more on the balances within each of them.

Sometimes, one or more of the parties will reach out to the mediator because they recognize that the status quo is no longer tenable or because they are looking for some breathing room in which to recoup losses. Typically, however, the mediator entering an intractable conflict is likely to confront a situation of stable and comfortable stalemate in which each side's leaders perceive (or at least claim to perceive) that time is on their side. The central challenges for the mediator now will be to find ways to shatter complacency or arrogance about power relations and sober up the sides and to act, if possible, in ways that reinforce stalemates while increasing discomfort. Overall, the mediator must identify ways and means of bringing home to the contending sides that the status quo with which they have become familiar is no longer sustainable and that the time for choice and decision is coming.

Turning Points and Timing

In an ideal world, the best moment for third-party intervention is at the preventive stage, before a conflict becomes violent. As noted at the beginning of this chapter, other points that offer potentially attractive openings are, first, shortly after violence has broken out, when minds may still be somewhat open and before the establishment of vested interests in wartime pursuits; second, in the immediate wake of a dramatic event such as a major military clash, the death or departure of a key leader, or a change in the regional configuration surrounding the conflict; third, after the parties have worn each other down to a status of reciprocal exhaustion, a circumstance that would logically imply that an intractable conflict might at last become tractable. The fourth moment—the introduction of a new third party —was discussed at the outset of the chapter as a special occasion due to the opportunity to maximize the leverage inherent in introducing a fresh third party.

There is more to be said about the third moment for intervention. A situation of grinding exhaustion will not by itself necessarily enhance the mediator's prospects for success. The leading scholarship on the subject of conflict "ripeness" suggests that the parties will be ready to negotiate only when the situation has reached the level of a "mutually hurting" stalemate and is likely to get worse: that is, the parties should have recently experienced very heavy costs or face the imminent prospect of such costs.[5] The clock can be important here: sometimes a sense of imminent disaster linked to an event or deadline can prompt the parties to consider fresh options. So, too, can a recent military disaster. The point is that stalemates, even bloody ones, can be all too comfortable for those in power. In order for the parties to consider talks, the hurt and the stalemate must be mutual—affecting both sides—and must be felt by top elites. The elites must come to recognize that their unilateral military options have failed to work and that their situations are at risk of deteriorating. While a mediator needs to know the objective facts about such stalemates, it is the parties' perceptions of those facts that shape their decisions.

The mediator makes these judgments and calculations to determine how best to intervene to help ripen the conflict. The mediator must not stand on the sidelines waiting for some magic moment to arrive. Instead, the mediator must analyze how best to shape perceptions, to coach and inform the parties, to warn decision makers and introduce fresh ideas, and even, in some circumstances, to use pressures and inducements that affect the parties' calculus of costs, rewards, fears, and confidence.

But even if the parties perceive the stalemate to be painful, the mediator's efforts will fail unless the parties also are capable of making bold decisions. They must, in other words, be strong and coherent enough to take a chance on peacemaking, placing at risk all the certainties, benefits, perquisites, positions, and sense of identity that have been created by and are nourished by the struggle. Hence, the mediator's analysis should include an assessment of the capacity of leaders and the cohesion of leadership groups in the context of their domestic political systems. Can they make decisions? Can they deliver their systems and societies? Do the sides believe in each other's ability to do so? The calculus of warring sides is not only, "Am I winning and do I need to settle now?" It is also, "Will I survive the decisions required to compromise? Can I deliver? And can *they* make the tough decisions and deliver on *their* side?" These are complex calculations, and mediators must acquire an acute sensitivity to the warring parties' mind-sets. The issues raised by such questions lie at the core of the collapse in 2000 of the Oslo phase of the Middle East peace process between Israelis and Palestinians. Weak or divided parties — and leaders so dependent on their "struggle" identity that they dare not risk all at the peace table — are not likely to be partners in peacemaking. And, of course, negotiations will always fail if only one side is objectively prepared to make peace or if one side is subjectively convinced that the other side is not prepared to do so. Here, too, the mediator's analysis should be guided by a sense of purpose, suggesting ways and means of shaping the parties' perceptions, strength, and coherence while pointing to what may be needed in order to achieve adequate symmetry between them so that both sides can move forward.

A mutually acceptable settlement formula must be available to the parties. "Acceptable," however, does not quite capture the point: the formula must be more attractive, more "enticing,"[6] than the status quo of war. Parties caught up in an intractable conflict cannot be considered amenable to a mediated solution unless there is the possibility of an outcome to which they are attracted and in which they can believe. The history of intractable conflicts is rife with cases in which past proposals or formulas have become discredited. Thus, a mediator considering engagement in an intractable case will want to examine closely the parties' views of the settlement ideas already on the table and to reflect deeply about possibilities for shaping a mutually acceptable formula for settlement.

Finally, the public must be ready to support a peace process or a nascent initiative. Sometimes, clear signs exist that the people of war-torn societies no longer support a continuation of the conflict and, unlike their leaders, are looking for a way out of a situation that has become unbearable because of an escalation of violence. When public attitudes undergo this kind of shift, it is important for mediators and other third parties to capitalize on the situation by impressing upon those who control the guns that their own constituents are looking to them for leadership in finding a political solution.

Even when the above conditions apply, much depends on whether or not there is an available mechanism for negotiating, reaching, and sealing a deal. The absence of such a negotiating mechanism is a serious matter: seldom do parties simply reach out and "find each other" with a series of reciprocal, bilateral moves and concessions. Mediators find work because parties need assistance with many aspects of their problem. However, the presence of rival, conflicting negotiating mechanisms can further entrench a conflict's intractability, because rival sponsors of negotiation acquire their own interests in the way the problem is addressed and foster illusions in the minds of the parties. This problem bedeviled the Sudan peace process during the 1990s and into 2001, as southern Sudanese leaders preferred a process led by neighboring states in the regional grouping known as IGAD (its full name is the Intergovernmental Authority on African Development), while the Khartoum authorities tended to prefer working with Arab neighbors Libya and Egypt as peace sponsors. One of the mediator's cardinal tasks will be to devise unified procedures, arrangements, and formats for making peace. A conflict will not ripen unless this is accomplished.

The purpose of the mediator's analysis is not to decide whether or not to engage. It is to assist in determining how best to engage. That the parties have not met one or more of the above conditions should not become an excuse for inaction. More often than not, third parties must work to create these conditions. If they had waited for ideal conditions, Americans, Britons, Norwegians, and Kenyans and other Africans would probably not have intervened in the conflict in Sudan, nor would British, EU, and U.S. officials have intervened in the India-Pakistan conflict over Kashmir.

History and Status of Negotiations

The first step in this part of the analysis is to construct a basic history of the conflict and of previous phases of negotiations. The analyst looks for key watersheds in fighting and peacemaking, seeking out major turning points and trends. A critical task is to identify what benchmarks have become clearly established in the parties' minds and what building blocks already exist with which to construct the edifice of peace. A peace process may extend over decades and include a number of significant past accomplishments that the parties — or at least one of the parties — are determined to retain and that the mediator would be crazy to abandon just because they are legacies of past efforts. The creative use of inherited building blocks can provide a source of leverage even as the mediator looks for other ways to restructure a stalled negotiation.

A useful supply of building blocks and benchmarks, however, does not in itself amount to a viable negotiating process. The newcomer must scrutinize the current negotiating environment and make a judgment about whether there is a mechanism and a process to work with, whether that process is more help than hindrance, and whether it will be feasible and advantageous to launch an entirely new negotiating initiative.

This element of the analysis reveals the circumstances that have produced gridlock or intractability. It sheds light on entrenched positions, redlines, and sticking points. But such analysis cannot be divorced from the fighting and the military balances on the ground. Most warring parties fight and talk simultaneously, and their talk reflects their fight. The new mediator must, therefore, become a military analyst as well as a diplomatic historian. This requires study of how the fighting has evolved, of whether it has acquired a stable, cyclical rhythm or is following some long-term trajectory that, over time, could produce a definitive result. There is little purpose in attempting to persuade parties that there is no military solution if, in reality, one side is clearly headed toward victory on the battlefield. Mediation in such circumstances soon shades into a form of coercive diplomacy. The decisive factor is the parties' perceptions of the military situation. This subjective element, as well as the objective facts on the ground, must be mastered by a new mediator.

The External Context

Conflicts vary tremendously in how they are linked to their external environments—regional and global. Some internal conflicts are almost overwhelmed by the stakes and involvement of outsiders. In their very different ways, the cases of Northern Ireland, Democratic Republic of Congo, Cyprus, and Nagorno-Karabakh illustrate this type: the conflict is heavily internationalized and the local parties' freedom of action is severely constrained or at least complicated by the necessity to consider and consult outside parties. Other internal struggles, such as the ones in Sri Lanka, Sudan, Colombia, Indonesia's Aceh region, and Russia's dissident Chechen republic—while certainly influenced in some measure by outside variables—are dominated to a greater degree by local actors. Interstate conflicts also vary in the degree of external leverage that can be brought to bear, and such external influence can vary greatly over time.

Careful assessment of a conflict's external context tells a mediator how others are likely to react to a fresh mediation initiative, whether there are key interested parties who could thwart or assist the effort, and how to broaden the base of the mediation. It is vitally important for the newly arrived mediator to know who else cares about this conflict and why. Similarly, the mediator needs to know what leverage other interested states could bring to the table if they became involved in the mediation. Knowing the external context means knowing where to find potentially useful sources of leverage. When U.S. mediators decided to mount a new peace effort in Sudan in 2001, one of their very first steps was to consult key Western and African partners with a stake in the outcome of the conflict and considerable influence on the Sudanese parties; this was the

genesis of what came to be known in mid-2002 as the "3+2+2" negotiating structure, which involved three Western players (the United
States, the United Kingdom, and Norway), two regional actors
(Egypt and Kenya), and the two parties to the conflict (the Sudan
government and SPLA/M).[7]

A serious mediator does not cultivate partners and recruit
"friends" of the mediation effort as a matter of diplomatic politesse
or simply to score points in bilateral relationships. Broadening the
base of a mediation makes sense if leaving other people out will
weaken or undercut its chances, and if bringing other people in will
bring the benefit of relevant relationships and bilateral or multilateral
leverage. It is important to be rigorously results oriented, to allow
the mediation process itself to drive the use that is made of such lat-
eral relations among outside parties.

The other reason for studying the external context of a conflict
is to discover who will behave as an ally or adversary of the conflict
parties, and to weigh the implications of this analysis for the mediation itself. U.S. and European mediators during the 1998–99 Kosovo
crisis went out of their way to deal with, and at a minimum neutralize, Belgrade's Russian friends, hoping in this manner to strip away
Slobodan Milosevic's illusions that Moscow would save him from
the full brunt of NATO coercive power. In the end, the Slavic links
between Moscow and Belgrade cut in both directions, serving the
NATO interest of sobering up Milosevic but also ensuring that he
did not face total defeat. In this instance of coercive mediation, the
negotiating structure offered Russian leaders (as well as the EU
presidency of Finnish leader Martti Ahtisaari) a central position.
This enabled them to help hammer out a political deal that preserved
Serbia's nominal sovereignty in Kosovo while inserting NATO-
Russian, UN, and OSCE troops into the dissident province without
having to conquer it from the Serbs with ground forces.

Mediation is generally less coercive than this. But the structure
of influence patterns may be parallel. Nongovernmental mediation
initiatives are quick to recognize the need for careful consultation
and coordination with the major states enjoying close relations with
the conflict parties. European, Latin American, and UN officials

working on the Colombia conflict appreciate the need to maintain a regular channel to Washington, whether or not they agree with U.S. policy on Colombia. For their part, U.S. officials working on Kashmir would miss a fundamental requirement of effective third-party action if they failed regularly to consult and—as appropriate—coordinate with the Chinese, Russian, and British governments.

A final reason for studying the external context is to identify sources of support that can make a settlement more attractive and help with its implementation. In most peacemaking interventions, there are a number of institutions—governments, NGOs, and international organizations (regional and global)—whose backing may be essential to keeping negotiations on track and moving them forward. Any peace process should show tangible gains for those people who have been most adversely affected by the conflict and its ongoing violence. Such gains can play a key role in building wider political support and underscoring the proposition that "peace pays." NGOs and international organizations can help in this respect by providing humanitarian relief and creating better living conditions for a beleaguered population. Donors play a critical role; however, securing their largesse is a daunting task at the best of times because donors will be reluctant to commit resources to a politically risky situation. Bringing these players along in a coordinated effort can be very difficult, particularly as these independent institutions have mandates of their own to fulfill. In involving other institutions, therefore, the mediator has constantly to remind them of the importance of working together.

GETTING READY TO MEDIATE

Good analysis, although vital, is just the beginning of the process of launching a fresh mediation initiative. The newly arrived mediator must be ready in other ways, too. Adequate institutional capacity and resources to undertake a generally long, difficult, and taxing peacemaking effort are essential elements of mediator readiness. All mediators, whether they represent governments and international organizations or are acting on behalf of NGOs and other private groups, face many of the same challenges, including obtaining adequate institutional resources and institutional support, dealing with competition from other actors and interests, and being able to project and deploy those resources while cultivating effective relationships with the parties to the conflict.

Readiness and Capacity Building

The newly arrived mediator must answer the question, "What's missing?" Intractable conflicts resist settlement in part because the most obvious sources of leverage are inadequate. But the presence or absence of leverage is only the beginning of an answer. The parties, or at least one of them, may be too fragmented or too dependent on the war to make peace. They may be too comfortable to have a genuine interest in peace, regardless of civilian suffering. Previous phases of peacemaking may have given all the good ideas a bad name, leaving decision makers cynical and strongly resistant to new information or new ideas. But it is also possible that the missing ingredient has been the absence of mediation skill, focus, and staying power. In other words, it may be that the problem has been with the mediation itself. To be effective, mediators must be capable of undertaking the task at hand, to be ready in every sense of the word.

Institutional readiness is hard to pinpoint and can be more apparent when it is absent than when it is present. According to Barbara McDougall, the Organization of American States (OAS) was not ready to undertake a peacemaking effort for Haiti in 1991.[8] Three years later the United States was ready, although the effort, which mixed coercion with persuasion, exemplifies mediation disjuncture. At the same time that former president Jimmy Carter, Senator Sam Nunn, and (at the time) retired general Colin Powell were negotiating the last elements of a deal to hand over power to President Jean-Bertrand Aristide, Washington deployed the Eighty-second Airborne Division to coerce General Raoul Cedras into giving up power. The mediation team knew that Washington was prepared to act but did not know that action had already been taken until they were ordered by President Clinton to leave the country.[9]

The concept of mediatory readiness requires some elaboration. We believe it encompasses three distinct dimensions: (1) having *operational and political capacity* for the extraordinary practical demands of the task and the leadership responsibilities of running a round-the-clock exercise for months and years; (2) having *strategic and diplomatic capacity* to place the mediation squarely in the center of one's policy concerns and to assemble an ad hoc or structured coalition of third parties willing to act as cooperating partners; and (3) being ready or capable in the sense of being *the right mediator for the job at hand*. Each of these dimensions is discussed below.

OPERATIONAL AND POLITICAL CAPACITY. Having operational and political capacity for mediation means being prepared to launch a sustained peacemaking initiative with the necessary leadership, mandate, bureaucratic resources, staff support, and personal/institutional staying power to establish a position as the lead channel for negotiation. Mediation is demanding work, and the prospective mediator needs to ask a number of searching questions before engaging. The starting place is to ask, Am I really serious about this and is my institution up to the challenge? A number of relevant bureaucratic, personnel, institutional, leadership, and political issues need to be considered.

◆ Can the requisite people and skills be made available and will they be dedicated to this task? One of the first actions of the lead mediator is to select and recruit a first-class team of people capable of mastering different aspects of the negotiating brief and devoting themselves to the initiative. For at least some of them, the mediation could become a full-time occupation. The mediator will need to recruit and retain a highly skilled team with the range of skills, experience, "presence" (i.e., stature and personal authority), and creativity to grab and hold the attention of highly experienced and focused conflict parties.

◆ Do I have the necessary resources? The mediation will require concrete institutional capacities and resources. The initiative needs to have an organizational base or home from which to operate, a center for digesting information and intelligence, for communicating with the parties and other interested players, for obtaining guidance and counsel from superiors, and for making decisions and obtaining spending authority. For instance, in seeking to play a peacemaking role in such places as the Middle East, Sri Lanka, and Colombia, Norway has established a fund specifically dedicated to supporting peacemaking efforts. The establishment of such a fund is a rare recognition of the fact that effective mediation demands not only time, dedication, and ingenuity but also more palpable ingredients, not the least of which is money. If the mediator's institution is not prepared to assume these kinds of burdens, the mediator should recognize such constraints and cede responsibility to others or forge a coalition to conduct a joint mediation.

◆ **Do I have a solid and durable mandate for the conduct of the mediation?** In mediations conducted by a state or group of states, it is imperative to develop and communicate a mandate for the conduct of the mediation. Without one, the mediator has no ground to stand on at home and can be blown off course or neutralized by the parties and by factions within his or her own country. Intractable conflicts have a tendency to export their divisions to other countries, making the job of the mediator a highly political task. Interested constituencies or interest groups will need to be consulted and reassured. Efforts to block the mediator or to steer the mediation process toward favoring one or another side in the conflict will need to be monitored and controlled.

The mediator's mandate provides a bedrock of institutional support. The mandate also spells out the elements of a mediation brief or terms of reference to guide its purposes, scope, and methods. Equally vital, the mandate provides authority to the mediator and serves to remind all others that the mediator speaks for the organization, institution, state, or group of states that have issued the mandate. A mandate implicitly enables the mediator to draw upon the support, as well as the counsel, of top political levels. But it should also include an appropriate mix of authority and independence, shielding the mediation process from unhelpful micromanagement or political interference so that a mediator can take initiatives and work creatively. Without such backing, the contending parties will turn the mediation into a leaf swept down a stream.

◆ Does the mediation have the leadership it will need to make an impact on an intractable conflict? The person leading a mediation requires certain professional and personal qualities. A mediator must know how to listen and hear across cultures and systems, and how to get inside the minds of unique and sometimes exotic political entities. A mediation's leader must have reservoirs of both persistence and intensity in order to dent the parties' natural resistance to making tough decisions. The leader will face the prospect of divisions and game-playing on all sides, as well as the certainty that many participants expect and hope for failure.

Another set of personal attributes relate to the politics of mediation. The long slog of trying to break an intractable conflict may not make for great press stories or serve to enhance short-term political standing. Mediation of intractable cases is for individuals who enjoy a high-stakes struggle and care about the results. For that reason, the effective mediator wants a strong team of players with whom tasks and credit can be shared. Open systems and flat hierarchies are essential in order to penetrate and understand the dynamics occurring within warring parties.

STRATEGIC AND DIPLOMATIC CAPACITY. The prospects for developing effective leverage and building the necessary staying power are affected by the place the conflict holds in the overall policies of the mediator's home base. A mediating entity is not ready to take on an intractable conflict if that conflict's settlement is not intrinsically important enough to warrant a central place in the entity's overall policy.

Intractable conflicts are no place for mediation initiatives undertaken as a substitute for clear policy or designed to conceal inaction and disarray in the ranks. A small power taking on a substantial role in an intractable conflict—such as Norway has done in Sudan and Sri Lanka—will not go far unless it is ready to give the conflict top priority. A group of states, such as the OAS member-states that led negotiations over Haiti in the early 1990s and the Bosnian "Contact Group" active in the early and mid-1990s, will have little impact in the absence of a truly common strategy whose successful implementation outweighs other regional interests of the participants. A major power mediator engaging in a tough, intractable case, such as Cyprus, Nagorno-Karabakh, or Western Sahara, will experience certain frustration unless the home state gives the conflict top billing—that is, the home state's desire for a settlement must at least equal the value of its privileged bilateral relations with the separate warring parties.

It will be difficult, if not impossible, to catalyze diplomatic coalitions and orchestrate coherent initiatives if numerous cross-cutting interests and rival agendas are in play, encouraging warring parties to discern mixed messages in the response of the international community. Some intractable cases have become yet more intractable as a result of policies and decisions that have made the mediator part of the conflict and an additional source of intractability.

FINDING THE RIGHT MEDIATOR FOR THE JOB AT HAND. As we have seen in chapter 3, some conflicts are forgotten or abandoned and some never connect with an appropriate third party capable of making a dent in the sources of intractability. But there are also cases that appear to respond better to certain types of intervention than to others. It is important to carefully consider up front the prospective "fit" between a conflict and a third party. We are talking here of the mediator's identity, image, cultural and geographic links, and overall relationship to the parties. The fit may grow out of historical relationships; prior relevant engagement in developmental or religious activities; colonial legacies and the institutional linkages they have generated (as, for example, in the case of the Commonwealth); spheres of influence or long-standing presence in a country or region; or a common educational, linguistic, or cultural bond that creates interpersonal links between the mediator and the warring parties.

A mediator in an intractable conflict will be called on to play a wide range of roles with the parties. Some roles demand tough talk and hardball strategies; others require deploying incentives and persuasion. But whatever part the mediator plays, it will be played more effectively if the mediator has an aura of legitimacy in the eyes of the protagonists and can develop and make use of relations of trust and familiarity with the parties. These characteristics of mediator identity and personal or institutional credibility will be highly case specific. They cannot be invented out of thin air. There are conflict arenas where mediating institutions and personalities have invested long years of work becoming the "natural" third-party players. These are the people and institutions who are already able to have frank and candid exchanges with top-level individuals on the warring sides. The implications for new, prospective mediators are, at a minimum, to develop the closest possible relationships to the veterans with the most intimate linkages to the parties; to shape a negotiating mechanism that includes roles for relevant insiders or side channels, which may further empower the mediation;[10] and to invest in acquiring a thorough grounding in the culture and history of the societies in question.

ROLLING OUT THE NEW STRATEGY

Few mysteries attend the launch of a new mediation initiative, which should occur only when all of the background research, spadework, policy reviews, and internal organizational moves have been accomplished. The rollout is straightforward if the ground has been prepared politically, administratively, and diplomatically.

The new mediation often begins with a phase of consultations to allow the mediator and the parties to listen to one another and exchange views. But the mediator will want to do more than take the parties' temperature. The purpose is to make an impact on the parties. The mediator, therefore, needs to test them, to place them in a new position in which they must make choices, to gauge their responses to different ideas and avenues of advance, and to gain a sharper sense of their priorities, fears, and political requirements. A mediator's job is to move the parties out of their dug-in positions and into a position where they will have to respond to fresh information, and at the same time to secure their commitment (whether seriously or tactically one learns only later) to working together within the reframed or relaunched peace process.

The precise sequence of visible and invisible third-party moves will depend on the circumstances of the conflict and the identity of the mediator. Typically, the newly arrived mediation team will mount a highly visible consultative process, orchestrated so as to highlight the freshness of the new approach while also permitting exchanges with the parties at an appropriately senior level about the status of the conflict and the major obstacles to moving forward. Mediation led by states or international organizations typically requires an elaborate, public choreography aimed at shaping domestic and foreign opinion and reaching a diverse—and polarized—set of constituencies. At times, such considerations predominate in a mediator's first steps. U.S.-led efforts in the Middle East to convene the Madrid conference of 1991[11] and to launch talks about the "road map" in 2002–3 relied heavily on public diplomacy and visible, albeit complex, consultative procedures. Mediation initiatives led by NGOs and other private organizations, as well as by small powers, may have the luxury of forgoing such activity and operating relatively quietly, or even secretly.

The assets and liabilities of different mediators at the launch of a fresh peace process need to be viewed within a long-term context. As the process advances over the following years, the qualities demanded of the mediators, and indeed the identity of the mediators, may well change. For this reason, gaining entry into the peace process and launching the new initiative successfully may be facilitated by a "layering" of mediators in which certain initial steps or early phases are undertaken in the shadows by low-profile players, while more powerful and conspicuous actors lend consistent but quiet support. Such layering—whether planned or accidental—can be detected in the interplay of third parties in such diverse post–Cold War hot spots as Indonesia-Aceh, Sri Lanka, the Middle East, Mozambique, Colombia, and the Philippines–Mindanao.

Often, preliminary, visible consultations should be preceded by extensive, confidential consultations with partners of the mediator and with friends and allies of the parties. This process is integral to the analytical, information-gathering process discussed earlier. The mediator will want to use these preliminary discussions for multiple purposes: to survey the political and military landscape, to cover the field and "surround" the parties so they have less chance to escape or to obstruct or outmaneuver the mediator, to identify promising channels that may be used in the future to pass indirect or supportive messages and information, to convey seriousness of purpose and perform professional due diligence, and to send indirect messages to the parties themselves about the gravitas and potential strength of the newly launched process.

As the fresh phase of a peace process unfolds, the mediator may be well advised to refrain from tabling a self-described "plan" or "solution" and instead enunciate certain broad, universal principles related to the search for an agreed-upon basis for settlement. This kind of self-restraint is especially important in cases in which old plans and solutions have been discredited in the eyes of the parties. In these situations, a sudden attempt to resurrect them will make the parties dive for cover. In confidential discussions, however, it will be essential to seize and hold the initiative through a series of probing questions designed to elicit answers to hypothetical "what if" questions about the conflict. For instance, the mediator might ask the government for its reaction to a scenario that would lead to the rebels dropping their demand for independence. What would the government be willing to put on the table? Would it go so far as to offer the rebels a guaranteed share of cabinet positions? The mediator's goal, as noted earlier, is to move the parties out of their defensive trenches. This can be done only with the use of fresh ammunition, creative new ideas, and conditional commitments from both sides. The challenge is to devise stratagems capable of breaking down two sets of defenses simultaneously.

CONCLUSION

In this chapter, we have counseled the newly arrived mediator to focus on the key judgments that must be made at the outset of a fresh initiative: Why have previous efforts fallen short? What is missing from the current conflict situation and what will be needed to ripen it? And what must be done by the mediator to assure readiness for the taxing work ahead? Posing these questions, admittedly, sets the bar fairly high and will doubtless yield some sobering and discouraging answers. But this is as it should be. Practitioners of all sorts should agree on some form of the Hippocratic oath to "do no harm" by their intervention and rise to the challenges of incremental learning in complex diplomatic-political interventions, just as they have learned to do in the fields of military and humanitarian intervention in complex emergencies.[12] Mediating entities have to assess realistically not only their good intentions and available resources but also their ability to activate those resources and to influence the warring parties. They must also be cognizant of the consequences of their actions, aware of how the success or failure of their mediation affects not only the particular phase of the conflict in which they are involved but also all succeeding phases.

6

Hanging On, Hunkering Down, and Bailing Out

IN ALMOST EVERY MEDIATION, there are moments when it looks as if the wheels have flown off. A terrorist attack or a sudden escalation of violence destroys months of painstaking negotiations. The unexpected death of a key leader leaves no legitimate interlocutor on one side. An election turfs out moderates who are willing to talk to the other side and puts extremists who don't want to negotiate into positions of power and influence. Even if negotiations are not derailed by some untoward event, failure to narrow outstanding differences on critical issues can engender feelings of mistrust that are rapidly followed by accusations, an uncontrollable spiral of mutual recriminations, and violence. One (or both) of the parties may decide that there is nothing more to talk about and abruptly terminate talks. In these circumstances, the mediator may become the subject of bitter personal attacks and public ridicule for having led the parties in a direction in which they apparently did not want to go or should not have gone. Any mediated intervention is a highly risky venture, and in intractable conflicts the odds are heavily weighted on the side of failure.

Confronted by calamity, the mediator faces some basic choices: identify some way to press on against the odds, back away from the engagement and hunker down, or pull out. The history of peacemaking is replete with stories of how different mediators have wrestled with this inescapable dilemma. In deciding what to do with a peace process that has gone wrong, mediators can try to maneuver

119

within the extraordinary constraints of a bad situation to try to put
a peace process back on track. This means taking advantage of critical
moments and exploiting them to their fullest—even a bad situation
may have unexploited potential for mediated intervention. Intractable conflicts yield to mediators in increments. These increments, at
first glance, may not appear to be much when measured against the
yardstick of a permanent settlement. But cumulatively they can (and
sometimes do) add up. To the extent that negotiations help to reduce
tensions and change perceptions, the possibility of changing an intractable situation may improve if the mediator remains engaged.

But making the best decision among difficult alternatives also
means having a keen sense of what is and what is not possible within
the constraints of the situation and keeping one's powder dry for
more auspicious moments. This sense of the possible includes recognizing when parties to a conflict are not capable of talking or of giving
up their commitment to armed victory. It also means recognizing a
number of other circumstances: when the situation on the ground will
not permit negotiation, when the everyday attacks on integrity and
motives that parties aim at every mediator finally manage to discredit
a mediation, when one's own institution ceases to support the effort,
and when another mediator is better placed to play an intermediary
role. In this case, clear-sightedness may lead a mediator to withdraw
from a peacemaking effort. Although exit is an option, it is not an
option to be taken lightly because it too has its costs. In considering
such basic choices, the mediator should think deeply and often about
the issues we looked at in chapter 2, especially the question of one's
own motives and interests. When conflict management is the prime
goal, this may argue for sustained engagement—at least on some
basis—even when the odds of achieving an actual settlement are
approaching zero. But if the critical objective is, indeed, to achieve
settlement, then the mediator's interest is less driven by visual evidence of a sustained diplomatic process, and other options may
become more attractive (or less unattractive).

This chapter explores these hard strategic choices mediators
confront when the wheels begin to fly off in an intractable conflict
situation. The basic choices when things get bad are to (1) hang on,

(2) hunker down, or (3) bail out. These represent distinct and viable separate options and they cover the waterfront: any mediator in a crisis has to do one of these three things. At first glance, all the options may look unattractive. But it is important that this choice be consciously framed and examined so that the mediator does not become committed blindly to clinging on during an impending train wreck. In other words, even when things are bad, the mediator must act and be seen to act as if it is possible to retain the strategic initiative rather than to become the prisoner of events.

Each strategic choice must also be informed by an understanding of what bargaining and negotiating tactics are appropriate and feasible once a fundamental strategic decision has been made. This requires not only clear strategic thinking but also clearheaded analysis of the specific case at hand. Mediation does not operate according to some generic cookbook of nostrums. Rather, it is context driven and heavily influenced by such factors as history, culture, personal experience, and societal and political structure. Indeed, contextual factors are so important—as we will show below—that they may shape strategic choices as well as negotiating tactics. In the following discussion of negotiating tactics, we argue that "bringing in other third parties" and "dealing with uncooperative leaders" relate directly to *hanging on*. "Seizing optimal moments'" and "protecting viable formulas'" most appropriately relate to a strategy of *hunkering down*. The device of managing multiple channels and using side channels and back channels can support either of these options. The strategic option of *exit* may be associated with quite different kinds of tactical advice, and there may be something to be said for leaving a dead cat, or incriminating evidence, on the doorstep of the truly intransigent party.

HANGING ON

Hanging on means continuing to keep the mediation effort alive with the intention of pushing along or ripening the process, even in the face of bad news. Hanging on becomes an appropriate choice for the third party when the possibility of a hiatus—a break in the peacemaking—brings the risk that the peace process will fall apart. But hanging on will not salvage a stuttering peace process unless the mediator can use the situation to put the wheels back on and gain some traction. There are, of course, various ways to hang on. The mediator can publicly reprimand the parties in the hope that they will be shamed (or shocked) into returning to their senses. Basically, this means speaking over the heads of official or formal parties to their constituents, the public, and other interested parties. The mediator can insist that the negotiation will not proceed until the parties have performed according to their commitments or the mediator can unilaterally suspend talks until the parties demonstrate that they are ready to behave and negotiate in good faith. But these kinds of negotiating tactics are unlikely to alter the fundamentals of a bad or worsening situation unless they are also informed by a more general strategy that simultaneously raises the costs of violence *and* the costs (to the parties) of exiting the negotiations. Essentially, what a mediator needs to do is raise the stakes and expand the range of the tests placed before the parties.

One way a mediator can do this is to secure support from external actors who are uniquely positioned to change the strategic calculus of the parties to the conflict because they represent additional relationships of significance to them and may have some capacity to impose pressures or offer positive incentives that will not only bring the parties to the negotiating table but also keep them there. The conflict in Cyprus provides an example of how the introduction of outside incentives can change the calculus of a peace process. Mediation in the Cyprus dispute has been a history of hanging on by an array of different mediators, who have tried to keep the parties engaged in an ongoing negotiation process.[1] Exhausting as this approach has been, it has served to contain a frozen intractable dispute and to ensure that the parties remain continuously engaged in dialogue and do not try to escalate the violence. None of the previous attempts by various third parties to mediate a comprehensive settlement to the conflict in Cyprus succeeded, but the process of sustaining ongoing negotiations kept a lid on the conflict and provided a much-needed means of defusing tensions when they flared up and of keeping the parties focused on their political, as opposed to military, options.

Following the Turkish invasion of the island in 1974, the United Nations repeatedly tried to resolve the intercommunal dispute through informal and formal negotiations. These continued intermittently until 1983, when UN negotiator Javier Pérez de Cuéllar led a new burst of activity. Pérez de Cuéllar sought a comprehensive approach to resolving the Cyprus problem. Although his initiative failed, it was succeeded by successive rounds of negotiations in the late 1980s and the 1990s. Despite the fact that each new chapter ended in failure, the United Nations persisted with its efforts to keep the two sides engaged in negotiations, and its efforts served to define and legitimize internationally certain parameters for the ultimate plan put to voters in 2004.

As frozen as the Cyprus conflict has been, its potential to drag in Turkey and Greece and to engage the rest of NATO makes it a high-stakes situation. The potential destructiveness of this conflict on the edge of Europe helps explain why the United Nations has continued to hang on. But as the case shows, simply continuing to show up will not necessarily move the parties to negotiate. Sometimes the movement away from violence occurs only with a change in the perceived costs and benefits to the parties of continuing to fight. One of the problems in reaching any kind of lasting settlement is that Turkish Cypriots historically have had a stronger attachment to the status quo than have the Greek Cypriots, because the former's security interests are looked after by the presence of Turkish troops on the island. At the same time, the Turkish Cypriots continue to harbor real concerns about being a minority under a plan for unification of the two zones. Nonetheless, the desire to join the European Union and the fear of being excluded changed the perceived costs to Cypriots on both sides of the so-called Green Line, which divides the two parts of the island, as well as to the Turks themselves. For these and other reasons, the Cyprus stalemate appears to be less intractable now than at any time since the island nation's independence in 1960. The lesson of this tale is that it is possible for mediators who remain available and engaged to help contain and suppress local combatants and to act as a buffer between their patrons, even when decades pass with only limited forward movement. If nothing else, the intervening years can serve to strengthen a number of core parameters — proposed or defined in earlier phases of the negotiation — for an eventual settlement plan. Mediators can hold the ring until such time as the broader geostrategic, economic, and political context shifts in ways that open a path to peace.

The ultimately unsuccessful attempts by the UN mediator to implement the 1991 Bicesse Accords in Angola provide an excellent example of hanging on but show the costs of doing so without sufficient leverage on the parties. UN Special Representative Margaret Anstee's efforts to soldier on against mounting odds is instructive about the kinds of bargaining strategies and tactics mediators can resort to in exceptionally difficult circumstances. At the same time, as a lesson in failure, it is instructive about the kinds of leverage and pressure that are required to deal with parties whose commitment to a negotiated peace process is, to say the least, questionable.

During the period that followed the mediation of the Bicesse Accords, Anstee was put in the difficult position of trying, first, to implement an intricate, multitrack settlement plan and, second, when it crumbled and the parties returned to war in the wake of failed elections, to pick up the pieces. When she accepted what she later described as "mission impossible," Anstee soon realized that she had few resources at her disposal and that Angola was not high on the priority list of the UN Security Council. In the eight-month period from November 1992 through June 1993, she chaired three successive mediation attempts aimed at salvaging the accords. In each, some progress was achieved, but every time a renewed outbreak of violence set the process back and destroyed the momentum that had been created.

Anstee's first meeting with the parties — UNITA and the government/MPLA — during which both sides agreed to a cease-fire and continued negotiations, was almost immediately followed by an outbreak of violence that rapidly escalated throughout the country. Even so, she pressed for a follow-on meeting, which was also disrupted by violence. This time she decided to lay the blame squarely on UNITA and suspended talks. At the same time, in an effort to acquire some leverage over the process, she reached out to the so-called Troika (the United States, the Soviet Union/Russia, and Portugal, who were the guarantors of the peace process) in an attempt to get the parties to return to the negotiating table. The effort was temporarily successful and talks resumed. But the bigger problem lay in the UN Security Council, which was unwilling to take decisive action and use tangible carrots and sticks to send a message to the parties, and to UNITA in particular, to stop all violence and comply with Security Council resolutions. The potential bilateral leverage of individual Troika governments was not applied coherently. Consequently, any commitments that were made at successive meetings quickly unraveled and efforts to secure a cease-fire fell on stony ground. Anstee's position was further undermined by the fact that the Security Council would not agree to commit troops to monitor a cease-fire until a cease-fire was in place. "Worse still," she recounts, "I was warned that, even if I managed to obtain a cease-fire, no UN troops could be provided to monitor it *until six or nine months later*, because of the overall crisis in peacekeeping. That left me, as the principal mediator, with no leverage whatsoever."[2]

Anstee's ultimately unsuccessful attempts to resuscitate the Bicesse Accords contain an important lesson. Although a mediator can resort to various tactics to cajole the parties to live up to their negotiated commitments—for instance, laying blame or suspending talks if the parties openly violate their negotiated commitments—these tactics will do little to stabilize the situation unless the mediator has *real* sources of leverage over the parties. In this particular instance, the critical sources of mediator leverage were missing: The Security Council was not willing to back up the word and work of the special representative on the ground through its various resolutions. Nor was it willing to commit peacekeeping forces to monitor a cease-fire—a commitment that was essential if the mediator was to have any real influence over the parties. Furthermore, the major outside states did not attach sufficient priority to the issue to lend Anstee the leverage she required, a central problem that must be resolved whenever a third-party coalition speaks through the agency of an international body such as the United Nations.

HUNKERING DOWN

At times, the approach of hanging on during a difficult mediation—
of continuing to try to move the parties forward through a variety of
means—is not possible. The parties are unwilling or unable to respond
to suggestions or prodding by the mediator because the situation on
the ground has changed, their constituencies have turned against
the peace process, or external events have frozen the peacemaking
effort. In these circumstances, the mediator may have no alternative
but to hunker down in what some would call a "porcupine mode"—
that is, keeping one's head down until the dust settles and more propitious conditions emerge. In porcupine mode, a third party accepts
that it has little leverage or control over the parties and understands
that the negotiations have reached an impasse. The mediator's position is essentially defensive—to protect the process from the antics
of the parties and to defend those gains (or concessions) that have
been achieved. When the situation changes, that is the time to move
forward again.

A strategy of hunkering down characterizes the strategic approach adopted by the United States in the Namibian-Angolan conflict during the mid-to-late 1980s. In practically every respect, the
1988 resolution of the conflict in Namibia and the subsequent achievement of that country's full independence on March 21, 1990, marked
the end of an intractable conflict that to all intents and purposes
began in 1959 with the founding of the South West Africa People's
Organization (SWAPO). From 1985 to mid-1987, the U.S. mediation effort was essentially becalmed due to internal turmoil, regional
tests of will, and debates within the United States and other Western
countries about sanctions. However, in 1987 the situation began to
change. First, the military equation began to display elements of a
strategic hurting stalemate in that neither side could hope unilaterally
to achieve a victory on the battlefield. Second, the economic and
military costs of the conflict were growing. The business community
and white opinion in South Africa were increasingly opposed to the
burdens of open-ended regional war at a time of growing international pressures against the apartheid system, and elements within

the South African government itself began to see the conflict as a quagmire; meanwhile, severe pressures mounted within the Angolan-Cuban-Soviet alliance and Castro made a successful bid to shape its decisions and obtain a dignified exit from the Angolan quagmire.

As the political situation began to change, the United States swung back into robust action, pressuring the parties into full-scale negotiations and, subsequently, in January 1988, resuming the regional peace process among Angola, South Africa, and Cuba—talks that paved the way for the New York Agreements on Namibia and Angola reached in December 1988. Had the United States pulled away from the table in the earlier period when talks bogged down, it would not have been able to perceive or seize the opportunity presented by changing political-military circumstances on the ground in Southern Africa and at the global level in the context of U.S.-Soviet relations. The fact that third-party mediated talks continued —and on two tracks, the local and the regional/global—helped bring about the withdrawal of Cuban troops from Angola, the withdrawal of South African forces from Angola and an end to other cross-border military actions, and the achievement of Namibian independence from South African rule.

Hunkering down doesn't always work. In the emotionally charged atmosphere of a badly decaying peace process, the parties may turn against the mediator, forcing the third party to leave. Even in these circumstances, however, the legacy of hunkering down may be the foundation of an ultimate settlement. Again, Angola provides an example. In 1998, following years of effort of both hanging on and hunkering down, the United Nations was essentially ejected after the peace talks broke down. Even after UNITA leader Jonas Savimbi was killed in 2002, the United Nations played no real role. Its long involvement in the 1990s had, however, left the legacy of a framework for peace. The 1994 Lusaka Protocol, painfully negotiated and never implemented, remained as a touchstone and point of reference that both parties recognized. In 2002, when the MPLA won its military victory, this framework emerged as the basis for an agreement between the government and the remnants of UNITA. As Paul Hare remarks, the parties did not "have to start from scratch, and the Lusaka agreement gave the loser a way of salvaging some dignity in the process."[3]

In discussing hanging on and hunkering down, we have used examples of state- and UN-based mediations, but the approaches apply equally to peacemaking efforts by other groups, including NGOs and so-called eminent persons. The International Body, composed of former U.S. senator George Mitchell, Canadian general John de Chastelain, and former Finnish prime minister Harri Holkeri, made an art of hanging on during the complicated and protracted Northern Ireland negotiations that led to the Good Friday Agreement in 1998. The work of the Inter-Tajik Dialogue, which has met dozens of times since its inception in 1993, not only paved the way for official peace talks but also provided a venue for the parties to the conflict to meet when the official talks faltered. Norwegian Church Aid, a Norwegian NGO with a long-term association with Guatemala, had to hunker down a number of times before successfully aiding the initiation of peace talks in 1990. Limited resources and competing demands from other areas in distress may affect whether a nonofficial body chooses or is able to hang on or hunker down, but when engaged, such bodies have been effective agents in keeping peace processes alive in seemingly hopeless cases.

BAILING OUT

At some point, mediators and other third-party intervenors may come under pressure to bail out of a peace process because it seems to be going nowhere and the political costs of staying involved or treading water are simply too high. What should the mediator do? Let nature take its course or pursue some of the strategies and tactics we have outlined above? How can the mediator be sure that the peace process is going nowhere and is possibly headed for disaster? Are there domestic, bureaucratic, and external considerations that must be taken into account when deciding whether to pull the plug?

There may be times when it is, indeed, prudent to use the exit option. But just as there are different ways of staying engaged in a negotiation process, there are also different ways to make an exit.

One way to exit is to throw in the towel and effectively terminate subsequent mediation efforts. The kind of political calculation
that informs an exit strategy is typically based on the following considerations: a recognition that there is no point in further mediation
because there is no apparent resolving formula to the conflict; the
parties, after repeated attempts to initiate dialogue, are no closer to
narrowing their differences than they were at the outset of negotiations (or prenegotiations); relations between the mediator and the
parties to the dispute have deteriorated to the point that the mediator
has little or no real credibility with, or leverage over, the parties; the
parties are resistant to any kind of third-party intervention and
appear comfortable with continuing in an existential test of wills;
and/or mediation is inflicting real and direct costs on the mediator—
costs that outweigh any foreseeable benefits that might come from
continuing with talks—and/or there are few perceived gains from
continuing with mediation.

There are remarkably few instances when an international
mediator has terminated negotiations with the parties to an intractable dispute. U.S. mediation prior to the outbreak of the Falklands
War is an example of bailing out when it is apparent—to the mediator
—that the parties will not settle their differences and that war is inevitable. The conflict between Great Britain and Argentina over
sovereignty of the Falkland/Malvinas Islands has some of the elements of an intractable dispute. Since Britain declared sovereignty
over the islands in 1840, Argentina has disputed British legal claims.
In the early 1960s, the two sides tried to negotiate a resolution to their
differences. Although no settlement was found, negotiations resumed
in the 1980s. In April 1982, Argentina seized the islands. The British
government, in response, deployed naval and ground forces to the
South Atlantic and recovered the territory. The UN Security Council
passed a special resolution (UN Resolution 502) urging the parties
to reach a negotiated settlement. The United States, led by Secretary
of State Alexander Haig, dispatched its own mediation mission to
avert war between its two allies. Although Haig tried to negotiate
with Argentina's military leaders, he made little headway: the Argen-
tines viewed his mission with suspicion, fearing that the United

States was biased toward Britain. Britain's prime minister, Margaret Thatcher, in turn, was angry that the United States was professing "neutrality" in the crisis. When it was apparent that war was inevitable, the United States pulled the plug on its mediation mission.[4]

More often, mediators are gently pushed aside or progressively marginalized by either choice or circumstance, as the Kashmir case illustrates. Following the Sino-Indian border war of 1962, the United States became actively involved in trying to mediate a solution to the Kashmir dispute between India and Pakistan. The moment seemed propitious. As Howard and Teresita Schaffer recall, "The Kennedy Administration saw the PLA [the Chinese Peoples' Liberation Army] rout of the Indian army as an opportunity to persuade New Delhi to take a more forthcoming attitude toward a Kashmir settlement on terms acceptable to Pakistan. It reckoned that India's concern about further Chinese moves would encourage it to seek better relations with Pakistan to avoid facing two hostile powers on its borders."[5] Washington also felt that it had some leverage over India because it had provided military assistance to India during the war with China. However, Washington's efforts to mediate a political settlement between India and Pakistan went nowhere. With China's unilateral withdrawal of its forces from India's border, India felt less pressured to reach any kind of accommodation with Pakistan. The United States was extremely active in the negotiations and offered its own formula for resolving the dispute, which would have seen the effective partition of Kashmir between Pakistan and India. However, the two sides scoffed at the U.S. proposals and remained at loggerheads. With the failure of these talks, the United States decided to disengage from any mediatory role in the conflict, a situation that endured for almost forty years, until 1998, as both India and Pakistan began conducting nuclear tests and tensions heightened with Pakistan's attacks along the Indian-controlled frontier of Kashmir. By the 1990s, it should be noted, the case of Kashmir was no longer a two-sided, interstate conflict but a far more complex one involving insurgency war and Kashmiri assertions of a right to self-determination or independence from both neighboring states.

In the intervening years before the nuclear tests, Washington clearly felt that resolution was not a viable political option and that it

was better to try to manage the conflict at a distance. As the Schaf-
fers argue, "For many years this looked like a good choice for U.S.
policymakers. Even as India and Pakistan moved toward developing nuclear weapons, the rationale was that neither side wanted to
stumble into a war, so that although neither had the political will to
solve the problem, both had a strong motivation to keep it below the
boiling point."[6]

The decision to exit can also flow from a quite different chain of
events when a third-party intervenor comes to the conclusion that the
costs of continued engagement are too high and outweigh the costs
of withdrawing from a conflict. This is especially likely to happen
when mediation is part of a wider strategy of engagement that could
involve costly commitments such as the deployment of peacekeeping
forces. The political elements of a mediated intervention can sometimes be compromised by the military aspects of a peacekeeping operation that has gone sour. When this happens, the third party may
come to believe that the costs of withdrawal and disengagement from
an intractable conflict are lower than the costs of continued involvement. This was essentially the calculation made in 1993 in Somalia
when the U.S. and UN mediatory, policing, and peacekeeping roles
became hopelessly confused and—being unwilling to master the strife-
torn country and impose peace—the outsiders cut their losses.

In the Sri Lanka case discussed in chapter 3, India found itself
in similar circumstances. In July 1987, the Indian government signed
an agreement with Sri Lanka that included a plan for an Indian
peacekeeping force to disarm the rebels in the north of Sri Lanka
and a plan for a devolution and greater autonomy for the northern
Tamils. However, opposition to the plan mounted in the southern,
Sinhalese-dominated areas of the country, and Indian peacekeeping
forces deployed in the north soon found themselves under attack by
Tamil insurgents. As in the Somalia example, the Indian peacekeeping efforts became conflated with other roles, and this confusion
worsened as Indian forces engaged in serious fighting, becoming
essentially parties to the conflict. This change in role increased the
costs of continuing Indian involvement to an unacceptable level for
the Indian government and its domestic constituents. Following the
assassination of Indian prime minister Rajiv Gandhi on May 21, 1991,

allegedly by extremist Tamil Tigers, India showed little appetite for any further direct peacekeeping/peacemaking interventions in the Sri Lankan conflict. Exit appeared to be the only defensible choice in a situation that had been made worse by India's intervention and that was increasingly difficult to defend in a domestic political context.

Sometimes, however, a third party does not have the luxury of exit. Although there may be good reasons to pull back and reduce the depth of one's involvement in an intractable dispute, terminal exit is sometimes not a serious option. This situation largely characterizes the nature of U.S. involvement as a third-party mediator in the Arab-Israeli conflict. To be sure, there have been recurring cycles of engagement and mediation that have been followed by disengagement or a lowered profile and a professed U.S. reluctance to press for talks between the parties. This cycle has been driven by the rhythms of the U.S. presidential electoral cycle, by extremist violence, by the fragility of domestic politics in the region (including the vagaries of Israel's own election cycle and parliamentary system), by changing views as to the nature of the parties (more specifically, changing views of who should speak for the Palestinians), and by the impact of changes in the broader regional and global context of the conflict. It may also be driven by the recognition that there are moments when it does not make a great deal of sense to flog shop-worn solutions on parties who themselves are experiencing mediation fatigue and who are vastly skilled in manipulating outside interventions for their own ends. As several commentators have noted, mediating in the Middle East is essentially about timing—timing and calibrating one's interventions for those moments when there is a real opportunity to push for a breakthrough because something on the ground has changed.

But as the world has witnessed on more than one occasion, when the United States has chosen to exercise its right of withdrawal and partial disengagement from the Middle East peace process, significant costs have been incurred. At the most basic level, it can be argued that the United States is so intimately linked to Israel's creation, security, and survival that exit is just not possible: it would be polit-

ically unacceptable to walk away and leave the local actors alone to
do what they choose. U.S. interests vis-à-vis Israel, as well as U.S.
interests in the surrounding Arab and Muslim worlds, are too high
to permit a real exit. The potential costs of disengagement may also
include the risk of other parties taking on intermediary roles and
introducing new agendas and timetables that are inimical to U.S.
interests and need to be reversed or resisted; the risk that U.S. disengagement will be used as an excuse by one (or more) of the parties
to unleash new rounds of violence; and the related risk that pulling
back to promote a ripening of the conflict and a reassessment by the
parties could lead unwittingly to uncontrolled conflagration throughout the entire region, making it even harder to pick up the pieces
later. The United States' own sense of mediation fatigue in both a
bureaucratic and a domestic political context therefore has to be
balanced against the risks of escalation and the fact that blame will
be laid at the U.S. president's doorstep.

All of this is to say that there is no easy exit for some third parties in particular conflict situations. Even a temporary withdrawal
of one's mediation services has a price. The risk may be worth taking
if a temporary exit provokes a reassessment of options and a renewed
interest and commitment to a peace process by the parties to the dispute, but this benefit has to be clearly weighed against the potential
(if unforeseen) ill effects of mediator inaction and retreat. Bailing out
should be an option taken only with extreme care.

NEGOTIATING TACTICS

Just as there are some fundamental strategic choices about what to
do in a fundamentally bad situation — hanging on, hunkering down,
or bailing out — there are also important tactical considerations that
come into play in mediating and negotiating in an environment where
the parties prefer violence to negotiation or are not clear themselves
about what they want out of a negotiation process. Hanging on and
hunkering down are dynamic strategies, requiring vigilance, a heightened sense of awareness about new possibilities that may emerge in
a seemingly hopeless situation, and a willingness to be flexible and

to explore (and even open) new avenues for dialogue when opportunity comes knocking.

The key to obtaining movement in stalled negotiations is to raise the price of stalemate or to lower the cost of exploring negotiated alternatives. In the most basic sense, what is needed is change. The mediator needs to be in possession of something new to lay before one or both parties to shatter existing assumptions, open jaded eyes, test basic motivations, and place serious choices in front of the sides. Change can come in many forms: new information or analysis that can be shared tactically to change perceptions; fresh knowledge of one side's innermost thinking; a new military situation on the ground created by the introduction of new technologies or new allies; a basic change in external circumstances creating an inexorable shift in perceptions and options (e.g., the impact of the 1991 defeat of Iraq on Palestinian calculations); the emergence of or announcement of fresh settlement ideas or the entry of an additional party to the negotiation; the breakup or fragmentation of a party's domestic political base; or the emergence of a new political dynamic that forces one or both sides to reprioritize its interests. In the remainder of this chapter, we concentrate on tactical devices and options that may help to strengthen the hand of the mediator when conditions in the negotiation appear to be going from bad to worse. One purpose of using these tactics may be to reframe the choices that lie at the root of a conflict. But the most important tactical goal is to isolate and focus on obstacles that account for the conflict's intractability, as distinguished from its basic causes. This point underscores the need constantly to bear in mind the intrinsic and extrinsic factors that contribute to intractability, as we discussed in the first chapter.

Exploiting Optimal Moments

One of the unfortunate characteristics of intractable conflicts is that the affected populace becomes inured to violence; consequently, the conflict never reaches a plateau—sometimes called a hurting stalemate—where the parties seriously begin to consider their political alternatives. But it is important to recognize that a sudden escalation in the level of violence in an intractable conflict can also bring about a rapid shift in key constituency attitudes, opening a new window of opportunity in a situation that otherwise seems hopeless This is especially true when the perpetrators of violence seriously miscalculate the impact that an act of eye-for-an-eye reprisal may have on public opinion and their own bases of political support. Such acts can also mobilize a moderate political center where none existed before or weaken the veto exercised by extremists who believe that a military victory over their opponents is the only possible "solution" to the conflict. Taking advantage of optimal moments is a negotiating tactic related directly to the strategy of hunkering down until the weather improves. The Northern Ireland conflict illustrates this pattern.

Throughout much of the 1970s and 1980s, efforts to reach an internal political settlement in Northern Ireland floundered because extremist groups in the Catholic and Protestant communities were consistently able to exercise a veto over successive efforts to do so. Although there were moderate voices in both camps, they were politically divided and weak. Negotiation efforts began with the dialogue between John Hume, leader of the moderate nationalist Social Democratic and Labor Party (SDLP), and Gerry Adams, leader of Sinn Féin, the political wing of the IRA. As Paul Arthur explains, although Hume was criticized for these contacts, he proceeded with the belief that this kind of dialogue was necessary to end IRA violence. He initiated talks in March 1988 after a bomb in Enniskillen killed eleven Protestants, horrifying not only the unionist community but many republican sympathizers as well.[7] Although these meetings were inconclusive, they nonetheless had enormous symbolic, political significance. The British and Irish governments took advantage of this situation and exploited the opening to push forward the peace process through secret negotiations between the British government and Sinn Féin and through multiparty talks in which both governments participated. The U.S. government also engaged, meeting with Adams. This, in turn, paved the way for formal negotiations in Belfast and the Good Friday Agreement of April 10, 1998—the foundation of the current peace process.

The Northern Ireland case is instructive as to how, at the very moment when the wheels appeared to have fallen off a nascent peace process, a series of terrorist acts or a dramatic escalation in the conflict may actually create an opening that allows third parties to gain traction and change the dynamics of a seemingly intractable situation.

In the wake of the terrorist attacks on the United States on September 11, 2001, Washington might have been tempted to focus its Sudan policy exclusively on pursuit of the war against terrorism and to abandon a recently launched initiative aimed at testing the Sudanese parties' interest in exploring whether there was any basis for negotiating an end to the civil war that has raged there for decades. But the Bush administration decided instead fully to exploit the new situation, using the Sudanese government's desire to get back into American good graces as a way to push both the antiterrorist agenda and the search for peace. Success in the latter is from far certain, but the striking dynamism in the Sudanese peace talks from late 2001 to the end of 2003 points to the possibility that it makes a difference when outsiders make good use of the clock.

Bringing in Other Third Parties and Changing the Subject

Hanging on as a negotiating strategy may also require special negotiating tactics. In a bad situation, as we indicated above, it may be necessary to multilateralize (or *further* multilateralize) the peacemaking process by recruiting additional third parties to strengthen leverage. These third parties may have the capacity not only to bring pressure to bear on them but also to ensure that the international community is working from the same script, or they may possess special attributes such as added perceived objectivity or—ironically—a special relationship with and access to one side that may be a necessary ingredient to breaking a bargaining impasse. Choosing exactly when to multilateralize a peacemaking process is a delicate matter, but a critical tactical issue. One critical juncture is the moment when the basis for negotiation is being hammered out and legitimized. Another is the crunch point when the parties begin asking the hardest questions about who will stand behind the accords and ensure the other side's compliance.

There are difficulties associated with reaching out to other third parties. The parties themselves may be opposed to broadening the cast of mediators or facilitators because they fear that such a step will undermine their own negotiating position and sources of external support. New regional powers or great powers with a direct interest in the conflict and its outcome may use the enlarged forum to grandstand and/or pursue their own interests, thereby undermining the whole enterprise. There are also real risks involved in enlarging a negotiating mechanism: the process may become unwieldy and bog down in endless procedural sideshows; decisions may be driven down to the lowest-common-denominator level; alternatively, expectations about what can be achieved (or acquired) at the negotiating table may be unrealistically inflated; and parties who have been excluded from negotiations in the past may demand a seat at the table. There is also the danger in any kind of multilateral venture that a broadened mediating alliance will trigger the formation of an opposing alliance, undermining the whole enterprise.

On the positive side, multilateralizing a mediated intervention may not only create new sources of leverage but also help share the costs and risks of peacemaking. In intractable conflict situations, creating an enlarged forum that puts the credibility and will of the parties to the test can push a stalled negotiation out of a rut. Ideally, a mediator can look to a strong coalition to create irresistible momentum and a coherent flow of influence on the parties. Such was the motivation of the United States when it convened the Madrid Peace Conference in 1991. Getting the key regional players to accept the idea of a conference was no easy task. James Baker conducted an intensive round of shuttle diplomacy and was eventually able to persuade the PLO, Israel, Syria, Saudi Arabia, Jordan, Egypt, and the members of the Gulf Cooperation Council to meet in Madrid along with the Soviet Union (as a cosponsor) and the United Nations (which attended as an observer). Although the achievements of the Madrid Conference were modest, the conference was nonetheless crucial in one key respect: it broke the long-standing taboo of direct talks between Israelis and Palestinians and fostered the beginnings of what became the Oslo process.

The creation and subsequent work of the International Body in the Irish peace process also demonstrates in a very different context that the parties to a conflict themselves may try to multilateralize a negotiation by bringing in outsiders who are perceived to be neutral and unbiased facilitators and who are seen as having the right skills and background to handle the most intractable issues in the negotiation. The International Body, charged with identifying "a suitable and acceptable method for full and verifiable decommissioning" of weapons, played a critical role in breaking a bargaining impasse that had stymied negotiations up to that point.[8]

When Australia turned to New Zealand to help mediate a resolution to the ethnonationalist conflict in the province of Bougainville in Papua New Guinea—an intractable conflict dating back to the 1960s, but which had become increasingly violent in the 1980s and 1990s[9]—it was with the explicit recognition that New Zealand brought critical assets to the table that Australia did not have, namely, no real stakes in the conflict (or in the Panguna copper mine in Bougainville). New Zealand played a critical role in facilitating and hosting negotiations. Wisely, at New Zealand's prompting, the parties began their negotiations by focusing on issues of process. Only after sufficient levels of trust had been established did the parties move on to more substantive (and contentious) issues. In turning to New Zealand to mediate the talks, Australia not only borrowed leverage but also was able to bring to the table a much-needed honest broker that enjoyed both the confidence and the trust of the parties.

Secret Channels, Side Channels, and Indirect Talks

When negotiations are deadlocked—or when the parties don't want to talk to each other—it may be difficult, if not impossible, for the mediator to know how to proceed. In the case of indirect or proximity talks, the mediator may find it hard to get the parties to "bid" and to respond to moves by the other side. The challenge in these situations is to try to get the parties involved in prenegotiations, that is to say, to get them to redefine the problem, develop a shared commitment to negotiate on the basis of agreed-upon principles, and eventually to arrange for further, direct negotiations. Although there are a number of different definitions (or conceptions) of prenegotiation, they all center on the notion that prenegotiation is the prelude to more formal, face-to-face negotiations and is marked by a decision by one or more parties to consider negotiation as an option.[10] It is the critical, exploratory phase in which parties typically will not or cannot meet directly but are willing to authorize — or at least tolerate — the activity of a third party that seeks to establish an agreed-upon basis for further negotiation.

Prenegotiation is useful to parties — especially those parties that are locked in an intractable dispute and refuse to openly acknowledge or negotiate with each other — because it promises lower exit costs than do formal negotiations should prenegotiation fail. Even if political elites are not interested in formal negotiations, prenegotiation may bring additional benefits, such as building public support for particular policies, deflecting or channeling pressures from key allies, or avoiding (or deescalating) a real crisis.

Even critics of the Oslo process recognize that secret diplomacy has a very real place in intractable conflicts, where the parties refuse to formally recognize each other and where negotiation itself is seen as a very high-risk option. For instance, Neil Lochery, a stern critic of the Oslo process, notes:

> Both parties considered the use of a secret channel to be essential in securing an initial peace agreement that included statements of mutual recognition. Secrecy allowed direct negotiations to take place despite an Israeli law forbidding direct contact with the PLO. Moreover, both sides agreed to complete deniability, making it easier to put forward ideas and discuss positions and potential trade-offs. The secret channel obviated the need for public posturing for domestic audiences that had marred previous public negotiations such as the Madrid Peace Conference in 1991. Finally, the secret nature of the talks helped to deepen relationships between the participants, enabling them to come up with creative solutions for previously intractable issues.[11]

Coping with Inevitable Antics and Procedural Roadblocks

Uncooperative leaders in an intractable conflict build roadblocks at every turn in a negotiation process. If their demands are met, they

will simply present new ones. Uncooperative behavior is also sometimes accompanied by a reluctance to meet directly with adversaries.
Mediators become accustomed to witnessing endless bickering about
the participants, the basis or framework of negotiations, and the format and procedures of the negotiation (including the role that third
parties are supposed to play). At times, warring parties exploit each
other's noncooperation in tactical gamesmanship aimed mainly at
buying time, avoiding decisions, and wrong-footing the other side.
Preconditions set by one or both sides (e.g., one side's insistence that
before talks can occur the other side must create a better atmosphere
for talks by ceasing hostile propaganda) are best rejected and cited
as evidence of a lack of seriousness. The parties must not be encouraged to view their agreement to talk as a favor or a quid pro quo for
some behavioral shift.

There are also cases, however, when such procedural gamesmanship masks a deeper ambivalence toward the terms and basis of
the talks being proposed. In such cases, procedural issues are substantive and may reflect the determination of all sides to achieve
unmet political requirements. Typically, these issues may involve
matters of status and recognition. Parties are also exceedingly sensitive to the slightest suggestion that their adversaries made fewer concessions or received privileged attention. Parties have zero tolerance
for allowing the other side to achieve things at the negotiating table
that do not reflect reality on the ground.

Given the various ways in which procedural hurdles may be
explained, the first job of the mediator is to determine what the real
problem is. This requires skillful testing of the parties' motives. It also
means that the mediator must develop a finely tuned ability to listen
and interpret the political and cultural context of the conflict. Expres-
sions of concern regarding issues of balance, equity, and face are not
necessarily mere macho tactical ploys: they may reflect deeply held
fears for survival and a sense that negotiation is the slippery slope
toward political extinction. In addition to listening carefully, the
mediator can coax intransigent interests to the negotiating table by
using a variety of tactics. For instance, the mediator can foster the
parties' trust and confidence by being clear about the ground rules

for dialogue at the outset and by defining a clear and specific basis for negotiation and an inclusive agenda that, once agreed to, will not later be changed. All of this takes stamina and patience.

It is sometimes necessary for the mediator to demonstrate to the parties that they bear the primary responsibility for making peace and that the mediator retains the option of placing the blame for failure squarely where it belongs. A mediator also must retain—but not lightly use—the threat to exit the process. When James Baker on the road to Madrid suddenly found himself confronting a set of reopened demands from the Palestinian delegation that it had previously agreed to defer, he exploded: "How many times have we done this?" he exclaimed. "The souk never closes. I've had it. Have a nice life."[12] Before he stomped out of the room, Baker also made it clear that he would not return unless the demand was dropped. The tactic worked and the Palestinians agreed to drop the issue.

A negotiation can grind to a halt before it has barely begun to move because no one wants to take the risk of being the first to agree to talks. Parties that are deeply and habitually averse to face-to-face meetings with a long-standing enemy will resort to just about any excuse not to climb aboard a new peace process. The mediator's challenge is to corral the parties by creating a sense of momentum and conveying to the parties that the train is about to leave the station with or without them, a tactic that works only when more than two parties are involved. Turning to the Madrid example again, Baker used this technique with his Middle East negotiating partners, working to persuade all parties that one of the other players "had undergone a significant change in attitude." Baker believed that his strongest point of leverage over the parties was to threaten to lay "the dead cat on their doorstep."[13]

Managing Factions, Spoilers, and Weak Parties

The compulsive spoiler who is addicted to violence because he believes that he can win—or because he believes that he is better off in the war than he would be under the settlement terms on offer— represents a unique challenge. When confronted with a strong leader who eschews negotiated solutions or enters into negotiated commitments only to renege on them at the next opportunity, the mediator has limited options. The third party can seek coercive means in order to shape directly the negotiating arena. It can, alternatively, play a waiting game, hunkering down in porcupine mode until the recalcitrant leader dies or is defeated, by which time mediation may no longer be required. This analysis does not argue necessarily for disengagement; rather, it may suggest that the mediator should be ready to seize the opportunity when a new leader or a new situation emerges.

A rising tide of violence that turns a peace process sour may mean that a sufficiently strong political center (or moderate middle) has not yet formed to control the political agenda. Given time and external support, moderate leaders who are strong enough to make concessions and control their own constituencies may emerge. But if there is a power vacuum or a leadership struggle at the top, pressing for negotiations and concessions will only encourage spoilers or other extremists to exploit the situation.

If the parties are divided and there is no political center of gravity among rival factions, it may be pointless for the mediator to press for negotiations. Rather, energy and effort may be better spent on cultivating and strengthening a new leadership that has the backing of rival factions and that can ultimately deliver its side at the bargaining table. As Australia soon discovered in its efforts to promote a negotiated settlement to the Bougainville conflict in Papua New Guinea, the political leadership in Bougainville was divided among rival factions, with no political center of moderate voices available to sustain negotiations. However, as a new political leadership began to emerge, Australia encouraged these individuals to bring their ideas to the negotiating table by providing logistical support for moderates who wanted to meet and by helping to host a peace conference in 1994 at a location in central Bougainville that could not be disrupted by hard-liners.

Weak leaders or leaders whose spheres of influence (and control) are limited (or eroding) pose a different kind of challenge. This is because they may be unable (or unwilling) to control outbreaks of violence that threaten the negotiation process. One tactic is to call for a time-out in the negotiation process — i.e., to suspend negotiations until the parties are willing to agree to abide by a cease-fire. A limited or interim cease-fire can sometimes be an important confidence-building mechanism and, if it holds, may actually strengthen the parties' respective commitment to the negotiation process. The risk, though, is that the parties may abuse it to catch their breath and, if the cease-fire breaks down, the relationship between them will worsen. This circumstance hands the enemies of peace a tool with which to disrupt talks and veto the creation or restoration of confidence.

In some situations, it may be possible to shore up the position of political leaders by conferring various kinds of symbolic rewards that strengthen their political legitimacy vis-à-vis domestic constituents while reinforcing the message that extremism does not pay. For example, a critical turning point in the Irish peace process was the decision by the Clinton administration to allow Gerry Adams to visit the United States to attend a conference organized by the National Committee on Foreign Policy in New York. As Paul Arthur notes, "Subsequent visas, the privilege of raising funds in the United States, invitations to the White House and Capitol Hill, and the continued support of the Clinton administration reinforced the call to Sinn Féin to engage in the process of political dialogue."[14] Sending a clear and consistent signal that moderation pays, and that the moderate leaders are the individuals with whom the international community can (and wants to) do business, can help to create a political center of gravity in a negotiation, especially if one side is highly factionalized.

Even so, circumstances may arise in which it is desirable to withhold these rewards because to confer political legitimacy on certain groups by including them in the peace process will undermine the prospects for a settlement in the longer run. This point is especially applicable to factions that have perpetrated major human rights abuses and/or whose commitment to a negotiated political settlement is questionable. The challenge for the mediator in these situations is to devise a process that allows these groups to participate in the negotiation process while simultaneously denying them the sort of symbolic recognition that they seek to attain. Establishing clearly defined rules that circumscribe the quality and level of their participation in the negotiation process can help strike a balance between the need for inclusion and the countervailing pressures not to give some groups too much legitimacy.

Richard Solomon describes how the five permanent members of the Security Council (the "Perm Five": the United States, Russia, China, the United Kingdom, and France) addressed the thorny problem of how to include the Khmer Rouge, which had perpetrated unspeakable horrors on the people of Cambodia, in the Paris peace process. "The issue of how to constitute the Supreme National Council embodied the highly contentious issue of whether to include in a settlement *at all* the feared Khmer Rouge—in the process giving it a measure of legitimacy and an opportunity to regain power through the UN-managed political process. . . . The issue was ultimately resolved for the Perm Five at the July session by agreeing that the Supreme National Council should be composed of *'individuals* representing the full range of Cambodian public opinion' . . . and by depriving the body of any operational authority. . . . By thus eliding the membership issue, and by creating a mechanism of only symbolic weight, we avoided recognizing the Khmer Rouge *as an organization*, even though Khieu Samphan, the Khmer Rouge's foreign minister, as an individual would represent the forces of Pol Pot as one of the guardians of Cambodia's sovereign rights."[15]

All things being equal, mediators prefer to deal with strong, coherent parties that are capable of taking tough decisions and making them stick. Parties must be strong to take the risks that peace entails —the risk of being disowned by one's own supporters as a sellout and outflanked by one's rivals, the risk that third parties will fail to hold the other side accountable for its actions, and the risk that the other side cannot be trusted. However, all things are *not* equal, and this nostrum needs to take into account the specific political and cultural context in which the conflict occurs. Autocratic societies —in which governance is organized in a top-down fashion, with heavy reliance on security institutions—will respond differently to third-party interventions than societies whose political institutions are more open to competing ideas advocated by multiple lobbies. Where space exists for civil society and the private sector to function with some autonomy, additional avenues of influence are open to the mediator.

As NATO powers sought to bed down the postwar arrangements in Kosovo flowing from their victory over Serb forces in 1999, they faced the probability of challenges from both the hard-line Kosovo Liberation Army and the Milosevic regime in Belgrade. The former had to be checked, confronted, and at the same time included in the ensuing process of political normalization in Pristina. As for the latter, once it became clear that civil society groups, especially the student movement, in Serbia were no longer quiescent about the huge toll Milosevic had imposed on his own people, the Western powers channeled appropriate types of support to the anti-Milosevic groups, helping to neutralize and ultimately change the regime. This admittedly unusual example of the potential link between "people power" and peacemaking underscores the central importance of peacemakers understanding the context in which they operate.

Sometimes, the domestic political structures of the parties to a conflict will contrast sharply, demanding asymmetrical strategies by a third party. The extraordinary contrast between Palestinian and Israeli political structures is one of the most widely noted examples of the phenomenon. For decades, American policymakers have had to deal with this disparity, treading delicately in the internal affairs of a highly fragmented, democratic ally with many influential friends in Washington while attempting to treat the Palestinians and their Arab neighbors in the manner normally reserved for autocratic, if not authoritarian, negotiating partners. But the Israeli example does not signify that democracies should necessarily be treated with kid gloves. There may be times when third parties must act decisively to compensate for weak or divided leadership in order to push forward the agenda of peaceful settlement.

In the case of the Ecuador-Peru border conflict, the mediators were the guarantors of the 1942 Rio de Janeiro Protocol (Argentina, Brazil, Chile, and the United States), an accord that had been widely accepted (but not by Ecuador) but not implemented by early 1995, when the brief Cenepa war broke out.[16] This was a 170-year-old intractable conflict that had erupted periodically, leaving the

parties deeply marked by issues of pride, status, and national grievance. It was a given that the sides would accept the assistance of the
guarantor powers, but it was also clear from the outset that profound
obstacles stood in the way of a settlement. Ecuador preferred a better
territorial deal than the one laid down in 1942, and its forces fared
well in 1995; Peru stuck to the letter of the 1942 territorial award
and simply wanted it implemented. Furthermore, a marked contrast
was evident between the "presidential diplomacy" of the autocratic
Fujimori government in Peru and the chaotically unstable democratic
politics of Ecuador, where no fewer than four presidents held office
in the three years leading up to the final peace agreement of 1998.

Given these circumstances, the four mediating powers found it
necessary to internationalize the negotiation and creatively to re-
shape the settlement agenda, breaking it down into bite-size pieces
and structuring it into a form that offered a fundamental quid pro
quo to the two sides and sufficient inducements to be reciprocally
attractive to them. The mediators were respectful of the parties and
reminded them that only they could make peace. But the mediators
also did not hesitate to insert themselves into the domestic affairs of
these relatively open societies, recruiting allies from local and external NGOs and from the private sector and civil society of the two
countries, especially Ecuador. In the end, success derived from many
factors, including the commitment of the four guarantor governments, the skills of the mediators, and the widespread desire of most
elites in Peru and Ecuador to see a transformation of their relationship and to enjoy the economic fruits of peace.

CONCLUSION

Are the strategies and tactics outlined above relevant to mediation
in various kinds of conflicts? Isn't it the case that mediators dealing
with any conflict—old or new, hot or frozen—may be faced with
dilemmas that will force them to make a decision of whether to stay
or go, to engage or hunker down? The obvious answer to these questions is "yes"; these strategies and tactics may of course be applicable to any conflict, depending on its trajectory.

Intractable conflicts, however, will almost certainly involve the mediator in major decisions of commitment or withdrawal. In situations in which the mediator is dealing with entrenched hatred, habits of war, and a never-ripening situation, the ability to decide on the most effective strategy or tactic will make the difference between a mediation that gains traction and one that becomes mired in the mud left by previous peacemaking efforts. Retaining the ability to make decisions under these circumstances is extremely hard, as events on the battlefield and in negotiating rooms, gatherings of dissidents, neighboring capitals, the UN Security Council, and the mediator's own institution will almost certainly throw the best-laid plans into chaos. Retaining some degree of independent action, however, is an essential element in a mediator's toolkit, as it makes the difference between gaining the respect of the parties to the conflict and being dragged about by their agendas. As we noted in chapter 5, readiness to mediate means more that marshaling adequate resources to do the job. It also entails a personal and institutional commitment to the process that will allow the mediator to endure long periods of inactivity or hostility in pursuit of peace while remaining clear about the viability of the mediation effort. If, in the mediator's assessment, the parties are stalling but haven't yet cut the phone lines to the negotiating forum, then a strategy of hanging on may be appropriate. If the lines are cut but the possibility of reconnecting them may still exist, then hunkering down may work. But when the parties refuse to answer the mediator's calls or all possible means of communication, including telegraph and roads, are destroyed, it may be time to bail out of a mediation effort. The clear-sightedness and critical assessment necessary for this kind of analysis require a brutal honesty on the part of the mediator, not just in the early phases of engagement but throughout the commitment to mediation in an intractable conflict.

7

Recipes for Securing
the Settlement

WHEN THE MOMENT FINALLY COMES that warring parties recognize their need for and interest in reaching a negotiated settlement, the mediator must pay special attention to certain themes we have identified in earlier chapters. These include how to manage spoilers who are intent on wrecking negotiations as one moves into the endgame; how to deal with the mediator's home environment as important, interested domestic constituencies in both political and bureaucratic environments flex their muscles; and how to mobilize the requisite resources and political support in the wider regional and international environment to sustain a negotiated agreement. In this chapter, we begin by discussing this checklist, the starting place for mediators to consider as the endgame unfolds. Thereafter, we identify the main ingredients that go into a settlement of the hardest cases.

There is no magic formula for concluding a settlement in intractable conflicts. A variety of elements will arise and will have to be dealt with if there is to be any hope of concluding an agreement. Although some of these elements are more salient to intractable conflicts than to other types of conflict, all are relevant to statecraft when a mediator is persuaded that the conflict parties have come to the table to explore seriously the possibility of a negotiated settlement.

Such moments may be hard to discern in the murky, churned-up waters of an intractable conflict. These moments emerge when the parties have experienced enough learning, prenegotiation, and downright pain that they are prepared to eschew zero-sum solutions, at least temporarily, and commit themselves to a serious discussion about their political options. At these moments, the rhetoric of the parties changes subtly. They will send signals that they are ready to test each other and not just manipulate and blame the other side. As we discussed in chapter 5, these changes may come about for a number of different reasons: a systemic change such as the end of the Cold War or the attacks of 9/11, a change of leadership, a change in conditions on the ground (for instance, one party may acquire resources that give it an advantage on the battlefield), or a change of perspective. It is to creating the last of these — a change of perspective on the desirability of fighting versus negotiation — that the mediator directs most of his or her attention.

These are delicate moments for the mediator and the parties alike. Each has to test and probe the others' intentions while assessing the pros and cons of a negotiated agreement. Key issues of substance and process have to be addressed. The challenge for all parties is to not lose sight of the primary agenda as they look to various confidence-building measures and intermediate steps to generate momentum. Incremental peacemaking is especially seductive in intractable conflicts, in which the gaps between the positions of the parties appear to be vast and neither party is prepared to make the major concessions that are ultimately required to conclude an agreement. But incrementalism will take the parties only so far. Stepping stones can became stopping places. Intractable conflicts become tractable only if the parties are prepared to take on the tough issues and make the substantive concessions necessary to reach a comprehensive political settlement. The mediator's challenge is to lead the parties to places where they do not want to go in order to talk about what they do not want to discuss with interlocutors they do not want to recognize.

THE MEDIATOR'S CHECKLIST

In preparing for this stage, mediators should keep a few basic principles in mind.

PROTECT AND EXPLOIT GOOD FORMULAS. Long, drawn-out conflicts tend, as we have seen, to erode and discredit the very ideas most necessary to form the basis for an ultimate accord. This happens when the sides lose confidence in proposals that did not bring peace in the past, associating them with failure and with the other side's perceived bad faith. The mediator's task as the endgame nears is to breathe life into the handful of viable and potentially winning ideas that have surfaced over the course of the conflict, repackaging them as required to inspire the parties' interest. Sometimes, this may require artfully linking old and new concepts, in the process changing the optics and balance of the terms contained in the overall negotiating package.

ANTICIPATE TROUBLESOME AND DESTRUCTIVE NEGOTIATING BEHAVIOR FROM THE PARTIES. Just because the parties agree to meet and appear to be genuinely interested in exploring a deal, the mediator should not expect smooth sailing. As we have seen in chapters 1 and 4, these parties may be led by hardened, cynical, and skeptical people who expect failure and are eagerly waiting for evidence of the other side's inability or unwillingness to make the necessary commitments and to carry them out. Each party may be held together by little more than its members' distrust and fear of the enemy. The endgame will place maximum strains on the unity of the negotiating sides.

The implications for the mediator are twofold. First, the mediator must devise stratagems for reinforcing the unity of the negotiating sides. The mediator should avoid overloading the parties' internal decision-making circuits with too many big issues clumsily sequenced. It is important to reinforce initiatives taken at the table with parallel supporting efforts back in the parties' own capitals, directly and through third parties. For example, U.S. and UN negotiators working on the Cyprus issue typically focus much of their effort on mobilizing their contacts in Athens and Ankara, who, in turn, can communicate in confidence with their Cypriot constituents. Second, the mediator needs steely nerves and tough-mindedness in the face of likely stunts and maneuvers by the sides aimed as much at testing the mediator's sense of direction as throwing the enemy off guard or off balance. Sometimes, parties will engage in theatrics intended essentially for home audiences. The challenge here is to become for each side the authoritative and trusted interpreter of what the other side is really up to. The more histrionic the sides' behavior, the greater the need for the mediator to stay cool and focused.

TEST AND ISOLATE SPOILERS. The endgame of a peace process is when the sides' true motivations and internal cohesion face their sternest test. It is also the time when decisions about the lofty issues of war and peace may be quietly—but lethally—shaped by the political economy of violent conflict, as leaders face the prospect of losing positions of power and tangible economic benefits that depend on war. For the mediator, the management of spoilers becomes a central concern. The key, at this decisive juncture, is for mediators to use the process aggressively to test each side's motives and willingness to consider proposals that would resolve its respective distrust of the other. The goal is to move the parties, using matched, conditional commitments ("yes, if"), to define the elements of a settlement. Success depends on the mediator's ability to read the sides' leaders and spokespersons, distinguishing tough, competent bargaining from outright obstructionism. When the latter occurs, the challenge will be to isolate and undermine spoilers within each negotiating side while rewarding the risk-takers prepared to imagine the possibility of peace. The currency for doing this depends on the mediator's success in extracting reciprocal, conditional offers from one side that can serve as ammunition for obtaining similar offers from the other.

MOBILIZE AND HARNESS THE TOOLS FOR TRANSFORMING THE POSTSETTLEMENT LANDSCAPE. During the intensive rounds of negotiations, the mediator's attention is often riveted by the challenges of getting specific leaders to the table to talk about a carefully constructed agenda. It is in this context that we have talked about spoilers. But a negotiated settlement can also be wrecked by the failure of the leadership to convince their broader constituencies to support the agreement. The settlement envisaged by negotiators cannot work if the locus of conflict remains a polarized and militarized countryside where unarmed civilians live in fear of the armed factions. This is why a well-designed settlement makes provision for changing reality on the ground — by introducing monitors, observers, media representation, institution- and capacity-builders, civil society groups, and assistance agencies. These are the people who will help a war-torn society heal itself while also undermining the possibility of spoiler games taking the sides back to war. Mediators (and their home institutions) can seldom actually deliver all these capacities themselves, but they can create networks of capable organizations (e.g., donors, postconflict reconstruction agencies, and other peacebuilders) and programmatic elements (e.g., the return of refugees and the creation of a system of transitional justice) that require the presence and assistance of relevant agencies. Although the mediator does not admit as much at the conference table, his or her goal is to get armed parties to sign agreements that will not only stop the fighting but also create conditions and a momentum that inexorably undercut the parties' political monopoly in the war-torn polity.

MAINTAIN THE SUPPORT OF THE HOME BASE. As discussed in chapter 4, the mediation process in intractable cases may become politicized in the mediator's domestic arena, creating exceptional challenges for policy management. This problem will grow more pronounced during the endgame as the zone of likely negotiability and trade-offs becomes clearer, media coverage intensifies, public opinion becomes activated, and political scrutiny mounts. Mediators need constantly to reacquaint themselves with how the process looks — and is playing in the media and among interest groups — back home. With advocacy groups mobilized in support of one side or another seeking to manipulate coverage of the process, mediators may need to erect backstopping mechanisms and special bureaucratic arrangements (e.g., broadened negotiating teams, new reporting channels, additional staff, and liaison arrangements within and between government agencies) to bolster support for the mediation; they may also find it necessary to expand public affairs outreach to place a more helpful spin on the story of the mediation and work the press to elicit sympathetic coverage.

KEEP AN EYE ON THE CLOCKS. With all the other challenges facing the mediator, he or she may have little inclination to think about all the clocks that are ticking. But timing is everything. Each of the sides has its own sense of timing, its reading of who has the initiative and who benefits from early progress or delay. It will be necessary to shape the way each side thinks about timing. Mediators must also understand how the specific conflict fits into the international context of other conflicts and peace processes. A settlement creates demands for political capital and tangible resources from the leading agencies dealing with issues of peacekeeping, postconflict reconstruction assistance, debt relief, and budget support. Ideally, the endgame should conclude in conditions that favor successful implementation. Moreover, the mediating agency may have its own domestic timing considerations related to political and other events. A settlement's key benchmarks should not be scheduled for times when the mediator's home base will be preoccupied with other concerns.

THE INGREDIENTS OF A NEGOTIATED SETTLEMENT

The settlement documents agreed upon by parties to a long-standing, deep-rooted military conflict can take many forms. The size and shape of the final documents will reflect the procedures used during the negotiations, the parties' political cultures, and the specific negotiating history leading to settlement. The most interesting questions for the practitioner and the student of mediation to explore are how to gather together the major building blocks of the settlement, how the parts should fit together, and in what sequence they should be negotiated. Where, in other words, should the mediator begin once the parties have agreed to explore seriously a negotiated outcome? And how should the mediator approach the key elements of a negotiated agreement, which, like volatile compounds, can explode at a moment's notice if they are not handled correctly?

To some degree, the answers are shaped by the specific conflict. Most of the substantive issues affecting the terms of negotiated settlement are very context specific, and the process of making a deal requires trading off demands and priorities.[1] Even so, some generally applicable principles of good tradecraft should be borne in mind, as should certain commonsense ideas about the structure of a settlement. These are especially valuable in intractable cases for the simple reason that such conflicts so often resist closure and successful implementation.

1. The starting place, for the mediator, is to develop with the parties *an agreed-upon definition of what the conflict is about, what needs to be settled, and what will appear on the endgame negotiating agenda.* This requires achieving explicit or tacit agreement on which issues belong in the settlement (and, by implication, which do not). The mediator should not be surprised if it takes time to get to this point. The question of how to manage the issue of the "right of return" of Palestinian refugees in the Israeli-Palestinian peace talks is a classic illustration of the problem. There can be no settlement of the conflict until this issue has been addressed in some fashion—whether by including it in an agreement, excluding it, or redefining it. The right of return has been elevated to a core principle by the Palestinian side, to the point that the Israelis or the mediator cannot simply say "forget about it," even if, in the end, it is addressed only at a symbolic level.

The negotiating agenda is determined by the issues in dispute, but not necessarily by *all* the issues in dispute. It must cover those issues that are politically essential to the sides and are logically essential to the viability of the settlement, but if a settlement is also required to cover relevant but nonessential items, the peace process may bog down. There is, in other words, a finite burden a settlement can bear if it is going to happen. There is, in effect, a "mini-max" loading principle that has to be invoked in considering not just the terms of a negotiated settlement but its overall design and structure. Core political issues that define the identities and key interests of the parties cannot be shunted aside (or fudged indefinitely); they must be included in the terms of a settlement if there is to be any hope of reaching a meaningful deal. However, putting everything on the table in an attempt to define a comprehensive (and politically definitive) agreement may place too many burdens on the parties and the settlement itself, virtually ensuring that it collapses from the weight of its political obligations. The challenge for the mediator is carefully to calculate how much the settlement can bear before attempting to secure critical concessions from the parties. In the end, however, the parties' own political requirements will govern the settlement's content.

2. The discussion of agendas (what is to be settled) leads to consideration of the negotiating sequence. The mediator's challenge is to *obtain an agreed-upon definition of the sequence in which issues will be addressed and the place (if any) of interim or partial agreements.* It is not possible to proceed toward settlement unless the parties and the mediator are working from similar assumptions about the decisions and commitments they are making. Will the sides seek to change conditions on the ground through interim steps that are intended to demonstrate good faith and create an improved climate for continuing negotiation? In other words, will they seek to create momentum for peace by achieving incremental progress? Or will they operate on the premise that individual parts of the package are only implemented after all issues have been agreed upon (i.e., "nothing is agreed upon until everything has been agreed upon")?

It is dangerous to drag out a series of partial settlements within the context of a single conflict structure. A string of partial deals may be useful if one is talking about a macroregional security complex such as Israel's broader relations with the Arab world. But for particular conflict dyads, as in the case of Israeli-Palestinian relations, the track record of incremental peacemaking is less than illustrious. Here, an approach of "nothing is agreed upon until everything has been agreed upon" may be desirable.

One reading of the Oslo process in the Middle East conflict is that it entailed a fundamental design flaw. By backloading the most difficult issues until a large number of interim measures had been achieved, Oslo placed a heavy burden on the continuity and staying power of leadership and on the implementation skills and intentions of all the players (including the third parties). Oslo's design also made the peace process a sitting duck for spoilers, assassins, and everyday political opportunists. In the event, the accords collapsed for a number of reasons: Rabin's assassination, mismanagement, dishonest implementation on both sides, miscalculation, cultural insensitivity, political instability, and the inability of a very weak Palestinian Authority to deliver on its promises.[2] But a strong case can also be made against the approach of beginning to implement interim measures before negotiating the basic outlines of an agreed-upon end state. The so-called Road Map promoted by the quartet of the United States, the European Union, the United Nations, and Russia, for instance, envisages implementation beginning before all major issues have been successfully negotiated. Such a method can succeed only if the third parties are prepared virtually to impose the steps and sequences on the parties. Most mediation is not conducted in a quasi-coercive fashion.

3. A related question concerns *the sequencing for negotiation of security measures and political issues: when should the parties work out the modalities of winding down hostile acts?* The mediator needs to induce the parties to come to a shared acceptance of a point at which the guns must fall silent and acts of violence come to an end. But when should this point occur? Is it good tradecraft to seek a truce or cease-fire early in the endgame in the belief that this will generate momentum and improve the climate for making tough political decisions? When the public and media focus on the need to bring costly violence under control, the sides may decide—perhaps for different reasons—to concentrate on immediate security objectives such as a cessation of hostilities or a cease-fire/disengagement deal. Mediators may even be tempted to adopt a narrow focus in order to stop the killing quickly, leaving aside other crucial issues that may appear to be less pressing, more open-ended, and less manageable. This appears to have been the case with the Norwegian-led negotiations in Sri Lanka in 2003, where the effort started with a "permanent cease-fire" that was supposed to be the prelude to more substantive political discussions over an agenda that was deliberately left vague and open-ended.

This approach has its risks, however. It encourages the parties to think in the short term and to engage in maneuvers and gambits aimed at buying time and gaining favorable security ground rules. The attempt to "sterilize" the military security issues when major political questions have not been dealt with can have the opposite effect of encouraging cheating and muscle-flexing on both sides, adding to the conflict's already massive scar tissue of distrust. The rush for a quick fix on security issues can also encourage party leaders to avoid facing up to deep-seated political questions that must be confronted if the core of the conflict is to be resolved and the terms of future coexistence defined. Procrastinating about the basic contours of the settlement also encourages political leaders to fudge and dissemble with their own domestic audiences about the real shape of an ultimate deal, a bad habit that can dangerously isolate leaders and negotiators when they most need a measure of public support.

In sum, the mediator is well advised to recall that the tradition of fight and talk is an ancient one, not confined to any specific culture. Equally ancient are the struggles between warring sides over this very issue. In the words of Fred Ikle, writing over thirty years ago about World Wars I and II, the Korean War, the war of Algerian independence, and the Greek civil war, "Sometimes, each side in a war refuses to negotiate for opposite reasons: one nation does not want to accept a cease-fire as a precondition to negotiation, while its enemy does not want to discuss a settlement as long as the fighting continues."[3] When considering proposals for early movement on military restraint, the mediator should have a watchful eye on the motives that may lurk behind them—for example, is one side (or both) eager merely for a breathing space, is the weaker side attempting to use the mediation to restrain the stronger side, is the dominant party attempting to force the weaker one to give up the military struggle before any political accord has been achieved, is one side trying to prove that the other cannot control its own commanders on the ground? While there are no rigid rules, experience suggests that cease-fires last longer when underpinned by a broad sense among the parties that a mutually acceptable framework for negotiation is coming within reach.

4. These considerations do not exclude a *significant role for confidence-building measures and political gestures aimed at shaping the negotiating environment.* Such measures can be useful at various stages of the mediation, including at the very outset of the endgame, when parties are just starting to explore each other's positions and flexibility. A mediator may choose to start the endgame by proposing reciprocal gestures related to humanitarian issues (establishing food corridors, releasing prisoners, and so forth) or by pressing the parties to tone down the shrill, polarized rhetoric in their public statements. Steps related to arms acquisition or ongoing military campaigns can also be undertaken as a means of signaling readiness to explore the negotiating track. Public statements to the home audiences of the parties tend to be closely watched by the two sides but are hard for mediators to shape and interpret across the negotiating table.

In general, intractable conflicts are fought by hardened and often skeptical parties whose leading players are more likely to view unilateral gestures by their adversaries as a form of propaganda or political theater than as a genuine signal of pacific intent. The mediators' best course, therefore, is to discourage unilateral actions and surprise moves and to work instead on tacitly agreed-upon avenues of cooperation or parallel gestures to improve the negotiating atmosphere.

5. Some of the most important ingredients of a settlement negotiation revolve around *how a settlement will be implemented, who will participate in facilitating and monitoring that process, what guarantees or verification measures will be available to the parties, and how to strengthen the credibility of commitments undertaken or proposed at the table.* The following chapter discusses the critical importance of the postsettlement, implementation phase of a peace process and outlines a wide range of measures that third parties can adopt to strengthen (or salvage) a settlement. Here, we focus on measures that can help assure that promises are kept, timetables respected, and matching commitments by the parties actually implemented. All of these measures aim at keeping the leading third party (or parties), who assisted the combatants in reaching a settlement, engaged in the settlement's implementation.

While these measures and provisions — sometimes called "guarantees" for short — do not come into effect until the implementation phase, *they have to be negotiated during the period leading up to settlement if they are to impress the parties and persuade them to take the risks of peace.* Bringing forward the discussion of guarantees enables them to acquire critical mass in the negotiating process. There are four types of measures for strengthening the credibility of a settlement.

The first is a variant of the diplomatic concept of "treaty powers," a historical term that refers to those states that gave assistance to, and put pressure on, the warring parties and helped bring about a negotiated settlement of their conflict. The conflict parties would ideally like such treaty powers to provide performance guarantees, a level of commitment exceeding the comfort level of most major states except in the rare case of a near-allied relationship with one of the signatories. The term "guarantors" — found in agreements such as the 1942 Rio Protocol, which sought to end the Ecuador-Peru border wars — has dropped away in more recent years in favor of such terms as "observers" who may "witness" an agreement and undertake to engage in consultations in the event of a violation.[4] In some accords, observers or facilitators sign or witness settlement documents in that capacity, thereby lending an aura of third-party engagement to the deal. Groups of "friends" and "contact groups" are another device for keeping alive the fabric of cooperation that may have developed during the settlement negotiations. Thus, *while performance guarantees are seldom available, parties to intractable conflicts will want to know — as they face up to life-and-death decisions at the presettlement stage — whether the third parties pushing peaceful settlement today will still be there tomorrow.* Mediators can expect such questions as they enter the endgame and should be ready to provide answers.

A second, more tangible and future-oriented measure is to *include in the settlement itself provision for the establishment of a specific mechanism to assist the conflict parties with coordination, troubleshooting and problem solving, and dispute management and resolution.* Such mechanisms are known by various names, including "roundtables," "joint committees," and "implementation councils." More important than the nomenclature is the concept that there is a first court of appeal and a sounding board that meets regularly, can take up issues brought to it by the parties, and includes key actors that participated in the negotiating process, as well as actors that may become part of the implementation phase. A mechanism of this sort is always useful to backstop a settlement. In the case of intractable conflicts, it could become indispensable, because the challenge of keeping an agreement on track is so much greater.

More specifically focused are certain settlement measures that provide for direct, external participation in the implementation process. Examples include human rights, election, and cease-fire/disarmament monitors, but the range of possibilities is wide. External observers may be called upon to render an opinion or even serve temporarily in an expert capacity in particular fields (e.g., military and police training, the judiciary, and banking) where controversy is inevitable and where the benefit of comparative, objective experience may be reassuring. Another variant of this approach is the participation of third parties in the process of verification and intelligence sharing with the warring parties on a basis negotiated between them. (This sort of undertaking can supplement the work of observers and peacekeepers deployed by international or regional agencies.) Less formal, but far from negligible, is the role of free media in the implementation of settlements: after all, one way to hold people to their word is to write about them when they cheat.

A fourth type of measure for buttressing settlements as they are being negotiated is the incorporation of external experts in working groups and commissions that will actually implement aspects of the accords. Provisions that call for the participation of electoral and constitutional experts, census specialists, economists, and reconstruction personnel can be inserted in an agreement. An area of especial salience in intractable conflicts is the question of how natural resources will be managed and revenues collected and allocated. An equitable basis for sharing resources and revenues should be developed in order to outflank spoilers and expand the opportunities for the parties to cooperate. When distrust is high, the participation of outsiders will be essential in creating confidence that customs services, public-sector employment commissions, criminal courts and truth commissions, state oil or agricultural boards, privatization agencies, and other official bodies will not become quagmires of corruption and partisan self-dealing.

Given the broader challenges of social and political engineering on complex matters such as creating truth and reconciliation commissions, designing constitutions, developing power sharing, holding elections, and reforming the judicial and security sectors, it may be desirable to make the parties aware of different models that have been tried and developed in other countries. Mediators clearly have a vital educational role to play in exposing parties to the knowledge and experience of those who have dealt with similar issues and challenges. This kind of educational function has been effectively performed by intermediaries such as Max van der Stoel, the former high commissioner for national minorities in the OSCE, and by countries such as Norway, which hosted discussions between the Sri Lankan government and the northern Tamil insurgents on different approaches to federalism. The United States Institute of Peace is regularly called upon to organize symposia, workshops, and training sessions whose explicit goal is the sharing of comparative experience and the marshaling of expertise from outside the immediate conflict zone on such issues as education and security-sector reform, the rule of law and transitional justice, and religious reconciliation. The goal of such third-party activity is to assist the parties in coming to grips with their own situations. Such efforts have been organized at the request of parties in the Balkans, Sudan, Rwanda, South Asia, Iraq, Afghanistan, Indonesia, and the Philippines.

6. All of the preceding ingredients—agenda, sequence and structure, cease-fire timing, confidence-building measures, guarantees during implementation—are important to the building of a settlement in an intractable conflict. *None of them, however, is as important as hammering out a framework of negotiation or a statement or declaration of principles.* This is the piece without which the puzzle will not be solved. It reflects those commitments in principle that are politically vital to the conflict parties and logically vital to the integrity of the settlement. Such a document can be as short as a page or much longer and more elaborate. A declaration of principles draws directly from the negotiating agenda and seeks to translate that agenda into a binding set of matching commitments according to which the parties enter into reciprocal, conditional undertakings ("I'll do this if you'll do that"). Its role is to describe—albeit typically in veiled and generalized language designed to meet each party's political requirements —the essential trade-offs that constitute the deal. Without such a statement, cease-fires have a tendency to collapse and negotiators lose sight of the basic purpose of the process and get bogged down in responding to diversions and tactical gamesmanship.

A declaration of principles or a negotiating framework does not, by any means, solve the conflict or conclude the mediation. It may, in fact, never appear explicitly in the final peace agreement; this is a matter of choice—some recent accords incorporate the basic principles as the first chapter of the peace treaty, while others may cite it in preambular language or simply repeat and elaborate on its main points. Rather, a declaration or framework serves as a lighthouse and series of guideposts to those seeking to navigate through the typically intricate and abstruse details of the deal. As the saying goes, the devil is always in the details, but the devil becomes especially satanic in the absence of a negotiating framework.

There is no abstract formula for creating one. Rather, the framework emerges from months, even years, of diplomacy and warfare as parties and mediators test each other and explore ideas and reactions. Among the items likely to appear in a framework or statement of principles are certain familiar principles drawn from international law relating to the universal rights of states and nations/peoples; the readiness of the sides to live together and to act on the basis of mutual respect; and some definition of the basic deal or outcome couched in very general and honorable language and described in terms that are salable both domestically (for the conflict parties) and internationally. The deal itself may be contained in separate, unlinked paragraphs, but each principle will typically be considered indispensable, so that no party is entitled to pick and choose. The deal is a package, based perhaps on a linkage of principal goals (e.g., "land for peace," "unity with self-determination," or mutual troop reductions), on a split-the-difference compromise among such values as timing and geography, or on some form of procedural mechanism such as arbitration or elections. In civil conflicts, the deal will often be defined under such broad rubrics as power and wealth sharing, constitutional process, security-sector reform, and respect for previously contested rights and freedoms (relating to, for example, religion, language, and schooling). In many cases, the framework will set target dates for the achievement of a specific state of affairs and will make clear what that end state should look like. Often, a declaration will describe the transition process for full implementation of the envisaged peace treaty and outline benchmarks for getting there, including the concept of a comprehensive and permanent cease-fire, building on de facto accords that may already be emerging.

CONCLUSION

The preceding discussion will have achieved its purpose if it helps the mediator to identify some of the component elements of the settlement and to think about how the parts fit together. The real meat of the mediation endgame will, of necessity, focus on translating the principles or framework just discussed into a set of binding commitments spelled out in sufficient detail as to satisfy the conflict parties and inspire confidence that the road to full implementation has been defined. As the next chapter makes clear, no one should have illusions that the settlement talks are the end of the mediation process. In reality, they are but the beginning of the next round of negotiations, this time about how to implement agreed-upon provisions, how to interpret them, how to deal with nonperformance, how to buttress the chances for faithful compliance, and, as necessary, how to adapt creatively the negotiated package to surmount obstacles and address issues not previously anticipated.

8

Making a Settlement Stick

THE FORMAL CEREMONY OF SIGNING A PEACE AGREEMENT is often accompanied by much public fanfare. Photographs of party leaders shaking hands — at long last — appear in newspapers all over the globe. In the background, the mediator and other friends of the process stand like proud parents at a graduation ceremony. The joint statements to the press by the former antagonists promise a new day in which mutual recriminations, recitation of grievances, and bloody attacks and reprisals will be things of the past. The promised new day, however, has all too often proved a false dawn, whose glimmerings of peace fade quickly into darkness as fighting resumes.[1] In the aftermath, the parties justify reverting to violence by pointing out that the other side broke the agreement first. They claim that their untrustworthy opponents brought the resumption of fighting on themselves — they could not control their radical fringes, they were using the cease-fire to rearm and reposition, they were never serious about living up to the agreement.

In this litany of complaints, parties rarely accuse the mediators of letting them down after the agreement was signed. And yet, the lack of continued third-party engagement during this period is almost a guarantee that the settlement will collapse. What can mediators do to help the parties implement a negotiated settlement and nail it down so that they do not go back to war? What specific lessons about securing a sustainable settlement can we learn from the all-too-common experience of watching the newfound optimism at the signing ceremony give way to old enmity on the morning after?

DEALING WITH INTRACTABILITY'S LEGACY: THIRD-PARTY ENGAGEMENT IN A DIFFICULT SETTING

Just as intractable conflicts differ from other conflicts during their long run as active wars, so do they differ in the postsettlement period. A long war is much more likely than a short one to leave behind a devastated economy, with little investment in anything but the business of war. The war also affects all types of social institutions — religion, education, and families — in ways that bequeath the parents' hostility and grievance to their children, grandchildren, and great-grandchildren. Lost generations of young people come of age without skills for peacetime, having spent their formative years in learning how to fight and survive. And many — often girls and young women — are denied an education altogether.

The same leaders who spent their careers trying to destroy each other now have to work out some sort of accommodation that will allow their societies to move forward. Political intransigence will have to yield to compromise. In some cases, parties will have to learn about governance, about running a country on a daily basis. In other cases, they in effect will have to go back to school, educating themselves about different political structures — power sharing or federalism, for instance — that offer solutions to postconflict governance dilemmas.

Protracted internal conflicts can leave a society and its leaders isolated from the rest of the world. Absorbed by their own problems, societies can emerge from many years of conflict only to find that their political, economic, and cultural ties with the rest of the world have atrophied. At the same time, their next generation either has had no real contact with the outside world or has moved away in search of a better life. Conflict can become the principal — or only — lens through which all other relationships are viewed. A conflict puts blinders on its participants, narrowing their field of vision and hampering the ability to exchange the information and develop the contacts that allow societies to function in the larger world.

The challenges, then, of the postsettlement period after an intractable conflict are immense, while the internal capacity to turn from a state of war to a state of peace is weak. The signed agreement may not provide guidance for very important elements of this transition. For instance, in many cases the question of demobilization is considered too fraught to take up during the peace negotiations and is put off to a future date.[2] In the interests of reaching an agreement, human rights issues are often left off the table entirely.[3] But both of these subjects can obstruct the implementation process because they contain issues of fundamental disagreement that may be deal-breakers for one of the adversaries or for the wider society. Left on their own, the conflict parties find it very difficult to chart a path for reconciliation or to work out their differences. The involvement of outside intermediaries becomes as critical at this stage as during the peace negotiations.

Facing different challenges in these intractable conflicts, intermediaries may need to revise and adapt their roles. A principal task for mediators in intractable conflicts is to set up a mechanism that includes actors who have an interest in the outcome and that actively engages them during the postsettlement phase. Although this effort can be very time-consuming, it heightens the chances that a broad range of interested parties will support and invest in the postconflict settlement. At the core of the implementation phase are those armed, adversarial leaders who previously directed the warring parties. Equally central in a well-designed settlement process is the continued engagement of the third party or coalition of third parties that helped the warring parties make peace.[4] In this postsettlement phase, third parties come in many sizes and shapes, and their role may or may not be formalized.

Postsettlement mediators also have to reach out to key allies, actors, and institutional interests in the wider international community. The objective of this engagement is not just to focus international attention and concern on a given conflict but also to marshal resources and critical bases of political and economic support at the point when they are needed most, namely, at the hour of decision, when the parties are ready to buy into a negotiated settlement. There are simply too many challenges, too many unfulfilled needs and ambitions among the parties, for a single, sparsely equipped team of negotiators to address without securing additional, external sources of support. Similarly, a central role for third parties at this point in the process is to create and sustain a focal point of coordination among these disparate actors: to make sure that promises are kept, timetables carefully respected, resource commitments lived up to, matching commitments by the former warring parties faithfully implemented, and fundamental disagreements and glaring cases of nonperformance addressed and resolved.[5]

Reaching out to and coordinating additional external actors is not enough. Mediators have to consider the unmet needs and ambitions of the local population, where the most enduring legacies of the conflict lie.[6] Strategies of peacemaking must be complemented early on in a settlement by actions and initiatives that provide concrete benefits to those have who have paid the greatest price for conflict.[7]

This chapter looks at the strategies and tools that mediators can employ during the postsettlement phase of the peace process. Because much has been written elsewhere about the wider challenges of peacebuilding, we have chosen to focus in this chapter on the most immediate and pressing choices about tradecraft that mediators confront once negotiations have gathered momentum and a potential settlement is within their grasp or already at hand. In this discussion, we do not assign particular options to particular actors, although some approaches will be more natural for powerful states and some for well-connected middle powers or NGOs. Our point is that all of these approaches must be considered in a postconflict setting for an intractable conflict. It is difficult to achieve coherence and to establish conflict-specific mechanisms for coordination, problem solving, and dispute management and resolution. The key third-party institutions—state based, international, or unofficial—must work together to provide the comprehensive and multifaceted assistance that parties need in the implementation phase.[8]

VARIETIES OF DIPLOMACY AND STATECRAFT IN PURSUIT OF PEACE

Students and practitioners of conflict management have too often viewed mediation in exclusionary terms, as involving a choice between, on the one hand, the adoption of coercive (or highly manipulative) bargaining strategies and, on the other hand, dialogue, facilitation, and a generous dosage of what is sometimes referred to as track-two—or unofficial—diplomacy. In the highly unsettled world of intractable conflicts, these are false choices. In terms of tactical approaches, mediators must be able to use a mixed strategy that involves a combination of coercive diplomacy and other, "softer," bargaining and negotiation strategies in order to lead the parties forward. Coercive diplomacy and the use of powerful sticks are sometimes necessary to get the parties back to the negotiating table (in whatever format makes the most sense now that the process has entered the postsettlement phase). On occasion, coercive measures are necessary to make peace stick. Coercion, however, is not enough. Mediators must also be able to employ positive inducements, reflected in concrete incentives, to establish and maintain peace. Equally important are innovative strategies that create space for previously ignored constituencies and that use tools of communication and dialogue to change social and psychological perceptions about the risks involved in buying into a political framework for settlement.[9]

The Use of Force in Inducing Peace

The experience of the 1990s illustrates the organic and sometimes indispensable linkage between force and diplomacy.[10] One important lesson of international diplomatic efforts in Bosnia is that mediators may require coercive diplomacy and the use of force to bring into line those elements that have no apparent interest in reaching a negotiated settlement because they do not fear the regional (or international) consequences of escalating a conflict or continuing with their armed struggle. The 1995 Dayton accords that ended the active, violent phase of the Bosnian conflict, were the product and to some extent the beneficiary of coercive mediation.[11] First, the prospect and then the reality of a changing military balance were required to get the parties to the table at Dayton and keep them there until terms were hammered out to bring the fighting to an end. Second, the credible prospect of a substantial, NATO-led peace enforcement operation being deployed immediately after agreements were signed made it possible to drive the parties to settlement and to keep the postconflict reconstruction and peace implementation effort from breaking down. This was an imposed peace, using sixty thousand troops from the world's most militarily capable states to stop the violence in its tracks, support complex and controversial new political arrangements negotiated among the parties, and gradually —over a period of years—establish a climate of stability that has led to further intergroup and regional political changes.

Obviously, Bosnia provides an exceptional model for peace implementation, as U.S. or NATO military assets are usually not available to mediators. The organizations that are frequently involved in postconflict reconstruction—the United Nations, regional organizations, and occasionally middle powers—have significant limitations in the field of peace enforcement and coercive diplomacy, and those limitations are often recognized by the warring parties. If there is neither the capacity nor the will to use coercion credibly, mediators should avoid commitments to future actions on which they may well be tested. By the same token, mediators also have to ensure that those who pledge to place troops on the ground once the settlement is concluded will make good on their commitments without delay.

An essential element for effective peace implementation is that specific conflicts and external actors are carefully matched and that the lead nation (or group of nations) shepherding a specific settlement or agreement into the implementation phase has the requisite sense of ownership of the peace process. Thus, for example, the Australians (backed by a UN mandate and the prospect of a follow-on, UN-led peace operation) successfully mounted a peace enforcement operation in East Timor—a conflict that was in their own neighborhood.[12] When an international or regional body is called upon to oversee peace implementation and deploy peacekeepers, a lead nation working alongside the operation may be required, as the British demonstrated in Sierra Leone, when they bolstered the shaky UNAMSIL operation in 2000–2003.[13] This pattern could be replicated in the case of the MONUC operation in the Democratic Republic of Congo. In such circumstances, limited peace enforcement operations provide support for the peacekeeping presence called for in negotiated settlements.

However, not every case requires NATO or U.S. military capabilities and the wielding of major coercive threats. Just as there is a range of third-party actors that can influence the security environment in which peacemaking takes place, there is a spectrum of coercive instruments. Peace implementation depends on such military-related tools and techniques as monitoring and observing cease-fire lines, buffering and separating forces, demobilizing and disarming combatants, and projecting an armed presence in support of civil authority to bolster stability and confidence. The term "coercive inducement" captures this spectrum of activities.[14] In the highly unstable security environment of a negotiated cease-fire in an intractable conflict setting, breaches of the peace are almost inevitable. If the conflict parties represent diffuse and fractured (or factionalized) constituencies, the eruption of violence is practically a foregone conclusion, because there will be spoilers who will want to derail the peace process before it generates any kind of momentum.

Nonmilitary Coercion

SANCTIONS AND THE POLITICAL ECONOMY OF VIOLENCE. Getting a peace process to stick while ensuring that the parties do not resume fighting when events move in directions they do not like calls for a strategy to suffocate the fires that drive intractable conflicts. Those parties that support negotiation efforts in intractable conflict zones need to think more broadly about the political economy of violence and the forces that sustain it. Easy access to arms through the illicit sale of contraband minerals and resources such as gold, diamonds, and oil is one of the endemic features of many intractable conflicts. Rentier economies controlled by guerrilla warlords or governments, or both, are likewise a critical element in the intractability equation. Those interested in promoting a peace process and weaning the parties from their addiction to violence have to make continued violence less profitable.[15]

Targeted sanctions have proved useful in helping to introduce some sort of control over the sources of wealth and arms that help fuel violence in intractable conflict zones. For example, the naming and shaming exercises in the United Nations over the sale of "blood diamonds," rare minerals, and timber products in such conflicted societies as Angola, Congo, Liberia, and Sierra Leone have put pressure on these countries' leaders and neighbors to control the illicit trading routes that have helped fund guerrilla movements and perpetuate predatory violence by state actors.[16] Building international (and regional) support for sanctions regimes that will cut the parties off from their international sponsors is an important aspect of a broader conflict management strategy directed at bringing intractable conflicts to an end. A related dimension is the growing international attention being paid by mediators and other third parties to the management and allocation of revenues derived from the exploitation of natural resources so that wealth and benefits are shared in ways that directly and forcefully support peace. This dimension of tradecraft applies to both the presettlement and postsettlement phases.[17]

DEALING WITH SPOILERS. In general, third parties helping to implement peace settlements have a clearly defined strategy for monitoring the security situation, investigating acts of violence, and ensuring that the parties do not take matters into their own hands through acts of reprisal that escalate tensions.[18] Sometimes this means placing observers on the ground who can quickly be deployed to investigate and report on cease-fire violations.[19] When peacekeepers are deployed, they should have the requisite authority not just to investigate cease-fire violations but also to operate under appropriate rules of engagement that do not jeopardize their mission. When no agreement exists for the deployment of observer or peacekeeping units, mediators may be tempted to put talks on hold until the security situation stabilizes. But such a move would send the wrong signal to those who want to strangle the peace process at birth. Mediators therefore have to mobilize all available resources and partners to place the parties on notice that a return to violence is not acceptable and will jeopardize the inducements that attracted them to the settlement in the first place.

DISARMAMENT AND DEMOBILIZATION. Another critical element in nailing a settlement down is getting the parties to disarm and demobilize (i.e., downsize or disband their forces) as laid down in the accord.[20] In many settlements, these two steps are followed by a restructuring of the security forces to create an ethnically or politically balanced national army. It is widely recognized that a peace process has a much greater chance of succeeding if security-based, confidence-building processes are completed on a tight schedule and ideally before an electoral process is set in motion. A peace process is much more likely to fail if the sequence of demilitarization initiatives falls too far behind political timetables. Outright refusal by the parties to respect security provisions of a settlement is a prescription for disaster. A settlement's long-term success ultimately hinges on the way that these issues are handled by the conflict parties and by external third parties in the early stages of the peace process.

In intractable conflicts, powerful political and psychological incentives encourage the parties to avoid, delay, and defer disarming and demobilizing their forces, and to renegotiate and default on provisions to do so, even if agreement is reached on other outstanding political issues. The acute security dilemma that the parties experience in an intractable conflict makes them extremely wary of their negotiating partners and reluctant to do anything that will compromise their security—even if offered security guarantees by external actors, in the form of peacekeeping deployments.[21]

The Angolan experience with the implementation of the 1992 Bicesse Accords starkly illustrates the point.[22] The demobilization of government (MPLA) and UNITA forces fell far behind the schedule outlined in the agreement. Over forty thousand troops were still not demobilized on the election date and the forces of both sides were more or less completely intact. Unrealistic timetables, along with a lack of cooperation by both parties, contributed to the failure of demobilization efforts in Angola and, thus, of the Bicesse Accords. The dearth of resources available to the UN peacekeeping force also undermined the process. But the broader lesson is that the United Nations was not able to nail the settlement down because demobilization did not occur before the critical political element in the peace process: countrywide elections. The continued existence of the two armies allowed violence to rapidly resurface once the

UNITA leader, Jonas Savimbi, decided he was dissatisfied with the election results. Similarly, in the case of the internationalized civil war in the Democratic Republic of Congo, both the internal and the regional parties consistently manipulated the agreed-upon timetables for implementation of cease-fire and troop-withdrawal commitments contained in the 1999 Lusaka Protocol.

These cases stand in sharp contrast to the experience in Namibia in 1989–90, where UNTAG—the UN peacekeeping force —was tasked with monitoring a cease-fire; confining South African and SWAPO forces to authorized locations; monitoring the withdrawal of some South African forces and confining to base the remainder until elections were completed; and monitoring the disbanding of various reserve and commando units.[23] Despite hiccups and challenges, these tasks were completed before UNTAG-supervised elections were held and the process of writing a constitution begun. The parallel security commitments to Cuban troop withdrawal from Angola, carried out under the authority of UN monitors known as UNAVEM, were similarly implemented in accordance with a precise and rigorous timeline. In the case of the UN operation in Mozambique in 1992–94, initial timetables were deliberately revised precisely in order to ensure that commitments could be implemented and that military and political components did not become unsynchronized.[24]

The most difficult and intractable issue in the conflict in Northern Ireland has been the "decommissioning" of all paramilitary arms (i.e., the process by which the paramilitaries would hand over their weapons).[25] The 1998 Good Friday Agreement, which established a political mechanism to link the governments of Ireland and the United Kingdom and a power-sharing framework to be followed by elections for an elected assembly for Northern Ireland, called for —but did not stipulate a schedule for—the decommissioning of weapons. Much of the negotiation centered on the practical modalities of decommissioning because concrete, firm timetables proved impossible to negotiate. As a consequence, the decommissioning issue remains a thorn in the side of the peace process. Although a number of symbolic acts have been staged in which small numbers of decommissioned weapons have been destroyed, various paramilitary forces are still in possession of most of their arms. This situation has left the peace process in limbo. On the positive side, however, those sponsoring ongoing negotiations between the parties have not given up on this issue. General John de Chastelain, one of the members of the original mediation team that helped negotiate the Good Friday Agreement, has continued to press the IRA not only to agree to a timetable for decommissioning but also to begin the process with more than symbolic gestures.

◆　◆　◆

As this brief discussion illustrates, the challenge for any third party assisting with the implementation of a settlement are formidable. Mediators have several options: ensuring that these troublesome issues are dealt with in a settlement, even if parties agree only to a commitment-in-principle to address them later; setting a clear timetable for subsequent negotiations linked to other elements of the overall settlement; creating and identifying external and local sources of leverage that can maintain pressure on the parties to fulfill their commitment to disarm; and delaying and renegotiating provisions of the accord if necessary in order to ensure that the parties do not get away with implementing it à la carte in order to obtain unilateral advantages. Parties will use almost any excuse to charge the other side with violating the terms of an agreement and, in the process, wiggle out of their own negotiated commitments and obligations. As negotiating timetables get pushed further and further back, the danger grows that the peace process will unravel. Mediators have to be prepared to negotiate (and renegotiate) timetables and the details of the agreement. It may be necessary to restructure the agreement to offset different obligations that the parties have failed to discharge. This is no easy task, but it is doable. However, at some point the mediator will have to tell the parties that enough is enough and that now it is time to move forward. The main point for the postsettlement mediator is straightforward: fudging the observance of security provisions will not work.

Breaking Defensive Investments

Intractable conflicts require special bargaining skills and often the use
of novel negotiating methods to change psychological dispositions
and break the cycle of violence.[26] As the terms of a settlement
emerge, negotiators have to convince the parties that the situation
can really change and that others have gone down the path of peace
successfully before.

Parties to an intractable conflict typically view their problems
and concerns as unique and immutable. They are unwilling to think
about alternative political futures because the warring status quo is
a way of life. Their sense of victimhood and grievance is usually
anchored in a reading of history that lays the blame entirely on the
other side.[27] People have invested in behaviors and routines that sym-
bolize their situation, and it is often difficult to persuade them to respect verbal cease-fires and to enter into new kinds of relationships
that allow them to overcome their anxieties and see change and new
processes in a positive light.[28] Mediators must find ways to overcome
the parties' defensive investments by challenging the view that it is
noble to be a victim.

As the parties begin to think seriously about an alternative
political future, a mediator may find it helpful to introduce the parties
to others who have been in a similar situation and have dealt with the
political risks associated with a settlement. Workshops that allow
potential or would-be peacemakers to learn from others help infuse
a sense of confidence in the peace process, breaking psychological
molds and inspiring the parties to think about their own situation in
a radically new light.[29] In the case of Northern Ireland, for example,
a series of workshops sponsored by the Institute for Democracy in
South Africa allowed key players in the peace process to compare
notes with their South African counterparts. These talks focused not
just on general experiences but on the practicalities of overcoming
intractable issues and getting from point A to point B in a peace process. The South Africans were also able to spot design flaws in the
Irish process. In a continuation of this chain of learning, both Irish

and South Africans have played the same role in the Sri Lankan peace process.

Nurturing a Moderate Middle

Although various kinds of hard-power inducements, including coercive measures, may be required to deal with spoilers who want to derail a negotiated settlement, the flip side of the coin is reconciliation and negotiation strategies that build, strengthen, and cement alliances between and among moderate political elements on all sides of the partisan divide.[30] This center of gravity has to be nurtured and maintained during all phases of the peace process, including the negotiation of the final details of a settlement and its implementation. Ultimately, the best defense against spoilers is a moderate political alliance that enjoys widespread and growing political legitimacy and support, has the authority to speak out against violence and acts of retribution, and is able to rally public opinion in support of the peace process and the terms of settlement. As Adrian Guelke notes, "The center is an alliance fused around the mutual recognition that settlement must be achieved 'come what may.'"[31]

Strengthening voices and interests at the moderate political center may be crucial to deflecting the various challenges and surmounting the numerous obstacles that spoilers erect in the path of a settlement. Sometimes this center is nurtured by the parties themselves, with largely indirect, symbolic political support from external actors. In South Africa, for example, the pact at the center was held together by President F. W. de Klerk and Nelson Mandela, the leaders, respectively, of the National Party and the African National Congress. Both leaders were firmly convinced that to avoid a national bloodbath they had to work closely together and ensure that the settlement worked. In other instances, mediators at both the track-one and track-two levels have created forums that have allowed groups to get together and build the kinds of interpersonal working relationships that are conducive to reaching an internal settlement. In Northern Ireland, new mediation techniques ultimately helped pave the way for John Hume's dialogue with Gerry Adams—a dialogue which, as Paul Arthur observes, was "necessary to end IRA violence."[32]

CREATING A COALITION FOR PEACE: REACHING OUT AND REACHING DOWN

Reaching Out

Intractable conflicts may be driven by a myriad of social, political, and economic forces and interests, some internal and some external. The chances of successfully implementing a settlement in an intractable conflict will be improved if mediators are able to reach out to other actors and interests—international and domestic—who see themselves as having a stake in the outcome of a peace process and the terms of a final settlement. Mediators cannot assume that a negotiated settlement will automatically generate political support on its own within either the immediate neighborhood or the wider international community. Mediators have to think holistically about the terms and modalities of a settlement. Their challenge is not just to help the parties to the conflict devise a new set of political arrangements that satisfy the major interests of elites but also to think about social, economic, and political mechanisms—beyond the immediate details and framework of the settlement itself—that will nurture and sustain the settlement not only from within (and below) but also from the outside.

Because most intractable conflicts are embedded in a wider system of subregional, regional, or even global interests, mediators have to be prepared to negotiate with multiple interests at multiple levels. It is essential to engage this panoply of actors and interests—sometimes supportive, sometimes hostile—in the negotiated outcome. They can actively undermine a settlement if they are not somehow co-opted or coerced into supporting it.

Establishing a negotiating forum or mechanism where key regional and international actors can meet and interact during the presettlement phase will encourage them to buy into the process. The fact that the five permanent members of the Security Council, all of whom had broader, systemic interests in the outcome of the Cambodian peace process in the early 1990s, were represented at the negotiating table in Paris was no accident. Their presence helped not only to ensure that the different Cambodian factions and regional actors (e.g., Vietnam) stayed the course in the negotiations but also to reduce the incentives to undermine the settlement once its main provisions were agreed upon.[33] The same can also be said about James A. Baker III's Middle East diplomacy, which paved the road to Madrid and helped create a supportive regional environment for the subsequent Oslo peace process.[34] Although the Americans were not directly involved in Oslo, Washington's broader efforts at regional engagement both before and after the Oslo accords lent a combination of legitimacy and direct support to that process—at least in its early phases. The Clinton administration's efforts in 2000–2001 to conclude a settlement between Israelis and Palestinians foundered, at least partly, on its failure sufficiently to engage regional players who were allies of PLO chairman Yassir Arafat and in a position to exert pressure on him.[35]

The multilevel nature of intractable conflicts places unusually severe pressures on mediators who are dealing directly with the parties while also engaging other regional and international players. Engaging this broader constituency, however, may prove to be essential not only in getting the parties to agree on a settlement but also in building up and sustaining the pressures and incentives required to get the parties to live up to the terms of their agreement.

A variant on this method of reaching out is for mediators to build into the settlement discussions a specific vehicle or institutional mechanism, which includes both the conflict parties and the key third parties, to help oversee the implementation of the settlement. A number of the African settlements of the late 1980s and 1990s included such devices as joint commissions and groups of "friends" or donors that were linked to the settlement and committed to participate in periodic meetings to review the process. The Namibia-Angola settlement of 1988, for example, established a tripartite joint commission of signatory parties plus observers from the United States and the Soviet Union (and later the United Nations) that met monthly for the duration of the agreed-upon implementation period to help keep the process on an even keel.[36] A different model was used in the 1942 Rio Protocol, which established four guarantor powers that went into action decades later, in 1995, when armed conflict flared up once again between Ecuador and Peru.[37]

A third dimension of reaching out involves domestic interest groups in the mediator's home country and foreign interest groups made up of overseas representatives of the conflict parties. For mediators working in a foreign ministry or the U.S. State Department, the most immediate challenge may come from individuals who represent different bureaucratic or political constituencies and are pursuing a range of policy initiatives that are working at cross-purposes to the mediator's own efforts. Domestic interest groups may also consist of powerful nongovernmental coalitions that favor one side in the conflict. The role that conservative Christian groups have played in the Sudan mediation of 2001–3 is an example of such a coalition. By mobilizing their membership, putting pressure on elected officials, and approaching the Bush administration directly, they have attempted to influence public debate about U.S. involvement in Sudan and to persuade the U.S. mediator to support the Christian southern Sudanese over the Islamist government in Khartoum. Navigating through this pressure has required U.S. diplomats to demonstrate considerable domestic political skill.

Diaspora communities and other mobilized domestic constituencies can also compromise the efforts of mediators who represent countries that are ethnically and culturally diverse. When different ethnic communities import partisan loyalties (and struggles) from their homelands and are prepared to lend their political and financial support to those struggles, they can greatly complicate the life of the mediator and the broader foreign policy environment within which he or she operates. For example, the sizable Haitian community in Canada forced the government's hand and encouraged a more proactive foreign policy when President Aristide, the first elected leader of Haiti's fledgling democracy, was overthrown in a bloodless coup in the early 1990s.[38] Members of the Armenian diaspora played a similar role in the conflict between Armenia and Azerbaijan over Nagorno-Karabakh.

It is also important to recognize that diaspora communities can play a crucial supporting role if they are encouraged to buy into the peace process. For example, President Bill Clinton's efforts to reach out to the Irish American community and to persuade them to curb the flow of arms and other kinds of illicit support for the IRA played a critical role in the peace process in Northern Ireland and greatly strengthened the hand of Senator George Mitchell as a mediator in this dispute.[39]

It is also critical to engage the international donor community. This community can provide funds to secure the requisite levels of humanitarian and development relief assistance and to channel it to those areas where it is needed most.[40] If a peace process is to gather momentum and generate political support, the local populace has to be persuaded that there are real, tangible gains that come from it. It is wrong to assume that a people wearied by war will automatically embrace a peace process. No matter how exhausted or shattered local communities are by recurring conflict and violence, they have to be shown that the peace process pays real (and not just theoretical) dividends. Otherwise, there will be strong incentives to return to fighting and warfare, especially in a populace that is all too prepared to use violence as a basic survival strategy. The peace dividend initially has to come in the form of direct humanitarian assistance and relief and rehabilitation programs, to be followed by longer-term economic and social development programs and incentives.

Mediators rarely have direct control over the kinds of resources that are necessary to create concrete incentives for the warring parties and their constituents to buy into a peace process. Mediators therefore have to reach out to potential allies in the donor community early on in the peace process to ensure that donors will pony up and put money and resources on the table. This requires a combination of diplomacy—especially if potential donors are other governments or international agencies—and lobbying. Donors are wary of throwing scarce resources into zones where the risks are high that they will not see a positive return on their investment. Regardless of whether they represent foreign ministries, NGOs, or international and regional organizations, mediators have to know which humanitarian, social, and economic ingredients are required to make a peace process work and must then devise a strategy to get the donors on board.

The International Monetary Fund, the World Bank, and regional international financial institutions are obviously key players in shaping development and economic reconstruction policies for war-torn societies. Although these institutions—and especially the World Bank—are likely to take the lead in designing recovery programs, they will also work closely with a range of bilateral donors and other actors. Because many donors will take their cues from the World Bank, it is important for the mediators to lay the groundwork and to identify priorities for social and economic reconstruction early on in the process.[41]

Reaching Down

One of the key challenges in building support for a peace process within a society, or from "below," is to put in place mechanisms that will address the security and other needs of the local communities. If violence is ongoing and different local groups feel threatened, it will be difficult—if not impossible—to build nationwide support for the peace process. Close attention, therefore, has to be paid both to maintaining physical security and to reforming the security sector at the local and not just the national level.[42] Some of the key questions to be addressed include: Are local police or military commanders responsible for human rights violations? If they are, what concrete measures can be taken to investigate these abuses and prevent violations from reoccurring? What are the main obstacles to security-sector reform at both the national and the local levels? What steps must be taken to ensure that reform and political transition keep potential spoilers in check and do not create a security vacuum that could all too easily be filled by criminals and disgruntled ex-combatants? How can the rule of law and judicial systems be strengthened and improved to make them more effective, more transparent, and more accountable so that human rights abuses are curtailed?[43]

Some peace accords are essentially political compacts negotiated between the leaders who control the guns. Such settlements will be far more durable if they are viewed as the first stage in a broader process of transformation that gradually changes the relationship between armed elites and the society as a whole. Thus, a second challenge is to find ways to empower the local populace in the peace process so that elites are accountable to their constituents.[44] Strengthening the links between civil societies and the state institutions is an important aspect of this process. Another is reducing the level of fragmentation and confrontation within civil society and between civil society and the government so that constructive dialogue can occur. The peace process in Guatemala, which began with the Contadora Declaration of August 1995 and concluded with a settlement in 1996 that was negotiated under UN auspices, illustrates the multiple difficulties of generating civil society engagement and public participation.[45] On the one hand, the immediate impact of the accords was positive. New public institutions were created, as mandated by the agreements. The human rights situation in the country improved dramatically. Violent internal armed conflict came to end and ex-combatants were disarmed and demobilized. A conscious and deliberate attempt was made to engage civil society by establishing the Civil Society Assembly, which contributed to the national dialogue and provided important input into the negotiations and the subsequent terms of the settlement. On the other hand, the political situation several years later remains extremely fragile, largely because of continuing fragmentation within civil society, a lack of accountability to the country's populace by political institutions and the élites who control them, and a weak and biased media that have made it difficult to debate issues and criticize the government. The peace process will move forward only if these shortcomings are rectified.

Pioneers of transformation in an intractable conflict all too often come under attack. As the assassinations of Anwar Sadat and Yitzhak Rabin illustrate, agents of transformation are risk takers who sometimes pay the supreme price.[46] Peace depends on the presence of such risk takers not only at the elite level but also at the community level. Track-two initiatives and other kinds of social and facilitation dialogues can help to identify these communal risk takers and to create forums that facilitate learning and allow the local community to engage in the kinds of behavioral and psychological change required to support a peace process from below. Key elements of civil society—and not just elites—ultimately have to share the political and social risks that come with peace.

CONCLUSION

In the previous chapter, we used the term "endgame" to signify the goal of achieving a signed agreement. This chapter makes clear that the signing of an agreement is not, in fact, the endgame, either for the signatories or for the mediator. Rather, it is an invitation to the next round of negotiations. These negotiations are, of course, rooted in and shaped by the actions taken and decisions made during the peace negotiations. The consequence is that the key to success in the implementation process lies partly in the past and partly in the present. The mediator may be required to assist the parties with negotiation and renegotiation of contentious issues or operational details that were glossed over, postponed, or ignored when the peace agreement was drawn up. A peace agreement is, after all, a relatively short document, stronger on general principles than on practical guidance for resolving specific disputes. Often, the third party involved in the implementation of an agreement is not the central player during the peace negotiations and has to translate the parties' general commitments into concrete activities without the benefit of direct participation in negotiating the terms. Handoffs between the two phases are rarely as well informed and well prepared as they should be. Connecting the negotiating phase of reaching an agreement with the implementation phase—when peacemaking is replaced by peacebuilding—may be the single most important step that friends and guarantors of a peace process can take to secure a settlement and make it stick.

9

Conclusion
LEARNING TO MEDIATE

THE HISTORY OF MANY INTRACTABLE CONFLICTS raises the question of whether they ever truly end. Conflicts in the Koreas, Cyprus, Sudan, Kashmir, and the Middle East have lasted many decades and sometimes appear destined always to elude settlement. And yet some intractable conflicts do end. Occasionally, they end on the battlefield. A leader is killed, a regime is overturned, or one side's commitment and doggedness manage to demoralize its opponent, as happened with North Vietnam in its wars with France and the United States. The circumstances that allow one side to finally gain a victory, however, are rare. In most intractable conflicts, military, financial, and political resources are sufficiently evenly matched between opposing parties so that no side can win.

These stalemated conflicts rarely move to settlement. Even though the stalemate may appear intolerable in these conflicts, antagonists show a great capacity for continuing on in hopes of an eventual military victory. In these situations in which the parties are locked in their continuing struggle, negotiation offers the only way out. When the conflict finally ended in Mozambique and South Africa, it was due to negotiation—arranged either directly between the parties or with the assistance of a mediator—rather than to military victory. Moreover, the record shows that more intractable conflicts end at the negotiating table than in the victory of one side over the other. When the guns were eventually silenced in El Salvador, Namibia, Guatemala, and Cambodia, critical roles were played by mediators who managed to establish sufficient levels of trust between the parties to allow face-to-face negotiations to take place and sufficient persuasiveness and leverage to help them thrash out the key details of a political settlement. More recently, long-festering struggles in Sri Lanka, East Timor, and Congo have succumbed, at least temporarily, to international pressure (including military pressure) and negotiated interventions by third parties.

We do not accept the notion that violent conflicts are best left to burn themselves out, and we believe that most intractable conflicts end only with considerable outside help. That has been our premise through this book. But our main point is subtler and more complex. We do not argue that concerted mediation inevitably brings peace. Rather, we think that the evidence confirms that third-party involvement is a necessary, if not sufficient, component of effective peace processes in intractable conflicts. When third parties engage in peacemaking—helping parties to recalculate the costs and benefits of continuing the fight, assisting parties in reframing the issues, nurturing a state of ripeness, developing "friends" of the process to help in implementation, working in the larger society to develop a vision of an alternative future, or bringing a forgotten conflict to the world's attention—they are putting pressure directly on the sources of intractability: namely, the deeply ingrained attitudes and modes of behavior of the parties and the conditions that have allowed the conflict to continue unchecked.

The preceding argument leads to prudent conclusions. First, one should be wary of taking on the hardest cases. There are sometimes powerful reasons to hang back or to place conflict management imperatives first, before mediation goals, as we have discussed in chapter 2. At the same time, we have pointed out that a decision to abstain from involvement in mediation also has consequences. Ignored or forgotten conflicts, as discussed in chapter 3, do not improve like vintage wines; they can become acidic and turn to vinegar. We have also stressed that mediators must prepare themselves to overcome major hurdles before plunging ahead, a task that includes assessing the dimensions of operational readiness discussed in chapter 5. To press ahead with a fresh mediation initiative in the face of significant impediments and weaknesses on the side of the mediation itself is likely to be counterproductive for the third party and to contribute irresponsibly to the conflict's own intractability.

Mediation has often been portrayed as an art, the skills for which are endowed at birth to a few gifted people. Our intention in this book has been to point out that mediation is a learned craft. It requires substantial tradecraft at every stage in the process; without this tradecraft, the mediator risks adding to the intractability of the conflict. Good mediation tradecraft can—and should—be practiced by many different institutions, both official and nonofficial. It should not, however, be practiced in a vacuum. A conflict, no matter how small or remote, affects its surrounding region. In an intractable conflict, this effect is magnified because long-enduring violence presents threats to regional stability in the form of refugee flows, arms smuggling, and other destabilizing transnational activities. Sometimes, the best policy is simply to stop the fighting—to freeze the conflict, separate the combatants, and, in certain kinds of cases, take necessary action to eliminate spoiler misbehavior. In other circumstances, it may mean getting out, either because conditions on the ground have deteriorated beyond repair or because another mediator may be better suited to act as an intermediary for this particular conflict. The argument, in a nutshell, is that parties and actors weighing whether or not to engage in mediation need to think strategically, clearly identifying priorities and the potential consequences of action and inaction. The decision to mediate should set in motion a series of analytic steps that are the building blocks of an effective mediation strategy.

When mediation appears called for, good tradecraft is needed to overcome the special obstacles and challenges that intractable conflicts present; its absence only makes things worse. Good tradecraft means knowing how to prepare for engagement and how to nurture relationships among the parties, when to apply pressure and when to back off, how to mobilize the comparative advantages of additional actors, and where to find reinforcements for a faltering process. Intractable conflicts demand that mediators be coherent and unified; anything less ensures failure. This does not mean that mediators must necessarily be unitary actors; coherence can be achieved in complex, layered mediations involving multiple parties. Although such complexity is hard to manage, it can help spread burdens and risks, and it may be essential in order to maximize leverage and boost potential resources for creating—and implementing—settlements.

This book will have served its purpose if it encourages professionals, policymakers, teachers, and tomorrow's practitioners to channel their attention toward these essential and practical tasks, to do their homework, to consult widely and listen openly, to consider drawing on the resources of a diverse portfolio of actors, to reach out across affected societies and institutions and, ultimately, to the victims of war-torn societies. If intractable conflicts need mediators to help them reach peace, then our best hope is to prepare good mediators.

Notes

1. MEDIATION AND INTRACTABLE CONFLICTS

1. For a review of this literature, see Roy Licklider, "Comparative Studies of Long Wars," in Chester A. Crocker, Fen Osler Hampson, and Pamela Aall, eds., *Grasping the Nettle: Analyzing Cases of Intractable Conflict* (Washington, D.C.: United States Institute of Peace Press, 2004). Also see Michael E. Brown, "Ethnic and Internal Conflicts: Causes and Implications," in Chester A. Crocker, Fen Osler Hampson, and Pamela Aall, eds., *Turbulent Peace: The Challenges of Managing International Conflict* (Washington, D.C.: United States Institute of Peace Press, 2001), 209–226; Michael E. Brown, ed., *Ethnic Conflict and International Security* (Princeton, N.J.: Princeton University Press, 1993); Michael E. Brown, *The International Dimensions of Internal Conflict* (Cambridge, Mass.: MIT Press, 1996); Paul Collier, "Economic Causes of Civil Conflict and Their Implications for Policy," in Crocker, Hampson, and Aall, eds., *Turbulent Peace*, 143–162; Ted Robert Gurr, *Peoples versus States: Minorities at Risk in the New Century* (Washington, D.C.: United States Institute of Peace Press, 2000); Ted Robert Gurr, "Minorities and Nationalists: Managing Ethnopolitical Conflict in the New Century," in Crocker, Hampson, and Aall, eds., *Turbulent Peace*, 163–188; David A. Lake and Donald Rothchild, eds., *The International Spread of Ethnic Conflict: Fear, Diffusion, and the Escalation Process* (Princeton, N.J.: Princeton University Press, 1998); Christopher R. Mitchell, *The Structure of International Conflict* (New York: St. Martin's, 1981); Janice Gross Stein, "Image, Identity, and the Resolution of Violent Conflict," in Crocker, Hampson, and Aall, eds., *Turbulent Peace*, 189–208; and Barbara F. Walter and Jack Snyder, eds., *Civil War, Insecurity, and Intervention* (New York: Columbia University Press, 1999).

2. See, for example, Melanie C. Greenberg, John H. Barton, and Margaret E. McGuinness, eds., *Words over War: Mediation and Arbitration to Prevent*

Deadly Conflict (Lanham, Md.: Rowman and Littlefield, 2000); Kevin M. Cahill, *Preventive Diplomacy: Stopping Wars before They Start* (New York: Routledge, 2000); Carnegie Commission on Preventing Deadly Conflict, *Preventing Deadly Conflict: Final Report* (New York: Carnegie Corporation of New York, 1997); David Cortright, *The Price of Peace: Incentives and International Conflict Prevention* (Lanham, Md.: Rowman and Littlefield, 1997); Fen Osler Hampson, "Preventive Diplomacy at the United Nations and Beyond," in Fen Osler Hampson and David M. Malone, eds., *From Reaction to Conflict Prevention: Opportunities for the UN System* (Boulder, Colo.: Lynne Rienner, 2002); Fen Osler Hampson and David M. Malone, eds., *From Reaction to Conflict Prevention: Opportunities for the UN System* (Boulder, Colo.: Lynne Rienner, 2002); Bruce W. Jentleson, *Opportunities Missed, Opportunities Seized: Preventive Diplomacy in the Post–Cold War World* (Lanham, Md.: Rowman and Littlefield, 1999); Bruce W. Jentleson, "Preventive Statecraft: A Realist Strategy for the Post–Cold War Era," in Crocker, Hampson, and Aall, eds., *Turbulent Peace*, 249–264; Michael S. Lund, *Preventing Violent Conflicts: A Strategy for Preventive Diplomacy* (Washington, D.C.: United States Institute of Peace Press, 1997); and Barnett R. Rubin, *Cases and Strategies for Preventive Action* (New York: Century Foundation Press, 1998).

3. See John de Chastelain, "The Good Friday Agreement in Northern Ireland," in Chester A. Crocker, Fen Osler Hampson, and Pamela Aall, eds., *Herding Cats: Multiparty Mediation in a Complex World* (Washington, D.C.: United States Institute of Peace Press, 1999), 431–468; and George J. Mitchell, *Making Peace* (New York: Alfred A. Knopf, 1999).

4. See, for example, Chester A. Crocker, *High Noon in Southern Africa: Making Peace in a Rough Neighborhood* (New York: W. W. Norton, 1992); Chester A. Crocker, "Peacemaking in Southern Africa: The Namibia-Angola Settlement of 1988," in Crocker, Hampson, and Aall, eds., *Herding Cats*, 207–244; Michael W. Doyle, Ian Johnstone, and Robert C. Orr, eds., *Keeping the Peace: Multidimensional UN Operations in Cambodia and El Salvador* (Cambridge: Cambridge University Press, 1997); William J. Durch, ed., *The Evolution of UN Peacekeeping: Case Studies and Comparative Analyses* (New York: St. Martin's Press, 1993); William J. Durch, *UN Peacekeeping, American Policy, and the Uncivil Wars of the 1990s* (New York: St. Martin's Press, 1996); Fen Osler Hampson, *Nurturing Peace: Why Peace Settlements Succeed or Fail* (Washington, D.C.: United States Institute of Peace Press, 1996); Janet Heininger, *Peacekeeping in Transition: The United Nations in Cambodia* (New York: Twentieth Century Fund Press, 1994); Cameron Hume, *Ending Mozambique's War: The Role of Mediation and Good Offices* (Washington, D.C.: United States Institute of Peace Press, 1996); Timothy D. Sisk, *Power Sharing and International Mediation in Ethnic Conflicts* (Washington, D.C.: United States Institute of Peace Press, 1996); Richard H. Solomon,

"Bringing Peace to Cambodia," in Crocker, Hampson, and Aall, eds., *Herding Cats*, 275–324; Richard H. Solomon, *Chinese Negotiating Behavior: Pursuing Interests through "Old Friends"* (Washington, D.C.: United States Institute of Peace Press, 2000); and Stephen John Stedman, Donald Rothchild, and Elizabeth M. Cousens, eds., *Ending Civil Wars: The Implementation of Peace Agreements* (Boulder, Colo.: Lynne Rienner, 2002).

5. Howard B. Schaffer and Teresita C. Schaffer, "Kashmir: Fifty Years of Running in Place," in Crocker, Hampson, and Aall, eds., *Grasping the Nettle*.

6. Edward Azar, for example, uses the terms "protracted" or "intractable" interchangeably to describe social conflicts that are "on-going and seemingly unresolvable." He argues that "the sources of protracted social conflict are the denial of those elements required in the development of peoples and societies, and whose pursuit is a compelling need in all. These are security, distinctive identity, social recognition of identity, and effective participation in the processes that determine conditions of security and identity and other such developmental requirements." Edward E. Azar, "Protracted International Conflicts: Ten Propositions," in Edward E. Azar and John W. Burton, *International Conflict Resolution: Theory and Practice* (Brighton, U.K.: Wheatsheaf Books, 1986), 28–29.

In a more recent discussion of the concept, Heidi and Guy Burgess argue: "'Intractability' is a controversial concept, which means different things to different people. Some people . . . intensely dislike the term, as they see it as too negative: intractable conflicts are impossible to resolve, they say, so people think they are not worth dealing with. . . . [A]s we see it, intractable conflicts are those that lie at the frontier of the field—the conflicts that stubbornly seem to elude resolution, even when the best available techniques are applied. . . . [T]hese conflicts are not hopeless, and they most certainly are worth dealing with. But they are very different from more tractable conflicts, such as most labor-management conflicts, some family conflicts, many workplace conflicts and even many international conflicts that can be successfully resolved through negotiation or mediation. Intractable conflicts need a different, more multifaceted, and more prolonged approach." Heidi Burgess and Guy Burgess, "The Meaning of Intractability," on "Beyond Intractability.Org," an online resource available at http://www.beyondintractability.org/iweb/index.htm.

7. For an important discussion of the different social, psychological, and political dimensions of intractability, see Louis Kriesberg, "Nature, Dynamics, and Phases of Intractability," in Crocker, Hampson, and Aall, eds., *Grasping the Nettle*. Also see Louis Kriesberg, *Constructive Conflicts: From Escalation to Resolution*, 2d ed. (Lanham, Md.: Rowman and Littlefield, 2003).

8. See Stephen John Stedman, "Spoiler Problems in Peace Processes," *International Security* 22, no. 2 (1997): 5–53.

9. See I. William Zartman, "Analyzing Intractability," in Crocker, Hampson, and Aall, eds., *Grasping the Nettle*.

10. For a discussion of the causes of intractability, see *Grasping the Nettle*.

11. See, for example, Robert D. Kaplan, "The Coming Anarchy," *Atlantic Monthly* 273, no. 2 (February 1994): 44–76; Edward N. Luttwak, "Give War a Chance," *Foreign Affairs* 78, no. 4 (1999): 36–44; and Edward N. Luttwak, "The Curse of Inconclusive Intervention," in Crocker, Hampson, and Aall, eds., *Turbulent Peace*, 265–272.

12. For earlier—pre-9/11—debates on this question, see Joseph S. Nye Jr., "Redefining the National Interest," *Foreign Affairs* 78, no. 4 (1999): 22–36; and Chester A. Crocker, "A Poor Case for Quitting: Mistaking Incompetence for Intervention," *Foreign Affairs* 79, no. 1 (2000): 183–186.

13. On this debate, see Stanley Hoffmann, "The Debate about Intervention," in Crocker, Hampson, and Aall, eds., *Turbulent Peace*, 273–284; and Leonard W. Doob, *Intervention: Guide and Perils* (New Haven, Conn.: Yale University Press, 1993).

14. On the United Nations' role and capacity for intervention, see Doyle, Johnstone, and Orr, *Keeping the Peace*; Durch, *UN Peacekeeping*; Bruce D. Jones, *Peacemaking in Rwanda: The Dynamics of Failure* (Boulder, Colo.: Lynne Rienner, 2001); Olara A. Otunnu and Michael W. Doyle, eds., *Peacemaking and Peacekeeping for the New Century* (Lanham, Md.: Rowman and Littlefield, 1998); Raimo Vayrynen, "The United Nations and the Resolution of International Conflict," *Cooperation and Conflict* 20, no. 3 (1985): 141–171; and Thomas G. Weiss, ed., *The United Nations and Civil Wars* (Boulder, Colo.: Lynne Rienner, 1995).

15. Mary B. Anderson, *Do No Harm: Supporting Local Capacities for Peace through Aid* (Cambridge, Mass.: Collaborative for Development Action, 1996); and Mary B. Anderson, "Humanitarian NGOs in Conflict Intervention," in Crocker, Hampson, and Aall, eds., *Turbulent Peace*, 637–648.

16. Pamela Aall, "What Do NGOs Bring to Peacemaking?" in Crocker, Hampson, and Aall, eds., *Turbulent Peace*, 365–384.

17. See, for example, Donald Rothchild and Caroline Hartzell, "Great and Medium Power Mediations: Angola," in I. William Zartman, ed., *Annals of the American Academy of Political and Social Science*, no. 518 (1991): 39–57.

18. On the role of NGOs and other civil society actors in mediation and conflict resolution in divided societies, see, for example, John Paul Lederach, *Preparing for Peace: Conflict Transformation across Cultures* (Syracuse: Syracuse University Press, 1996); John Paul Lederach, *Building Peace: Sustainable Reconciliation in Divided Societies* (Washington, D.C.: United States Institute of Peace

Press, 1998); John Paul Lederach, *The Journey towards Reconciliation* (Scottdale, Penn.: Herald Press, 1999); John Paul Lederach, "Civil Society and Reconciliation," in Crocker, Hampson, and Aall, eds., *Turbulent Peace*, 841–854; John W. McDonald Jr. and Diane B. Bendahamne, eds., *Conflict Resolution: Track-Two Diplomacy* (Washington, D.C.: Foreign Service Institute, U.S. Department of State, 1985); Harold H. Saunders, "The Multilevel Peace Process in Tajikistan," in Crocker, Hampson, and Aall, eds., *Herding Cats*, 159–180; and Harold H. Saunders, "Prenegotiation and Circum-negotiation: Arenas of the Multilevel Peace Process," in Crocker, Hampson, and Aall, eds., *Turbulent Peace*, 483–496.

2. WHEN POWERFUL STATES MEDIATE

1. Christopher R. Mitchell and K. Webb, eds., *New Approaches to International Mediation* (New York: Greenwood Press, 1988). See also Jacob Bercovitch, ed., *Studies in International Mediation: Essays in Honor of Jeffrey Z. Rubin* (Houndsmills, Basingstoke, U.K.: Palgrave/Macmillan, 2002); and Jacob Bercovitch, ed., *Resolving International Conflicts: The Theory and Practice of Mediation* (Boulder, Colo.: Lynne Rienner, 1996).

2. See Saadia Touval, "Mediation and Foreign Policy," *International Studies Review* 5, no. 4 (2003): 91–96; and I. William Zartman and Maureen R. Berman, *The Practical Negotiator* (New Haven, Conn.: Yale University Press, 1982). For a scholar-practitioner account drawn from a U.S. policy perspective, see Richard N. Haass, *Conflicts Unending: The United States and Regional Disputes* (New Haven and London: Yale University Press, 1990).

3. Marieke Kleiboer, "Great Power Mediation: Using Leverage to Make Peace?" in Bercovitch, ed., *Studies in International Mediation*, 127–140.

4. On the concept and variants of coercive diplomacy, see Alexander George, *Forceful Persuasion: Coercive Diplomacy as an Alternative to War* (Washington, D.C.: United States Institute of Peace Press, 1991).

5. Stephen Morrison and Alex de Waal, "Can Sudan Escape Its Intractability?" in Crocker, Hampson, and Aall, eds., *Grasping the Nettle*.

6. Shibley Telhami, "Beyond Resolution? An Essay on the Palestinian-Israeli Conflict," and Stephen Cohen, "Intractability and the Israeli-Palestinian Conflict," both in Crocker, Hampson, and Aall, eds., *Grasping the Nettle*.

7. A cogent statement of this perspective is in Haass, *Conflicts Unending*, 57–77.

8. John J. Maresca, "The Conflict over Nagorno-Karabakh," in Bruce W. Jentleson, ed., *Opportunities Missed, Opportunities Seized* (New York: Rowman and Littlefield, 1999), 82–84.

9. Richard Holbrooke, *To End a War*, rev. ed. (New York: Random House, 1999).

10. On the African political security and political context of the Congo war, see John F. Clark, ed., *The African Stakes of the Congo War* (New York: Palgrave/Macmillan, 2002).

11. Maresca, "The Conflict over Nagorno-Karabakh."

3. OUT OF SIGHT, OUT OF MIND

1. Saunders, "Prenegotiation and Circum-negotiation."

2. Roy Licklider, "The Consequences of Negotiated Settlements in Civil Wars, 1945–1993," *American Political Science Review* 39, no. 3 (1995): 259–273.

3. See, for instance, Carnegie Commission on Preventing Deadly Conflict, *Preventing Deadly Conflict;* David A. Hamburg, *No More Killing Fields: Preventing Deadly Conflict* (Lanham, Md.: Rowman and Littlefield, 2002); and Barnett R. Rubin, *Cases and Strategies for Preventive Action* (New York: Century Foundation Press, 1998).

4. Herman J. Cohen, *Intervening in Africa: Superpower Peacemaking in a Troubled Continent* (New York: St. Martin's Press, 2000), 165.

5. Ibid., 178.

6. Barnett R. Rubin, *The Search for Peace in Afghanistan: From Buffer State to Failed State* (New Haven, Conn.: Yale University Press, 1995), 30.

7. Ibid., 125.

8. Frederick S. Starr, "Making Eurasia Stable," *Foreign Affairs* 70, no. 1 (1996): 89–92.

9. Rubin, *Search for Peace in Afghanistan*, 143.

10. Licklider, "The Consequences of Negotiated Settlements in Civil Wars."

11. Charles King, "The Uses of Deadlock: Intractability in Eurasia," in Crocker, Hampson, and Aall, eds., *Grasping the Nettle.*

12. For instance, in the case of Moldova, King points out that "even though it now appears that most Russian troops will eventually leave Moldova . . . the Russian Federation's 'presence' will remain in other ways. With the vast numbers of retired Russian military personnel who have elected to stay in Transnistria—where they and their families have lived for years and where their military pensions go further than in parts of Russia—the Transnistrians have a ready supply of mobilizable soldiers." Ibid.

13. See Okello Lucima, ed., "Protracted Conflict, Elusive Peace: Initiatives to End Violence in Northern Uganda," in *Accord: An International Review of*

Peace Initiatives 11 (2002); and Human Rights Watch, "LRA Conflict in Northern Uganda and Southern Sudan, 2002," *Human Rights Watch News*, October 29, 2002.

14. The UN Charter gives the Security Council the responsibility of dealing with threats to international peace and security. In other words, the council members have a treaty obligation to act when a threat arises. This action may be in the form of fact-finding missions, open debates, or measures such as mediation or arbitration based on Article 33 of the Charter on the "Pacific Settlement of Disputes." Despite this obligation under international law, the powerful states on the Security Council have often failed to provide adequate support for these actions and equally often have declined to take up their treaty-based responsibilities.

15. Meeting organized by the United States Institute of Peace on practitioner perspectives on mediation, Washington, D.C., September 17–18, 1998.

16. Adekeye Adebajo, *Building Peace in West Africa: Liberia, Sierra Leone, and Guinea-Bissau* (Boulder, Colo.: Lynne Rienner, 2002), 44. For a comprehensive analysis of ECOMOG's strengths and shortcomings, see Herbert Howe, "Lessons of Liberia: ECOMOG and Regional Peacekeeping," *International Security* 21, no. 3 (Winter 1996–97): 145–176.

17. Zartman, "Analyzing Intractability."

18. Margaret J. Anstee, "The United Nations in Angola: Post-Bicesse Implementation," in Crocker, Hampson, and Aall, eds., *Herding Cats*, 615–642.

19. Andrea Bartoli, "Mediating Peace in Mozambique: The Role of the Community of Sant'Egidio," in Crocker, Hampson, and Aall, eds., *Herding Cats*, 245–274.

20. For a discussion of the varieties of power that a mediator brings to a peacemaking context, see Jeffrey C. Rubin, "Conclusion: International Mediation in Context," in Jacob Bercovitch and Jeffrey C. Rubin, eds., *Mediation and International Relations* (New York: St. Martin's Press, 1992), 249–272.

21. See also Diana Chigas, "Negotiating Intractable Conflicts: The Contribution of Unofficial Intermediaries," in Crocker, Hampson, and Aall, eds., *Grasping the Nettle*.

22. Jan Egeland, "The Oslo Accord: Multiparty Facilitation through the Norwegian Channel," in Crocker, Hampson, and Aall, eds., *Herding Cats*, 527–546.

23. For an extended discussion of comparative advantage among mediators, see Chester A. Crocker, Fen Osler Hampson, and Pamela Aall, "Multiparty Mediation and the Conflict Cycle," in Crocker, Hampson, and Aall, eds., *Herding Cats*, 19–46.

4. THE MEDIATOR'S ENVIRONMENT

1. The term "environment" is used loosely here to capture the various settings in which the mediator must operate. For more on the effect of culture on negotiations, see Peter Berton, Hiroshi Kimura, and I. William Zartman, eds., *International Negotiation: Actors, Structure/Process, Values* (New York: St. Martin's Press, 1999); Raymond Cohen, *Negotiating across Cultures: Communication Obstacles in International Diplomacy* (Washington, D.C.: United States Institute of Peace Press, 1991); Scott Snyder, *Negotiating on the Edge: North Korean Negotiating Behavior* (Washington, D.C.: United States Institute of Peace Press, 1999); Richard H. Solomon, *Chinese Negotiating Behavior: Pursuing Interests through "Old Friends"* (Washington, D.C.: United States Institute of Peace Press, 1999); and Guy Olivier Faure, "Nonverbal Negotiation in China: Cycling in Beijing," *Negotiation Journal* 11, no. 1 (1995): 11–18.

2. Richard H. Solomon, *Exiting Indochina: U.S. Leadership of the Cambodia Settlement and Normalization with Vietnam* (Washington, D.C.: United States Institute of Peace Press, 2000), 59–69.

3. This chapter draws on a number of excellent practitioner accounts of working within a specific conflict, including Ahmedou Ould-Abdallah. *Burundi on the Brink, 1993–95: A UN Special Envoy Reflects on Preventive Diplomacy* (Washington, D.C.: United States Institute of Peace Press, 2000); Margaret J. Anstee, *Orphan of the Cold War: The Inside Story of the Collapse of the Angolan Peace Process, 1992–95* (New York: St. Martin's Press, 1996); Paul Hare, *Angola's Last Best Chance for Peace: An Insider's Account of the Peace Process* (Washington, D.C.: United States Institute of Peace Press, 1998); Mitchell, *Making Peace;* and Solomon, *Exiting Indochina.*

4. For example, both his Mauritanian background and his long experience in public service in Mauritania and the United Nations were extremely helpful to Ahmedou Ould-Abdallah in his work as the UN secretary-general's special representative SRSG to Burundi. See Ould-Abdallah, *Burundi on the Brink,* 38.

5. Mitchell, *Making Peace,* 28.

6. Ould-Abdallah, *Burundi on the Brink,* 39.

7. Bartoli, "Mediating Peace in Mozambique."

8. Quoted in Jane Perlez, "CIA Chief Going to Israel in Effort to Maintain Calm," *New York Times,* June 6, 2001.

9. William B. Quandt, *Camp David: Peacemaking and Politics* (Washington, D.C.: Brookings Institution, 1986), 322.

10. Egeland, "The Oslo Accord."

11. James A. Baker III, "The Road to Madrid," in Crocker, Hampson, and Aall, eds., *Herding Cats*, 185–186.

12. Paul Arthur, "Multiparty Mediation in Northern Ireland," in Crocker, Hampson, and Aall, eds., *Herding Cats*, 478.

13. Ann Lesch, "Negotiations in Sudan," in David R. Smock, ed., *Making War and Waging Peace: Foreign Intervention in Sub-Saharan Africa* (Washington, D.C.: United States Institute of Peace Press, 1993), 130–131.

14. Baker, "The Road to Madrid," 188.

15. Fabienne Hara, "Burundi: A Case of Parallel Diplomacy," in Crocker, Hampson, and Aall, eds., *Herding Cats*, 151–152.

16. Crocker, "Peacemaking in Southern Africa," 217.

17. Arthur, "Multiparty Mediation in Northern Ireland," 482.

18. Serge Schmemann, "Israeli Raids Kill 17 Palestinians in Tel Aviv, 3 Die in Shooting," *New York Times*, March 5, 2002, 1.

19. Cohen, *Negotiating across Cultures*, 56.

20. Mitchell, *Making Peace*, 32.

21. Arthur, "Multiparty Mediation in Northern Ireland," 479. Also see John Darby, *Intimidation and the Control of the Conflict in Northern Ireland* (Dublin: Gill and Macmillan, 1986).

22. Data from the International Conflict Management (ICM) Project, 2000 version, directed by Jacob Bercovitch, University of Canterbury, New Zealand.

23. Louis Kriesberg, "Coordinating Intermediary Peace Efforts," *Negotiation Journal* 2, no. 4 (1986): 341–352.

24. For further discussion of ripeness in resolving conflict, see I. William Zartman, *Ripe for Resolution: Conflict and Intervention in Africa* (New York: Oxford University Press, 1985).

5. BUILDING A NEGOTIATING STRATEGY

1. See the helpful overview of leverage in mediation in Carnevale, "Mediating from Strength," in Bercovitch, ed., *Studies in International Mediation*, 25–40. The discussion here concentrates primarily on leverage derived from what Carnevale terms "strategic strength" (what the mediator brings to the table) as distinguished from "tactical strength" (what the mediator does at the table using maneuver, technique, and procedural moves). In practice, of course, a skilled and purposeful mediator will deploy strategic leverage assets at

the table once the parties have engaged in the process, so that strategic and tactical leverage merge into a coherent arsenal. A normative critique of leverage-based mediation is in Kleiboer, "Great Power Mediation."

2. A classic discussion of this dynamic is by Fred Charles Ikle, *Every War Must End* (New York: Columbia University Press, 1971), esp. chaps. 4 and 5.

3. Schaffer and Schaffer, "Kashmir."

4. Cynthia Arnson and Teresa Whitfield, "Third Parties and Intractable Conflicts: The Case of Colombia," in Crocker, Hampson, and Aall, eds., *Grasping the Nettle*.

5. See Saadia Touval and I. William Zartman, "International Mediation in the Post–Cold War Era," in Crocker, Hampson, and Aall, eds., *Turbulent Peace*, 427–444; Haass, *Conflicts Unending;* and Jeffrey Z. Rubin, "The Timing of Ripeness and the Ripeness of Timing," in Louis Kriesberg and Stuart J. Thorson, eds., *Timing the De-escalation of International Conflicts* (Syracuse: Syracuse University Press, 1991), 237–246.

6. I. William Zartman, "Ripeness: The Hurting Stalemate and Beyond," in Paul C. Stern and Daniel Druckman, eds., *International Conflict Resolution after the Cold War* (Washington, D.C.: National Academy Press, 2000), 241–243.

7. Morrison and de Waal, "Can Sudan Escape Its Intractability?"

8. Barbara McDougall, "Haiti: Canada's Role in the OAS," in Crocker, Hampson, and Aall, eds., *Herding Cats*, 387–404.

9. Robert A. Pastor, "More and Less Than It Seemed: The Carter-Nunn-Powell Mediation in Haiti, 1994," in Crocker, Hampson, and Aall, eds., *Herding Cats*, 505–526.

10. An interesting discussion of the roles and styles of "outsiders" and "insiders" as mediators is by Paul Wehr and John Paul Lederach, "Mediating Conflict in Central America," *Journal of Peace Research* 28, no. 1 (1991): 85–98.

11. For an example of such choreography, see Baker, "The Road to Madrid."

12. Anderson, *Do No Harm.*

6. HANGING ON, HUNKERING DOWN, AND BAILING OUT

1. See Hampson, *Nurturing Peace*, 27–52.

2. Anstee, "The United Nations in Angola," 603.

3. Paul Hare, "Angola: The Lusaka Peace Process," in Crocker, Hampson, and Aall, eds., *Herding Cats*, 643–662.

4. See Margaret Thatcher, *The Downing Street Years* (New York: Harper Collins, 1993), 191–230.

5. Schaffer and Schaffer, "Kashmir."

6. Ibid.

7. Arthur, "Multiparty Mediation in Northern Ireland," 484–485.

8. November 28, 1995, communiqué issued by the British and Irish governments. Quoted in de Chastelain, "The Good Friday Agreement in Northern Ireland," 438.

9. On the history of the Bougainville conflict and various peacemaking efforts, see Donald Denoon, *Getting under the Skin: The Bougainville Copper Agreement and the Creation of the Panguna Mine* (Melbourne: University of Melbourne Press, 2000); and Pat Howley, *Breaking Spears and Mending Hearts: Peacemakers and Restorative Justice in Bougainville* (London: Zed Books, 2003).

10. On prenegotiation, see Janice Gross Stein, ed., *Getting to the Table* (Baltimore: Johns Hopkins University Press, 1990); and Harold H. Saunders, *Sinai II: The Politics of International Mediation, 1974–1975* (Washington, D.C.: Foreign Policy Institute, SAIS, Johns Hopkins University, 1993).

11. Neill Lochery, "Oslo's Lessons," *Jerusalem Post*, May 12, 2002, 6.

12. Baker, "The Road to Madrid," 203.

13. Ibid., 188.

14. Arthur, "Multiparty Mediation in Northern Ireland," 485.

15. Solomon, "Bringing Peace to Cambodia," 295. Also see Solomon, *Exiting Indochina*.

16. See Luigi R. Einaudi, "The Ecuador-Peru Peace Process," in Crocker, Hampson, and Aall, eds., *Herding Cats*, 405–430; and Monica Herz and Joao Pontes Nogueira, *Ecuador vs. Peru: Peacemaking amid Rivalry* (Boulder, Colo.: Lynne Rienner, 2002).

7. RECIPES FOR SECURING THE SETTLEMENT

1. The reader may wish to consult the discussion of varied roads to settlement in Louis Kriesberg, *Constructive Conflicts: From Escalation to Resolution*, 2d ed. (Lanham, Md.: Rowman and Littlefield, 2003), chap. 9; and Dean G. Pruitt, "Mediator Behavior and Success in Mediation," in Bercovitch, ed., *Studies in International Mediation*, 41–55.

2. Two interesting accounts are in Ron Pundak, "From Oslo to Taba: What Went Wrong?" *Survival* 43, no. 3 (2001): 31–46; and Yuval Elizur, "Israel Banks on a Fence," *Foreign Affairs* 82, no. 2 (2003): 106–119.

3. Ikle, *Every War Must End*, 87.

4. See Herz and Nogueira, *Ecuador vs. Peru*, 28–36.

8. Making a Settlement Stick

1. See Roy Licklider, "Obstacles to Peace Settlements," in Crocker, Hampson, and Aall, eds., *Turbulent Peace*, 697–718; and Licklider, "The Consequences of Negotiated Settlements."

2. This has been the case in Northern Ireland. See de Chastelain, "The Good Friday Agreement in Northern Ireland"; and Mitchell, *Making Peace*.

3. On the tensions between peacemaking and democratic governance/ rule of law issues, see Pauline Baker, "Conflict Resolution versus Democratic Governance: Divergent Paths to Peace?" in Crocker, Hampson, and Aall, eds., *Turbulent Peace*, 753–764.

4. See Hampson, *Nurturing Peace*.

5. On these and other challenges, see Stephen John Stedman, "International Implementation of Peace Agreements in Civil Wars: Findings from a Study of Sixteen Cases," in Crocker, Hampson, and Aall, eds., *Turbulent Peace*, 737–752; and Stedman, Rothchild, and Cousens, eds., *Ending Civil Wars*.

6. On these challenges, see Kriesberg, *Constructive Conflicts*; and Lederach, *Building Peace*.

7. See Sisk, *Power Sharing and International Mediation*.

8. Bruce D. Jones, "The Challenges of Strategic Coordination," in Stedman, Rothchild, and Cousens, eds., *Ending Civil Wars*, 89–116.

9. On the psychology and identity of conflict and peacemaking, see Stein, "Image, Identity, and the Resolution of Violent Conflict"; and Marc Howard Ross, *The Management of Conflict: Interpretations and Interests in Comparative Perspective* (New Haven, Conn.: Yale University Press, 1996).

10. On the more general relationship between the use of force and diplomacy in U.S. foreign policy, see George, *Forceful Persuasion*.

11. See Richard C. Holbrooke, "The Road to Sarajevo," in Crocker, Hampson, and Aall, eds., *Herding Cats*, 325–344; and Holbrooke, *To End a War*.

12. See Ian Martin, *Self-Determination in East Timor: The United Nations, the Ballot, and International Intervention* (Boulder, Colo.: Lynne Rienner, 2001).

13. See John L. Hirsch, *Sierra Leone: Diamonds and the Struggle for Democracy* (Boulder, Colo.: Lynne Rienner, 2001.)

14. See Donald C. F. Daniel and Bradd C. Hayes with Chantal De Jonge Oudraat, eds., *Coercive Inducement and the Containment of International Crises* (Washington, D.C.: United States Institute of Peace Press, 1999).

15. Mats Berdal and David M. Malone, eds., *Greed and Grievance: Economic Agendas in Civil Wars* (Boulder, Colo.: Lynne Rienner, 2001); Paul Collier, *Economic Causes of Civil Conflict and Their Implications for Policy* (Washington, D.C.: World Bank, 2000); and Collier, "Economic Causes of Civil Conflict and Their Implications for Policy."

16. See Simon Chesterman and Beatrice Pouligny, "Are Sanctions Meant to Work? The Politics of Creating and Implementing Sanctions through the United Nations," *Global Governance* 9, no. 4 (2003): 503–518; David Cortright and George A. Lopez, eds., *The Sanctions Decade: Assessing UN Strategies in the 1990s* (Boulder, Colo.: Lynne Rienner, 2000); and David Cortright and George Lopez, *Sanctions and the Search for Security: Challenges to UN Action* (Boulder, Colo.: Lynne Rienner, 2002).

17. See Collier, *Economic Causes of Civil Conflict;* Collier, "Economic Causes of Civil Conflict"; Berdal and Malone, *Greed and Grievance;* and Morrison and de Waal, "Can Sudan Escape Its Intractability?"

18. See Stephen John Stedman, "Spoiler Problems in Peace Processes," *International Security* 22, no. 2 (1997): 5–53.

19. See Doyle, Johnstone, and Orr, *Keeping the Peace;* and Otunnu and Doyle, *Peacemaking and Peacekeeping.*

20. On the challenges of disarmament and demobilization, see Joanna Spear, "Disarmament and Demobilization," in Stedman, Rothchild, and Cousens, eds., *Ending Civil Wars,* 141–182; and Barbara F. Walter, "Designing Transitions from Civil War: Demobilization, Democratization, and Commitments to Peace," *International Security* 24, no. 1 (1999): 127–155.

21. Barbara F. Walter, "A Critical Barrier to Civil War Settlement," *International Organization* 51, no. 3 (1997): 335–364.

22. See Anstee, *Orphan of the Cold War;* Anstee, "The United Nations in Angola"; and Hare, "Angola: The Lusaka Peace Process."

23. Crocker, "Peacemaking in Southern Africa."

24. Aldo Ajello, "Mozambique: Implementation of the 1992 Peace Agreement," in Crocker, Hampson, and Aall, eds., *Herding Cats,* 615–642.

25. De Chastelain, "The Good Friday Agreement in Northern Ireland."

26. On these challenges, see Louis Kriesberg, *Constructive Conflicts: From Escalation to Resolution*, 2d. ed. (Lanham, Md.: Rowman and Littlefield, 2003).

27. On the psychology of victimization, see Vamik Volkan and Joseph Montville, eds., *The Psychodynamics of International Relationships* (Lanham, Md.: Rowman and Littlefield, 1991).

28. The classic description of these problems is found in Morton Deutsch, *The Resolution of Conflict* (New Haven, Conn.: Yale University Press, 1973).

29. See Ronald J. Fisher, "Third-Party Consultation," *Journal of Conflict Resolution* 16, no. 1 (1972): 67–94; and Fisher, *The Social Psychology of Intergroup Conflict and International Conflict Resolution* (New York: Springer-Verlag, 1990).

30. In the long term, various kinds of power-sharing agreements may be required to cement the political center and create a stable political modus vivendi. On the challenges of power sharing, see Donald Horowitz, *Ethnic Groups in Conflict* (Berkeley: University of California Press, 1985); Joseph Rothschild, *Ethnopolitics: A Conceptual Approach* (New York: Columbia University Press, 1981); and Sisk, *Power Sharing and International Mediation*.

31. Quoted in Arthur, "Multiparty Mediation in Northern Ireland," 484.

32. Ibid.

33. Solomon, "Bring Peace to Cambodia"; Solomon, *Exiting Indochina*.

34. Baker, "The Road to Madrid."

35. See Dennis Ross, "Unmasking Arafat," *Foreign Policy* (July-August 2000); and Ross, *The Missing Peace: The Inside Story of the Fight for the Middle East Peace* (New York: Farrar, Straus and Giroux, forthcoming).

36. Crocker, "Peacemaking in Southern Africa."

37. Einaudi, "The Ecuador-Peru Peace Process."

38. McDougall, "Haiti: Canada's Role in the OAS."

39. See de Chastelain, "The Good Friday Agreement in Northern Ireland"; and Mitchell, *Making Peace*.

40. On donor roles, see Nicole Ball, "The Challenges of Rebuilding War-Torn Societies," in Crocker, Hampson, and Aall, eds., *Turbulent Peace*, 719–736; Organization for Economic Co-operation and Development (OECD)/Development Assistance Committee, *DAC Guidelines on Conflict, Peace, and Development Co-operation* (Paris: Development Assistance Committee of the OECD, 1997); and World Bank, *Post-Conflict Reconstruction: The Role of the World Bank* (Washington, D.C.: World Bank, 1998).

41. See Collier, *Economic Causes of Civil Conflict*; Paul Collier and Anke Hoeffler, *Greed and Grievance in Civil War* (Washington, D.C.: World Bank,

2000); Paul Collier, Anke Hoeffler, and Mans Sonderbom, "On the Duration of Civil Wars" (paper for World Bank, Washington, D.C., 2001); Patricia Cleves, Nat Colletta, and Nicholas Sambanis, "Addressing Conflict: Emerging Policy at the World Bank," in Fen Osler Hampson and David M. Malone, eds., *From Reaction to Conflict Prevention: Opportunities for the UN System* (Boulder, Colo.: Lynne Rienner, 2002), 297–320; Licklider, "Obstacles to Peace Settlements"; and Susan L. Woodward, "Economic Priorities for Successful Peace Implementation," in Stedman, Rothchild, and Cousens, eds., *Ending Civil Wars*, 183–214.

42. Walter, "A Critical Barrier to Civil War Settlement"; and Stedman, "International Implementation of Peace Agreements."

43. On these challenges, see Center for Strategic and International Studies, *Play to Win: The Commission on Post-Conflict Reconstruction* (January 2003); Center for Strategic and International Studies and the Association of the United States Army, *Post-Conflict Reconstruction: A Joint Project of the Task Framework* (May 2002); Neil J. Kritz, "The Rule of Law in the Postconflict Phase: Building a Stable Peace," in Crocker, Hampson, and Aall, eds., *Turbulent Peace*, 801–820; and Tonya L. Putnam, "Human Rights and Sustainable Peace," in Stedman, Rothchild, and Cousens, eds., *Ending Civil Wars*, 237–272.

44. On strategies for meeting the challenges of intercommunal reconciliation, see Lederach, *Building Peace*; John Paul Lederach and Janice Moomaw Jenner, *A Handbook of International Peacebuilding: Into the Eye of the Storm* (San Francisco: Jossey-Bass, 2002); Louis Kriesberg, *International Conflict Resolution: The US-USSR and Middle East Cases* (New Haven, Conn.: Yale University Press, 1992); Kriesberg, *Constructive Conflicts*; and Saunders, "Prenegotiation and Circum-negotiation."

45. William Stanley and David Holiday, "Broad Participation, Diffuse Responsibility: Peace Implementation in Guatemala," in Stedman, Rothchild, and Cousens, eds., *Ending Civil Wars*, 421–462.

46. On the role of leadership and risk-taking in peacemaking, see Janice Gross Stein, "Structures, Strategies, and Tactics of Mediation: Kissinger and Carter in the Middle East," *Negotiation Journal* 1, no. 4 (1985): 331–347; Stein, "Image, Identity, and the Resolution of Violent Conflict"; and Michael Watkins and Susan Rosegrant, *Breakthrough International Negotiation: How Great Negotiators Transformed the World's Toughest Post–Cold War Conflicts* (San Francisco: Jossey-Bass, 2001).

Bibliography

The following works were consulted during the course of writing this book.

Aall, Pamela. "What Do NGOs Bring to Peacemaking?" In Chester A. Crocker, Fen Osler Hampson, and Pamela Aall, eds., *Turbulent Peace: The Challenges of Managing International Conflict*, 365–384. Washington, D.C.: United States Institute of Peace Press, 2001.

———. "Non-governmental Organizations and Conflict Prevention: Roles, Capabilities, Limitations." In David Carment and Albrecht Schnabel, eds., *Conflict Prevention from Rhetoric to Reality: Opportunities and Innovations*, 168–185. Lanham, Md.: Lexington Books, forthcoming.

Adebajo, Adekeye. *Building Peace in West Africa: Liberia, Sierra Leone, and Guinea-Bissau*. Boulder, Colo.: Lynne Rienner, 2002.

Ajello, Aldo. "Mozambique: Implementation of the 1992 Peace Agreement." In Chester A. Crocker, Fen Osler Hampson, and Pamela Aall, eds., *Herding Cats: Multiparty Mediation in a Complex World*, 615–642. Washington, D.C.: United States Institute of Peace Press, 1999.

Albin, Cecilia. "Negotiating Intractable Conflicts: On the Future of Jerusalem." *Cooperation and Conflict: Nordic Journal of International Studies* 32, no. 1 (1997): 29–77.

Anderson, Mary B. *Do No Harm: Supporting Local Capacities for Peace through Aid*. Cambridge, Mass.: Collaborative for Development Action, 1996.

———. "Humanitarian NGOs in Conflict Intervention." In Chester A. Crocker, Fen Osler Hampson, and Pamela Aall, eds., *Turbulent Peace: The Challenges of Managing International Conflict*, 637–648. Washington, D.C.: United States Institute of Peace Press, 2001.

Anstee, Margaret J. *Orphan of the Cold War: The Inside Story of the Collapse of the Angolan Peace Process, 1992–93.* New York: St. Martin's Press, 1996.

———. "The United Nations in Angola: Post-Bicesse Implementation." In Chester A. Crocker, Fen Osler Hampson, and Pamela Aall, eds., *Herding Cats: Multiparty Mediation in a Complex World,* 615–642. Washington, D.C.: United States Institute of Peace Press, 1999.

Appleby, R. Scott. *The Ambivalence of the Sacred: Religion, Violence, and Reconciliation.* Lanham, Md.: Rowman and Littlefield, 2000.

———. "Religion as an Agent of Conflict Transformation in Peacebuilding." In Chester A. Crocker, Fen Osler Hampson, and Pamela Aall, eds., *Turbulent Peace: The Challenges of Managing International Conflict,* 821–840. Washington, D.C.: United States Institute of Peace Press, 2001.

Arnson, Cynthia, and Teresa Whitfield. "Third Parties and Intractable Conflicts: The Case of Colombia." In Chester A. Crocker, Fen Osler Hampson, and Pamela Aall, eds., *Grasping the Nettle.* Washington, D.C.: United States Institute of Peace Press, 2004.

Arthur, Paul. "Multiparty Mediation in Northern Ireland." In Chester A. Crocker, Fen Osler Hampson, and Pamela Aall, eds., *Herding Cats: Multiparty Mediation in a Complex World,* 469–502. Washington, D.C.: United States Institute of Peace Press, 1999.

Assefa, Hiskias. *Mediation of Civil Wars: Approaches and Strategies: The Sudan Conflict.* Boulder, Colo.: Westview Press, 1987.

Azar, Edward E. "Protracted International Conflicts: Ten Propositions." In Edward E. Azar and John W. Burton, *International Conflict Resolution: Theory and Practice,* 28–39. Brighton: Wheatsheaf Books, 1986.

———. *The Management of Protracted Social Conflict: Theory and Cases.* Aldershot, U.K.: Dartmouth Publishing, 1990.

Bailey, Sydney Dawson. *Four Arab-Israeli Wars and the Peace Process.* Basingstoke, U.K.: Macmillan, 1990.

Baker, James A., III. "The Road to Madrid." In Chester A. Crocker, Fen Osler Hampson, and Pamela Aall, eds., *Herding Cats: Multiparty Mediation in a Complex World,* 183–206. Washington, D.C.: United States Institute of Peace Press, 1999.

Baker, Pauline. "Conflict Resolution versus Democratic Governance: Divergent Paths to Peace?" In Chester A. Crocker, Fen Osler Hampson, and Pamela Aall, eds., *Turbulent Peace: The Challenges of Managing International Conflict,* 753–764. Washington, D.C.: United States Institute of Peace Press, 2001.

Ball, Nicole. "The Challenge of Rebuilding War-Torn Societies." In Chester A. Crocker, Fen Osler Hampson, and Pamela Aall, eds., *Turbulent Peace: The Challenges of Managing International Conflict*, 719–736. Washington, D.C.: United States Institute of Peace Press, 2001.

Bartoli, Andrea. "Mediating Peace in Mozambique: The Role of the Community of Sant'Egidio." In Chester A. Crocker, Fen Osler Hampson, and Pamela Aall, eds., *Herding Cats: Multiparty Mediation in a Complex World*, 245–274. Washington, D.C.: United States Institute of Peace Press, 1999.

Bell-Fialkoff, Andrew. *Ethnic Cleansing*. New York: St. Martin's Press, 1996.

Bercovitch, Jacob. *Social Conflicts and Third Parties: Strategies of Conflict Resolution*. Boulder, Colo.: Westview Press, 1984.

———. "International Mediation: A Study of the Incidence, Strategies and Conditions of Successful Outcomes." *Cooperation and Conflict: Nordic Journal of International Politics* 21 (1986): 155–168.

———, ed. *Resolving International Conflicts: The Theory and Practice of Mediation*. Boulder, Colo.: Lynne Rienner, 1996.

———, ed. *Studies in International Mediation: Essays in Honor of Jeffrey Z. Rubin*. Houndsmills, Basingstoke: Palgrave/Macmillan, 2002.

———. "Mediation in the Most Resistant Cases." In Chester A. Crocker, Fen Osler Hampson, and Pamela Aall, eds., *Grasping the Nettle*. Washington, D.C.: United States Institute of Peace Press, 2004.

Bercovitch, Jacob, and Jeffrey Langley. "The Nature of the Dispute and the Effectiveness of International Mediation." *Journal of Conflict Resolution* 37, no. 4 (1993): 670–691.

Bercovitch, Jacob, and Jeffrey Rubin, eds. *Mediation in International Relations: Multiple Approaches to Conflict Management*. New York: St. Martin's Press, 1992.

Berdal, Mats, and David M. Malone, eds. *Greed and Grievance: Economic Agendas in Civil Wars*. Boulder, Colo.: Lynne Rienner, 2001.

Berton, Peter, Hiroshi Kimura, and I. William Zartman, eds. *International Negotiation: Actors, Structure/Process, Values*. New York: St. Martin's Press, 1999.

Bloomfield, David. *Political Negotiations in the Brooke Initiative in Northern Ireland, 1988–1992*. Houndsmills, Basingstoke, U.K.: Palgrave/Macmillan, 1996.

———. *Peacemaking Strategies in Northern Ireland: Building Complementarity in Conflict Management Theory*. New York: St. Martin's Press, 1997.

Botes, Johannes, and Christopher Mitchell. "Constraints on Third-Party Flexibility." *Annals of the American Academy of Political and Social Science*, no. 542 (1995): 168–184.

Brett, J. M. "Mediator Style and Mediation Effectiveness." *Negotiation Journal* 2, no. 3 (1986): 277–285.

Brown, Michael E., ed. *Ethnic Conflict and International Security.* Princeton, N.J.: Princeton University Press, 1993.

————, ed. *The International Dimensions of Internal Conflict.* Cambridge, Mass.: MIT Press, 1996.

————. "Ethnic and Internal Conflicts: Causes and Implications." In Chester A. Crocker, Fen Osler Hampson, and Pamela Aall, eds., *Turbulent Peace: The Challenges of Managing International Conflict,* 209–226. Washington, D.C.: United States Institute of Peace Press, 2001.

Burgess, Heidi, and Guy Burgess. "The Meaning of Intractability." 2003. In "Beyond Intractability.Org," an online resource available at http://www .beyondintractability.org/iweb/index.htm.

Cahill, Kevin M. *Preventive Diplomacy: Stopping Wars before They Start.* New York: Routledge, 2000.

Carnegie Commission on Preventing Deadly Conflict. *Preventing Deadly Conflict: Final Report.* New York: Carnegie Corporation of New York, 1997.

Carnevale, Peter. "Strategic Choice in Mediation." *Negotiation Journal* 2, no. 1 (1986): 41–56.

————. "Mediating from Strength." In Jacob Bercovitch, ed., *Studies in International Mediation: Essays in Honor of Jeffrey Z. Rubin,* 25–40. London: Palgrave/Macmillan, 2002.

Carnevale, Peter J., and Sharon Arad. "Bias and Impartiality in International Mediation." In Jacob Bercovitch, ed., *Resolving International Conflicts: The Theory and Practice of Mediation,* 39–56. Boulder, Colo.: Lynne Rienner, 1996.

Center for Strategic and International Studies (CSIS). *Play to Win: The Commission on Post-Conflict Reconstruction* (January 2003). Available at http:// csis.org/ isp/pcr/playtowin.pdf.

Center for Strategic and International Studies (CSIS) and the Association of the United States Army (AUSA). *Post-Conflict Reconstruction: A Joint Project of the Task Framework* (May 2002). Available at http://csis.org/isp/ pcr/framework.pdf.

Chan, Steve, and Vivienne Jabri, eds. *Mediation in Southern Africa.* London: Macmillan, 1993.

Chayes, Abram, and Antonia Handler Chayes. *The New Sovereignty: Compliance and International Regulatory Agreements.* Cambridge, Mass.: Harvard University Press, 1995.

Chesterman, Simon, and Beatrice Pouligny. "Are Sanctions Meant to Work? The Politics of Creating and Implementing Sanctions through the United Nations." *Global Governance* 9, no. 4 (2003): 503–518.

Chigas, Diana. "Negotiating Intractable Conflicts: The Contribution of Unofficial Intermediaries." In Chester A. Crocker, Fen Osler Hampson, and Pamela Aall, eds., *Grasping the Nettle*. Washington, D.C.: United States Institute of Peace Press, 2004.

Clark, John F., ed. *The African Stakes of the Congo War*. New York: Palgrave/Macmillan, 2002.

Cleves, Patricia, Nat Colletta, and Nicholas Sambanis. "Addressing Conflict: Emerging Policy at the World Bank." In Fen Osler Hampson and David M. Malone, eds., *From Reaction to Conflict Prevention: Opportunities for the UN System*, 297–320. Boulder, Colo.: Lynne Rienner, 2002.

Cohen, Herman J. *Intervening in Africa: Superpower Peacemaking in a Troubled Continent*. New York: St. Martin's Press, 2000.

Cohen, Raymond. *Negotiating across Cultures: Communication Obstacles in International Diplomacy*. Washington, D.C.: United States Institute of Peace Press, 1991. Revised ed., 1997.

Cohen, Stephen. "Intractability and the Israeli-Palestinian Conflict." In Chester A. Crocker, Fen Osler Hampson, and Pamela Aall, eds., *Grasping the Nettle*. Washington, D.C.: United States Institute of Peace Press, 2004.

Collier, Paul. *Economic Causes of Civil Conflict and Their Implications for Policy*. Washington, D.C.: World Bank, 2000.

———. "Economic Causes of Civil Conflict and Their Implications for Policy." In Chester A. Crocker, Fen Osler Hampson, and Pamela Aall, eds., *Turbulent Peace: The Challenges of Managing International Conflict*, 143–162. Washington, D.C.: United States Institute of Peace Press, 2001.

Collier, Paul, and Anke Hoeffler. *Greed and Grievance in Civil War*. Washington, D.C.: World Bank, 2000.

Collier, Paul, Anke Hoeffler, and Mans Soderbom. "On the Duration of Civil Wars." Paper for the World Bank Development Research Group. Washington, D.C.: World Bank, 2001. Available at http//www.worldbank.org/research/conflict/duration.

Corbin, Jane. *The Norway Channel: The Secret Talks That Led to the Middle East Peace Accord*. New York: Atlantic Monthly Press, 1994.

Cortright, David. *The Price of Peace: Incentives and International Conflict Prevention*. Lanham, Md.: Rowman and Littlefield, 1997.

Cortright, David, and George A. Lopez, eds. *The Sanctions Decade: Assessing UN Strategies in the 1990s.* Boulder, Colo.: Lynne Rienner, 2000.

Cortright, David, and George Lopez. *Sanctions and the Search for Security: Challenges to UN Action.* Boulder, Colo.: Lynne Rienner, 2002.

Coy, Patrick, and Lynne M. Woehrle. *Social Conflicts and Collective Identities.* Lanham, Md.: Rowman and Littlefield, 2000.

Crocker, Chester A. *High Noon in Southern Africa: Making Peace in a Rough Neighborhood.* New York: W. W. Norton, 1992.

———. "Peacemaking in Southern Africa: The Namibia-Angola Settlement of 1988." In Chester A. Crocker, Fen Osler Hampson, and Pamela Aall, eds., *Herding Cats: Multiparty Mediation in a Complex World*, 207–244. Washington, D.C.: United States Institute of Peace Press, 1999.

———. "A Poor Case for Quitting: Mistaking Incompetence for Intervention." *Foreign Affairs* 79, no. 1 (2000): 183–186.

———. "Intervention: Towards Best Practices and a Holistic View." In Chester A. Crocker, Fen Osler Hampson, and Pamela Aall, eds., *Turbulent Peace: The Challenges of Managing International Conflict*, 229–248. Washington, D.C.: United States Institute of Peace Press, 2001.

Crocker, Chester A., Fen Osler Hampson, and Pamela Aall, eds. *Herding Cats: Multiparty Mediation in a Complex World.* Washington, D.C.: United States Institute of Peace Press, 1999.

———. "Multiparty Mediation and the Conflict Cycle." In Chester A. Crocker, Fen Osler Hampson, and Pamela Aall, eds., *Herding Cats: Multiparty Mediation in a Complex World*, 19–46. Washington, D.C.: United States Institute of Peace Press, 1999.

———, eds. *Turbulent Peace: The Challenges of Managing International Conflict.* Washington, D.C.: United States Institute of Peace Press, 2001.

———, eds. *Grasping the Nettle: Analyzing Cases of Intractable Conflict.* Washington, D.C.: United States Institute of Peace Press, 2004.

Daniel, Donald C., Bradd C. Hayes, Chantal De Jonge Oudraat, eds. *Coercive Inducement and the Containment of International Crises.* Washington, D.C.: United States Institute of Peace Press, 1999.

Darby, John. *Intimidation and the Control of the Conflict in Northern Ireland.* Dublin: Gill and Macmillan, 1986.

De Chastelain, John. "The Good Friday Agreement in Northern Ireland." In Chester A. Crocker, Fen Osler Hampson, and Pamela Aall, eds., *Herding*

Cats: Multiparty Mediation in a Complex World, 431–468. Washington, D.C.: United States Institute of Peace Press, 1999.

De Soto, Alvaro. "Ending Violent Conflict in El Salvador." In Chester A. Crocker, Fen Osler Hampson, and Pamela Aall, eds., *Herding Cats: Multiparty Mediation in a Complex World*, 345–385. Washington, D.C.: United States Institute of Peace Press, 1999.

Denoon, Donald. *Getting under the Skin: The Bougainville Copper Agreement and the Creation of the Panguna Mine.* Melbourne: University of Melbourne Press, 2000.

Deutsch, Morton. *The Resolution of Conflict: Constructive and Destructive Processes.* New Haven, Conn.: Yale University Press, 1973.

Dixon, William J. "Third-Party Techniques for Preventing Conflict Escalation and Promoting Peaceful Settlement." *International Organization* 50, no. 2 (1996): 653–681.

Doob, Leonard W. *Intervention: Guide and Perils.* New Haven, Conn.: Yale University Press, 1993.

Doyle, Michael W., Ian Johnstone, and Robert C. Orr, eds. *Keeping the Peace: Multidimensional UN Operations in Cambodia and El Salvador.* Cambridge: Cambridge University Press, 1997.

Druckman, Daniel, and Christopher J. Mitchell, eds. "Flexibility in International Negotiation and Mediation." *Annals of the American Academy of Political and Social Science*, no. 542 (1995): 10–218.

Durch, William J., ed. *The Evolution of UN Peacekeeping: Case Studies and Comparative Analyses.* New York: St. Martin's Press, 1993.

———, ed. *UN Peacekeeping, American Policy, and the Uncivil Wars of the 1990s.* New York: St. Martin's Press, 1996.

Edmead, Frank. *Analysis and Prediction in International Mediation.* Geneva: UNITAR, 1971.

Egeland, Jan. "The Oslo Accord: Multiparty Facilitation through the Norwegian Channel." In Chester A. Crocker, Fen Osler Hampson, and Pamela Aall, eds., *Herding Cats: Multiparty Mediation in a Complex World*, 527–546. Washington, D.C.: United States Institute of Peace Press, 1999.

Einaudi, Luigi R. "The Ecuador-Peru Peace Process." In Chester A. Crocker, Fen Osler Hampson, and Pamela Aall, eds., *Herding Cats: Multiparty Mediation in a Complex World*, 405–430. Washington, D.C.: United States Institute of Peace Press, 1999.

Elizur, Yuval. "Israel Banks on a Fence." *Foreign Affairs* 82, no. 2 (2003): 106–119.

Etzioni, Amitai. "Mediation as a World Role for the United States." *Washington Quarterly* 18, no. 3 (1995): 75–87.

Faure, Guy Olivier. "Nonverbal Negotiation in China: Cycling in Beijing." *Negotiation Journal* 11, no. 1 (1995): 11–18.

Fearon, James, and David Laitin. "Explaining Interethnic Cooperation." *American Political Science Review* 90, no. 4 (1996): 715–735.

Fisher, Ronald J. "Third-Party Consultation: A Method for the Study and Resolution of Conflict." *Journal of Conflict Resolution* 16, no. 1 (1972): 67–94.

———. *The Social Psychology of Intergroup Conflict and International Conflict Resolution.* New York: Springer-Verlag, 1990.

George, Alexander. *Forceful Persuasion: Coercive Diplomacy as an Alternative to War.* Washington, D.C.: United States Institute of Peace Press, 1991.

Gordon, Dennis R. "The Paralysis of Multilateral Peacekeeping: International Organizations and the Falkland/Malvinas War." *Peace and Change* 12, nos. 1–2 (1987): 51–63.

Greenberg, Melanie C., John H. Barton, and Margaret E. McGuinness, eds. *Words over War: Mediation and Arbitration to Prevent Deadly Conflict.* Lanham, Md.: Rowman and Littlefield, 2000.

Gurr, Ted Robert. *Peoples versus States: Minorities at Risk in the New Century.* Washington, D.C.: United States Institute of Peace Press, 2000.

———. "Minorities and Nationalists: Managing Ethnopolitical Conflict in the New Century." In Chester A. Crocker, Fen Osler Hampson, and Pamela Aall, eds., *Turbulent Peace: The Challenges of Managing International Conflict,* 163–188. Washington, D.C.: United States Institute of Peace Press, 2001.

Haass, Richard N. *Conflicts Unending: The United States and Regional Disputes.* New Haven and London: Yale University Press, 1990.

———. "Using Force: Lessons and Choices for U.S. Foreign Policy." In Chester A. Crocker, Fen Osler Hampson, and Pamela Aall, eds., *Turbulent Peace: The Challenges of Managing International Conflict,* 295–308. Washington, D.C.: United States Institute of Peace Press, 2001.

Hadden, Tom. "The Role of International Agencies in Conflict Resolution: Some Lessons from the Irish Experience." *Bulletin of Peace Proposals* 18, no. 4 (1987): 567–572.

Hamburg, David A. *No More Killing Fields: Preventing Deadly Conflict.* Lanham, Md.: Rowman and Littlefield, 2002.

Hampson, Fen Osler. *Nurturing Peace: Why Peace Settlements Succeed or Fail.* Washington, D.C.: United States Institute of Peace Press, 1996.

———. "Parent, Midwife, or Accidental Executioner? The Role of Third Parties in Ending Violent Conflict." In Chester A. Crocker, Fen Osler Hampson, and Pamela Aall, eds., *Turbulent Peace: The Challenges of Managing International Conflict*, 387–406. Washington, D.C.: United States Institute of Peace Press, 2001.

———. "Preventive Diplomacy at the United Nations and Beyond." In Fen Osler Hampson and David M. Malone, eds., *From Reaction to Conflict Prevention: Opportunities for the UN System*, 139–159. Boulder, Colo.: Lynne Rienner, 2002.

Hampson, Fen Osler, and David M. Malone, eds. *From Reaction to Conflict Prevention: Opportunities for the UN System*. Boulder, Colo.: Lynne Rienner, 2002.

Hampson, Fen Osler, and Brian S. Mandell. "Managing Regional Conflict: Security Cooperation and Third Party Mediators." *International Journal* 45, no. 2 (1990): 191–201.

Hara, Fabienne. "Burundi: A Case of Parallel Diplomacy." In Chester A. Crocker, Fen Osler Hampson, and Pamela Aall, eds., *Herding Cats: Multiparty Mediation in a Complex World*, 135–158. Washington, D.C.: United States Institute of Peace Press, 1999.

Hare, Paul J. *Angola's Last Best Chance for Peace: An Insider's Account of the Peace Process*. Washington, D.C.: United States Institute of Peace Press, 1998.

———. "Angola: The Lusaka Peace Process." In Chester A. Crocker, Fen Osler Hampson, and Pamela Aall, eds., *Herding Cats: Multiparty Mediation in a Complex World*, 643–662. Washington, D.C.: United States Institute of Peace Press, 1999.

———. "Angola: An Intractable Conflict?" In Chester A. Crocker, Fen Osler Hampson, and Pamela Aall, eds., *Grasping the Nettle*. Washington, D.C.: United States Institute of Peace Press, 2004.

Heininger, Janet. *Peacekeeping in Transition: The United Nations in Cambodia*. New York: Twentieth Century Fund Press, 1994.

Hermann, Margaret G. "Leaders, Leadership, and Flexibility: Influences on Heads of Government as Negotiators and Mediators." *Annals of the American Academy of Political and Social Science*, no. 542 (1995): 148–167.

Herz, Monica, and Joao Pontes Nogueira. *Ecuador vs. Peru: Peacemaking amid Rivalry*. Boulder, Colo.: Lynne Rienner, 2002.

Hirsch, John L. *Sierra Leone: Diamonds and the Struggle for Democracy*. Boulder, Colo.: Lynne Rienner, 2001.

Hoffmann, Stanley. "The Debate about Intervention." In Chester A. Crocker, Fen Osler Hampson, and Pamela Aall, eds., *Turbulent Peace: The Challenges of Managing International Conflict*, 273–284. Washington, D.C.: United States Institute of Peace Press, 2001.

Holbrooke, Richard C. "The Road to Sarajevo." In Chester A. Crocker, Fen Osler Hampson, and Pamela Aall, eds., *Herding Cats: Multiparty Mediation in a Complex World*, 325–344. Washington, D.C.: United States Institute of Peace Press, 1999.

———. *To End a War*, rev. ed. New York: Random House, 1999.

Hopmann, P. Terrence. *The Negotiation Process and the Resolution of International Conflicts*. Columbia, S.C.: University of South Carolina Press, 1996.

Horowitz, Donald. *Ethnic Groups in Conflict*. Berkeley: University of California Press, 1985.

Howe, Herbert. "Lessons of Liberia: ECOMOG and Regional Peacekeeping." *International Security* 21, no. 3 (Winter 1996–97): 145–176.

Howley, Pat. *Breaking Spears and Mending Hearts: Peacemakers and Restorative Justice in Bougainville*. London: Zed Books, 2003.

Human Rights Watch. "LRA Conflict in Northern Uganda and Southern Sudan, 2002." *Human Rights Watch News*, October 29, 2002.

Hume, Cameron. *Ending Mozambique's War: The Role of Mediation and Good Offices*. Washington, D.C.: United States Institute of Peace Press, 1996.

Ikle, Fred Charles. *Every War Must End*. New York: Columbia University Press, 1971.

Jabri, Vivienne. *Mediating Conflict: Decision-Making and Western Intervention in Namibia*. Manchester, U.K.: Manchester University Press, 1990.

Jentleson, Bruce W. *Opportunities Missed, Opportunities Seized: Preventive Diplomacy in the Post–Cold War World*. Lanham, Md.: Rowman, and Littlefield, 1999.

———. "Preventive Statecraft: A Realist Strategy of the Post–Cold War Era." In Chester A. Crocker, Fen Osler Hampson, and Pamela Aall, eds., *Turbulent Peace: The Challenges of Managing International Conflict*, 249–264. Washington, D.C.: United States Institute of Peace Press, 2001.

Jones, Bruce D. *Peacemaking in Rwanda: The Dynamics of Failure*. Boulder, Colo.: Lynne Rienner, 2001.

———. "The Challenges of Strategic Coordination." In Stephen John Stedman, Donald Rothchild, and Elizabeth M. Cousens, eds., *Ending Civil Wars: The Implementation of Peace Agreements*, 89–116. Boulder, Colo.: Lynne Rienner, 2002.

Kaplan, Robert D. "The Coming Anarchy." *Atlantic Monthly* 273, no. 2 (February 1994): 44–76.

Katz, Mark, ed. *Soviet-American Conflict Resolution in the Third World.* Washington, D.C.: United States Institute of Peace Press, 1991.

Kaufman, Chaim. "Possible and Impossible Solutions to Ethnic Wars." *International Security* 20, no. 4 (1996): 136–175.

Kim, Sung Hee, Dean G. Pruitt, and Jeffrey Z. Rubin. *Social Conflict: Escalation, Stalemate, and Settlement,* 2d ed. New York: McGraw-Hill, 1994.

King, Charles. "The Uses of Deadlock: Intractability in Eurasia. " In Chester A. Crocker, Fen Osler Hampson, and Pamela Aall, eds., *Grasping the Nettle.* Washington, D.C.: United States Institute of Peace Press, 2004.

Kleiboer, Marieke. "Ripeness of Conflict: A Fruitful Notion?" *Journal of Peace Research* 31, no. 1 (1994): 109–116.

———. "Understanding Success and Failure of International Mediation." *Journal of Conflict Resolution* 40, no. 2 (1996): 360–389.

———. "Great Power Mediation: Using Leverage to Make Peace?" In Jacob Bercovitch, ed., *Studies in International Mediation: Essays in Honor of Jeffrey Z. Rubin,* 127–140. London: Palgrave/Macmillan, 2002.

Kleiboer, Marieke, and Paul Hart. "Time to Talk? Multiple Perspectives on Timing of International Mediation." *Cooperation and Conflict* 30, no. 4 (1995): 307–348.

Kremenyuk, Victor A., ed. *International Negotiation: Analysis, Approaches, Issues.* 2d ed. San Francisco: Jossey-Bass, 2002.

Kressel, Kenneth, and Dean Pruitt, eds. *Mediation Research: The Process and Effectiveness of Third-Party Intervention.* San Francisco: Jossey-Bass, 1989.

Kriesberg, Louis. "Coordinating Intermediary Peace Efforts." *Negotiation Journal* 2, no. 4 (1986): 341–352.

———. "Formal and Quasi-Mediators in International Disputes: An Exploratory Analysis." *Journal of Peace Research* 28, no. 1 (1991): 19–27.

———. *International Conflict Resolution: The US-USSR and Middle East Cases.* New Haven, Conn.: Yale University Press, 1992.

———. "The Growth of the Conflict Resolution Field." In Chester A. Crocker, Fen Osler Hampson, and Pamela Aall, eds., *Turbulent Peace: The Challenges of Managing International Conflict,* 407–426. Washington, D.C.: United States Institute of Peace Press, 2001.

———. *Constructive Conflicts: From Escalation to Resolution,* 2d ed. Lanham, Md.: Rowman and Littlefield, 2003.

————. "The Nature of Intractability" (2003). In "Beyond Intractability.Org," an online resource available at http://www.beyondintractability.org/iweb/index.htm.

————. "Nature, Dynamics, and Phases of Intractability." In Chester A. Crocker, Fen Osler Hampson, and Pamela Aall, eds., *Grasping the Nettle.* Washington, D.C.: United States Institute of Peace Press, 2004.

Kriesberg, Louis, Terrell A. Northrup, and Stuart J. Thorson, eds. *Intractable Conflicts and Their Resolution.* Syracuse: Syracuse University Press, 1989.

Kriesberg, Louis, and Stuart J. Thorson, eds. *Timing the De-escalation of International Conflicts.* Syracuse: Syracuse University Press, 1991.

Kritz, Neil J. "The Rule of Law in the Postconflict Phase: Building a Stable Peace." In Chester A. Crocker, Fen Osler Hampson, and Pamela Aall, eds., *Turbulent Peace: The Challenges of Managing International Conflict,* 801–820. Washington, D.C.: United States Institute of Peace Press, 2001.

Kusnitz, Leonard. "The United Nations and Orphan Conflicts: The Guatemalan Case." *National Security Studies Quarterly* 2, no. 2 (1996): 33–56.

Lake, David A., and Donald Rothchild, eds. *The International Spread of Ethnic Conflict: Fear, Diffusion, and the Escalation Process.* Princeton, N.J.: Princeton University Press, 1998.

Lall, Arthur S., ed. *Multilateral Negotiation and Mediation: Instruments and Methods.* New York: Pergamon Press, 1985.

Lederach, John Paul. *Preparing for Peace: Conflict Transformation across Cultures.* Syracuse: Syracuse University Press, 1996.

————. *Building Peace: Sustainable Reconciliation in Divided Societies.* Washington, D.C.: United States Institute of Peace Press, 1998.

————. *The Journey towards Reconciliation.* Scottdale, Penn.: Herald Press, 1999.

————. "Civil Society and Reconciliation." In Chester A. Crocker, Fen Osler Hampson, and Pamela Aall, eds., *Turbulent Peace: The Challenges of Managing International Conflict,* 841–854. Washington, D.C.: United States Institute of Peace Press, 2001.

Lederach, John Paul, and Janice Moomaw Jenner. *A Handbook of International Peacebuilding: Into the Eye of the Storm.* San Francisco: Jossey-Bass, 2002.

Lesch, Ann. "Negotiations in Sudan." In David R. Smock, ed., *Making War and Waging Peace: Foreign Intervention in Sub-Saharan Africa,* 107–131. Washington, D.C.: United States Institute of Peace Press, 1993.

Licklider, Roy. *Stopping the Killing: How Civil Wars End.* New York: New York University Press, 1993.

———. "The Consequences of Negotiated Settlements in Civil Wars, 1945–1993." *American Political Science Review* 39, no. 3 (1995): 259–273.

———. "Obstacles to Peace Settlements." In Chester A. Crocker, Fen Osler Hampson, and Pamela Aall, eds., *Turbulent Peace: The Challenges of Managing International Conflict*, 697–718. Washington, D.C.: United States Institute of Peace Press, 2001.

———. "Comparative Studies of Long Wars." In Chester A. Crocker, Fen Osler Hampson, and Pamela Aall, eds., *Grasping the Nettle*. Washington, D.C.: United States Institute of Peace Press, 2004.

Lochery, Neill. "Oslo's Lessons." *Jerusalem Post*, May 12, 2002, 6.

Lucima, Okello, ed. "Protracted Conflict, Elusive Peace: Initiatives to End Violence in Northern Uganda." In *Accord: An International Review of Peace Initiatives* 11 (2002).

Lund, Michael. *Preventing Violent Conflicts: A Strategy for Preventive Diplomacy.* Washington, D.C.: United States Institute of Peace Press, 1997.

Luttwak, Edward N. "Give War a Chance." *Foreign Affairs* 78, no. 4 (1999): 36–44.

———. "The Curse of Inconclusive Intervention." In Chester A. Crocker, Fen Osler Hampson, and Pamela Aall, eds., *Turbulent Peace: The Challenges of Managing International Conflict*, 265–272. Washington, D.C.: United States Institute of Peace Press, 2001.

Mandell, Brian S., and Brian W. Tomlin. "Mediation in the Development of Norms to Manage Conflict: Kissinger in the Middle East." *Journal of Peace Research* 28, no. 1 (1991): 43–55.

Maresca, John J. "The Conflict over Nagorno-Karabakh." In Bruce W. Jentleson, ed., *Opportunities Missed, Opportunities Seized*, 82–84. New York: Rowman and Littlefield, 1999.

Martin, Ian. *Self-Determination in East Timor: The United Nations, the Ballot, and International Intervention.* Boulder, Colo.: Lynne Rienner, 2001.

Mason, Paul E., and Thomas F. Marsteller Jr. "UN Mediation: More Effective Options." *SAIS Review* 5, no. 2 (1985): 271–284.

McDonald, John W., Jr., and Diane B. Bendahmane, eds. *Conflict Resolution: Track-Two Diplomacy.* Washington, D.C.: Foreign Service Institute, U.S. Department of State, 1985.

McDougall, Barbara. "Haiti: Canada's Role in the OAS." In Chester A. Crocker, Fen Osler Hampson, and Pamela Aall, eds., *Herding Cats: Multiparty Mediation in a Complex World*, 387–404. Washington, D.C.: United States Institute of Peace Press, 1999.

Miall, Hugh, Oliver Ramsbotham, and Tom Woodhouse. *Contemporary Conflict Resolution: The Prevention, Management, and Transformation of Deadly Conflict.* Oxford: Polity Press, 1999.

Mitchell, Christopher R. *The Structure of International Conflict.* New York: St. Martin's Press, 1981.

———. "The Motives for Mediation." In Christopher R. Mitchell and K. Webb, eds., *New Approaches to International Mediation,* 29–51. New York: Greenwood Press, 1988.

Mitchell, Christopher R., and K. Webb, eds. *New Approaches to International Mediation.* New York: Greenwood Press, 1988.

Mitchell, George J. *Making Peace.* New York: Alfred A. Knopf, 1999.

Mooney, Terrance Lorne, ed. *The Challenge of Development within Conflict Zones.* Paris: Development Centre of the Organization for Economic Cooperation and Development, 1995.

Morrison, Stephen, and Alex de Waal. "Can Sudan Escape Its Intractability?" In Chester A. Crocker, Fen Osler Hampson, and Pamela Aall, eds., *Grasping the Nettle.* Washington, D.C.: United States Institute of Peace Press, 2004.

Munck, Gerardo, and Chetan Kumar. "Civil Conflicts and the Conditions for Successful International Intervention: A Comparative Study of Cambodia and El Salvador." *Review of International Studies* 21, no. 2 (1995): 159–181.

Nye, Joseph S., Jr. "Redefining the National Interest." *Foreign Affairs* 78, no. 4 (1999): 22–36.

———. "Soft Power and Conflict Management in the Information Age." In Chester A. Crocker, Fen Osler Hampson, and Pamela Aall, eds., *Turbulent Peace: The Challenges of Managing International Conflict,* 353–364. Washington, D.C.: United States Institute of Peace Press, 2001.

Oakley, Robert B., Michael J. Drziedzic, and Eliot M. Goldberg, eds. *Policing the New World Disorder: Peace Operations and Public Security.* Washington, D.C.: National Defense University Press, 1998.

Organization for Economic Co-operation and Development (OECD)/ Development Assistance Committee. *DAC Guidelines on Conflict, Peace, and Development Co-operation.* Paris: Development Assistance Committee of the OECD, 1997.

Ott, Marvin. "Mediation as a Method of Conflict Resolution: Two Cases." *International Organization* 26, no. 4 (1972): 596–618.

Otunnu, Olara A., and Michael W. Doyle, eds. *Peacemaking and Peacekeeping for the New Century*. Lanham, Md.: Rowman and Littlefield, 1998.

Ould-Abdallah, Ahmedou. *Burundi on the Brink, 1993–95: A UN Special Envoy Reflects on Preventive Diplomacy*. Washington, D.C.: United States Institute of Peace Press, 2000.

Pape, Robert A. "Partition: An Exit Strategy for Bosnia." *Survival* 39, no. 4 (1997–98): 25–28.

Pastor, Robert A. "More and Less Than It Seemed: The Carter-Nunn-Powell Mediation in Haiti, 1994." In Chester A. Crocker, Fen Osler Hampson, and Pamela Aall, eds., *Herding Cats: Multiparty Mediation in a Complex World*, 505–526. Washington, D.C.: United States Institute of Peace Press, 1999.

Perlez, Jane. "CIA Chief Going to Israel in Effort to Maintain Calm." *New York Times*, June 6, 2001, A1.

Princen, Thomas. *Intermediaries in International Conflict*. Princeton, N.J.: Princeton University Press, 1992.

Pruitt, Dean G. "Mediator Behavior and Success in Mediation." In Jacob Bercovitch, ed., *Studies in International Mediation: Essays in Honor of Jeffrey Z. Rubin*, 41–55. London: Palgrave/Macmillan, 2002.

Pundak, Ron. "From Oslo to Taba: What Went Wrong?" *Survival* 43, no. 3 (2001): 31–46.

Putnam, Tonya L. "Human Rights and Sustainable Peace." In Stephen John Stedman, Donald Rothchild, and Elizabeth M. Cousens, eds., *Ending Civil Wars: The Implementation of Peace Agreements*, 237–272. Boulder, Colo.: Lynne Rienner, 2002.

Quandt, William B. *Camp David: Peacemaking and Politics*. Washington, D.C.: Brookings Institution, 1986.

Quandt, William B., and Michael H. Armacost. *Peace Process: American Diplomacy and the Arab-Israeli Conflict since 1967*, rev. ed. Berkeley: University of California Press, 2001.

Rabie, Mohammed. *U.S.-PLO Dialogue: Secret Diplomacy and Conflict Resolution*. Gainsville: University of Florida Press, 1995.

Ramsbotham, Oliver, and Tom Woodhouse. *Humanitarian Intervention in Contemporary Conflict: A Reconceptualization*. London: Blackwell Publishers, 1996.

Ross, Dennis. "Unmasking Arafat." *Foreign Policy* (July-August 2002). Available at http://www.foreignpolicy.com/issue_julyaug_2002/ross.html.

———. *The Missing Peace: The Inside Story of the Fight for the Middle East Peace*. New York: Farrar, Straus and Giroux, forthcoming.

Ross, Marc Howard. *The Management of Conflict: Interpretations and Interests in Comparative Perspective.* New Haven, Conn.: Yale University Press, 1996.

Rothchild, Donald, and Caroline Hartzell. "Great and Medium Power Mediations: Angola." In I. William Zartman, ed., *Annals of the American Academy of Political and Social Science,* no. 518 (1991): 39–57.

Rothman, Jay. *From Confrontation to Cooperation: Resolving Ethnic and Regional Conflict.* Thousand Oaks, Calif.: Sage Books, 1992.

———. *Resolving Identity Based Conflicts in Nations, Organizations, and Communities.* San Francisco: Jossey-Bass, 1997.

Rothschild, Joseph. *Ethnopolitics: A Conceptual Approach.* New York: Columbia University Press, 1981.

Rubin, Barnett R. *The Search for Peace in Afghanistan: From Buffer State to Failed State.* New Haven, Conn.: Yale University Press, 1995.

———. *Cases and Strategies for Preventive Action.* New York: Century Foundation Press, 1998.

Rubin, Jeffrey Z., ed. *Dynamics of Third-Party Intervention: Kissinger in the Middle East.* New York: Praeger Publishers, 1981.

———. "The Timing of Ripeness and the Ripeness of Timing." In Louis Kriesberg and Stuart J. Thorson, eds, *Timing the De-escalation of International Conflicts,* 237–246. Syracuse: Syracuse University Press, 1991.

———. "Conclusion: International Mediation in Context." In Jacob Bercovitch and Jeffrey C. Rubin, eds., *Mediation and International Relations,* 249–272. New York: St. Martin's Press, 1992.

Rubin, Jeffrey Z., Dean G. Pruitt, and Sung Hee Kim. *Social Conflict: Escalation, Stalemate, Settlement.* New York: McGraw-Hill, 1994.

Sandole, Dennis J. D., and Hugo Van Der Merwe, eds. *Conflict Resolution: Theory and Practice: Integration and Application.* Manchester: Manchester University Press, 1993.

Saunders, Harold H. *Sinai II: The Politics of International Mediation, 1974–1975.* Washington, D.C.: Foreign Policy Institute, SAIS, Johns Hopkins University, 1993.

———. "The Multilevel Peace Process in Tajikistan." In Chester A. Crocker, Fen Osler Hampson, and Pamela Aall, eds., *Herding Cats: Multiparty Mediation in a Complex World,* 159–180. Washington, D.C.: United States Institute of Peace Press, 1999.

———. "Prenegotiation and Circum-negotiation: Arenas of the Multilevel Peace Process." In Chester A. Crocker, Fen Osler Hampson, and Pamela

Aall, eds., *Turbulent Peace: The Challenges of Managing International Conflict*, 483–496. Washington, D.C.: United States Institute of Peace Press, 2001.

Schaffer, Howard B., and Teresita C. Schaffer. "Kashmir: Fifty Years of Running in Place." In Chester A. Crocker, Fen Osler Hampson, and Pamela Aall, eds., *Grasping the Nettle*. Washington, D.C.: United States Institute of Peace Press, 2004.

Schmemann, Serge. "Israeli Raids Kill 17 Palestinians in Tel Aviv, 3 Die in Shooting." *New York Times*, March 5, 2001, A1.

Shrock-Shenk, Carolyn, and Lawrence Ressler, eds. *Making Peace with Conflict: Practical Skills for Conflict Transformation*. Scottdale, Penn.: Herald Press, 1999.

Sisk, Timothy D. *Power Sharing and International Mediation in Ethnic Conflicts*. Washington, D.C.: United States Institute of Peace Press, 1996.

Smock, David R., and Chester A. Crocker, eds. *African Conflict Resolution: The U.S. Role in Peacemaking*. Washington, D.C.: United States Institute of Peace Press, 1995.

Snyder, Scott. *Negotiating on the Edge: North Korean Negotiating Behavior*. Washington, D.C.: United States Institute of Peace Press, 1999.

———. "'Intractable' Confrontation on the Korean Peninsula: A Contribution to Regional Stability?" In Chester A. Crocker, Fen Osler Hampson, and Pamela Aall, eds., *Grasping the Nettle*. Washington, D.C.: United States Institute of Peace Press, 2004.

Solomon, Richard H. "Bringing Peace to Cambodia." In Chester A. Crocker, Fen Osler Hampson, and Pamela Aall, eds., *Herding Cats: Multiparty Mediation in a Complex World*, 275–324. Washington, D.C.: United States Institute of Peace Press, 1999.

———. *Chinese Negotiating Behavior: Pursuing Interests through "Old Friends."* Washington, D.C.: United States Institute of Peace Press, 1999.

———. *Exiting Indochina: U.S. Leadership of the Cambodia Settlement and Normalization with Vietnam*. Washington, D.C.: United States Institute of Peace Press, 2000.

Spear, Joanna. "Disarmament and Demobilization." In Stephen John Stedman, Donald Rothchild, and Elizabeth M. Cousens, eds., *Ending Civil Wars: The Implementation of Peace Agreements*, 141–182. Boulder, Colo.: Lynne Rienner, 2002.

Stanley, William, and David Holiday. "Broad Participation, Diffuse Responsibility: Peace Implementation in Guatemala." In Stephen John Stedman, Donald Rothchild, and Elizabeth M. Cousens, eds., *Ending Civil Wars:*

The Implementation of Peace Agreements, 421–462. Boulder, Colo.: Lynne Rienner, 2002.

Starr, S. Frederick. "Making Eurasia Stable." *Foreign Affairs* 75, no. 1(1996): 80–92

———. "Twenty Theses on Afghanistan." Brookings Institution/Asia Society Conference, May 18, 2001, available at http://www.cacianalyst.org/Publications/Afghanistan_Theses.htm.

Stedman, Stephen John. *Peacemaking in Civil War: International Mediation in Zimbabwe*. Boulder, Colo.: Lynne Rienner, 1991.

———. "Spoiler Problems in Peace Processes." *International Security* 22, no. 2 (1997): 5–53.

———. "International Implementation of Peace Agreements in Civil Wars: Findings from a Study of Sixteen Cases." In Chester A. Crocker, Fen Osler Hampson, and Pamela Aall, eds., *Turbulent Peace: The Challenges of Managing International Conflict*, 737–752. Washington, D.C.: United States Institute of Peace Press, 2001.

Stedman, Stephen John, Donald Rothchild, and Elizabeth M. Cousens, eds. *Ending Civil Wars: The Implementation of Peace Agreements*. Boulder, Colo.: Lynne Rienner, 2002.

Stein, Janice Gross. "Structures, Strategies, and Tactics of Mediation: Kissinger and Carter in the Middle East." *Negotiation Journal* 1, no. 4 (1985): 331–347.

———, ed. *Getting to the Table*. Baltimore: Johns Hopkins University Press, 1990.

———. "Image, Identity, and the Resolution of Violent Conflict." In Chester A. Crocker, Fen Osler Hampson, and Pamela Aall, eds., *Turbulent Peace: The Challenges of Managing International Conflict*, 189–208. Washington, D.C.: United States Institute of Peace Press, 2001.

Stern, Paul C., and Daniel Druckman, eds. *Conflict Resolution after the Cold War*. Washington, D.C.: National Academy Press, 2000.

Suhrke, Astri, and Bruce Jones. "Preventive Diplomacy in Rwanda: Failure to Act or Failure of Actions?" In Bruce W. Jentleson, ed., *Opportunities Missed, Opportunities Seized: Preventive Diplomacy in the Post–Cold War World*, 238–264. Lanham Md.: Rowman and Littlefield Publishers, 2000.

Telhami, Shibley. "Beyond Resolution? An Essay on the Palestinian-Israeli Conflict." In Chester A. Crocker, Fen Osler Hampson, and Pamela Aall, eds., *Grasping the Nettle*. Washington, D.C.: United States Institute of Peace Press, 2004.

Thatcher, Margaret. *The Downing Street Years*. New York: Harper Collins, 1993.

Touval, Saadia. *The Peace Brokers: Mediators in the Arab-Israeli Conflict, 1948–1979*. Princeton, N.J.: Princeton University Press, 1982.

———. "Coercive Mediation on the Road to Dayton. *International Negotiation* 1, no. 3 (1996): 547–570.

———. "Mediation and Foreign Policy." *International Studies Review* 5, no. 4 (2003): 91–96.

Touval, Saadia, and I. William Zartman. eds. *International Mediation in Theory and Practice*. Boulder, Colo.: Westview Press, 1985.

———. "International Mediation in the Post–Cold War Era." In Chester A. Crocker, Fen Osler Hampson, and Pamela Aall, eds., *Turbulent Peace: The Challenges of Managing International Conflict*, 427–444. Washington, D.C.: United States Institute of Peace Press, 2001.

Umbricht, Victor H. *Multilateral Mediation: Practical Experiences and Lessons*. Dordrecht, Netherlands: Martinus Nijoff Publishers, 1989.

Vayrynen, Raimo. "The United Nations and the Resolution of International Conflict." *Cooperation and Conflict* 20, no. 3 (1985): 141–171.

Volkan, Vamik D., and Joseph V. Montville, eds. *The Psychodynamics of International Relationships: Concepts and Theories*. Lanham, Md.: Rowman and Littlefield, 1991.

Wallensteen, Peter. *Understanding Conflict Resolution: War, Peace and the Global System*. Thousand Oaks, Calif.: Sage Publications, 2002.

Walter, Barbara F. "A Critical Barrier to Civil War Settlement." *International Organization* 51, no. 3 (1997): 335–364.

———. "Designing Transitions from Civil War: Demobilization, Democratization, and Commitments to Peace." *International Security* 24, no. 1 (1999): 127–155.

Walter, Barbara F., and Jack Snyder, eds. *Civil War, Insecurity, and Intervention*. New York: Columbia University Press, 1999.

Watkins, Michael, and Susan Rosegrant. *Breakthrough International Negotiation: How Great Negotiators Transformed the World's Toughest Post–Cold War Conflicts*. San Francisco: Jossey-Bass, 2001.

Weeks, Dudley. *The Eight Essential Steps to Conflict Resolution: Preserving Relationships at Work, at Home, and in the Community*. New York: Putnam, 1994.

Wehr, Paul, and John Paul Lederach. "Mediating Conflict in Central America." *Journal of Peace Research* 28, no. 1 (1991): 85–98.

Weiss, Thomas G., ed. *The United Nations and Civil Wars*. Boulder, Colo.: Lynne Rienner, 1995.

Woodward, Susan L. "Economic Priorities for Successful Peace Implementation." In Stephen John Stedman, Donald Rothchild, and Elizabeth M. Cousens, eds., *Ending Civil Wars: The Implementation of Peace Agreements*, 183–214. Boulder, Colo.: Lynne Rienner, 2002.

World Bank. *Post-Conflict Reconstruction: The Role of the World Bank*. Washington, D.C.: World Bank, 1998.

Yarrow, C. H. Mike. *Quaker Experiences in International Conciliation*. New Haven, Conn.: Yale University Press, 1993.

Young, Oran. *The Intermediaries: Third Parties in International Crises*. Princeton, N.J.: Princeton University Press, 1967.

Zartman, I. William. *Ripe for Resolution: Conflict and Intervention in Africa*. New York: Oxford University Press, 1985.

———. "Ripening Conflict, Ripe Moment, Formula, and Mediation." In Diane Bendahmane and John McDonald, eds., *Perspectives on Negotiation*, 205–228. Washington, D.C.: Foreign Service Institute, 1986.

———, ed. "Resolving Regional Conflicts: International Perspectives." *Annals of the American Academy of Political and Social Science*, no. 518 (1991): 8–187.

———, ed. *Elusive Peace: Negotiating an End to Civil Wars*. Washington, D.C.: Brookings Institution, 1995.

———. "Ripeness: The Hurting Stalemate and Beyond." In Paul C. Stern and Daniel Druckman, eds., *International Conflict Resolution after the Cold War*. Washington, D.C.: National Academy Press, 2000.

———. "Analyzing Intractability." In Chester A. Crocker, Fen Osler Hampson, and Pamela Aall, eds., *Grasping the Nettle*. Washington, D.C.: United States Institute of Peace Press, 2004.

Zartman, I. William, and Maureen R. Berman. *The Practical Negotiator*. New Haven, Conn.: Yale University Press, 1982.

Zartman, I. William, and Louis Rasmussen, eds. *Peacemaking in International Conflict: Methods and Techniques*. Washington, D.C.: United States Institute of Peace Press, 1999.

Zartman, I. William, and Saadia Touval. "International Mediation: Conflict Resolution and Power Politics." *Journal of Social Issues* 41, no. 2 (1985): 27–45.

Index

About the Authors

Chester A. Crocker is the James R. Schlesinger Professor of Strategic Studies at Georgetown University and chairman of the board of directors of the United States Institute of Peace. From 1981 to 1989 he was assistant secretary of state for African affairs; as such, he was the principal diplomatic architect and mediator in the prolonged negotiations among Angola, Cuba, and South Africa that led to Namibia's transition to democratic governance and independence, and to the withdrawal of Cuban forces from Angola. He is the author of *High Noon in Southern Africa: Making Peace in a Rough Neighborhood*, and coeditor of *Turbulent Peace: The Challenges of Managing International Conflict; Managing Global Chaos: Sources of and Responses to International Conflict; African Conflict Resolution: The U.S. Role in Peacemaking;* and *Herding Cats: Multiparty Mediation in a Complex World*. He is also an adviser on strategy and negotiation to U.S. and European firms.

Fen Osler Hampson is professor of international affairs and director of the Norman Paterson School of International Affairs, Carleton University, Ottawa, Canada. He is the author of five books, including *Nurturing Peace: Why Peace Settlements Succeed or Fail,* and coeditor of twenty others, including *Turbulent Peace: The Challenges of Managing International Conflict; Managing Global Chaos: Sources of and Responses to International Conflict;* and *Herding Cats: Multiparty Mediation in a Complex World*. His most recent book is *Madness in the Multitude: Human Security and World Disorder*. Hampson was a peace fellow at the

239

United States Institute of Peace in 1993–94. He is chair of the Human Security Track of the Helsinki Process on Globalization and Democracy, a joint initiative of the governments of Finland and Tanzania.

Pamela Aall is director of the Education Program at the United States Institute of Peace. Before joining the Institute, she worked for the President's Committee on the Arts and the Humanities, the Institute of International Education, the Rockefeller Foundation, the European Cultural Foundation, and the International Council for Educational Development. She is president of Women in International Security. She is coeditor of *Turbulent Peace: The Challenges of Managing International Conflict; Managing Global Chaos: Sources of and Responses to International Conflict;* and *Herding Cats: Multiparty Mediation in a Complex World,* and coauthor of *Guide to IGOs, NGOs, and the Military in Peace and Relief Operations.*

United States Institute of Peace

The United States Institute of Peace is an independent, nonpartisan federal institution created by Congress to promote the prevention, management, and peaceful resolution of international conflicts. Established in 1984, the Institute meets its congressional mandate through an array of programs, including research grants, fellowships, professional training, education programs from high school through graduate school, conferences and workshops, library services, and publications. The Institute's Board of Directors is appointed by the President of the United States and confirmed by the Senate.

TAMING INTRACTABLE CONFLICTS

This book is set in Cochin; the display type is also Cochin. Hasten Design Studio designed the book's cover; Mike Chase designed the interior. Helene Y. Redmond made up the pages, which were proofread by Karen Stough. The index was prepared by Sonsie Conroy. The book's editor was Nigel Quinney.